CAPTAIN AMERICA

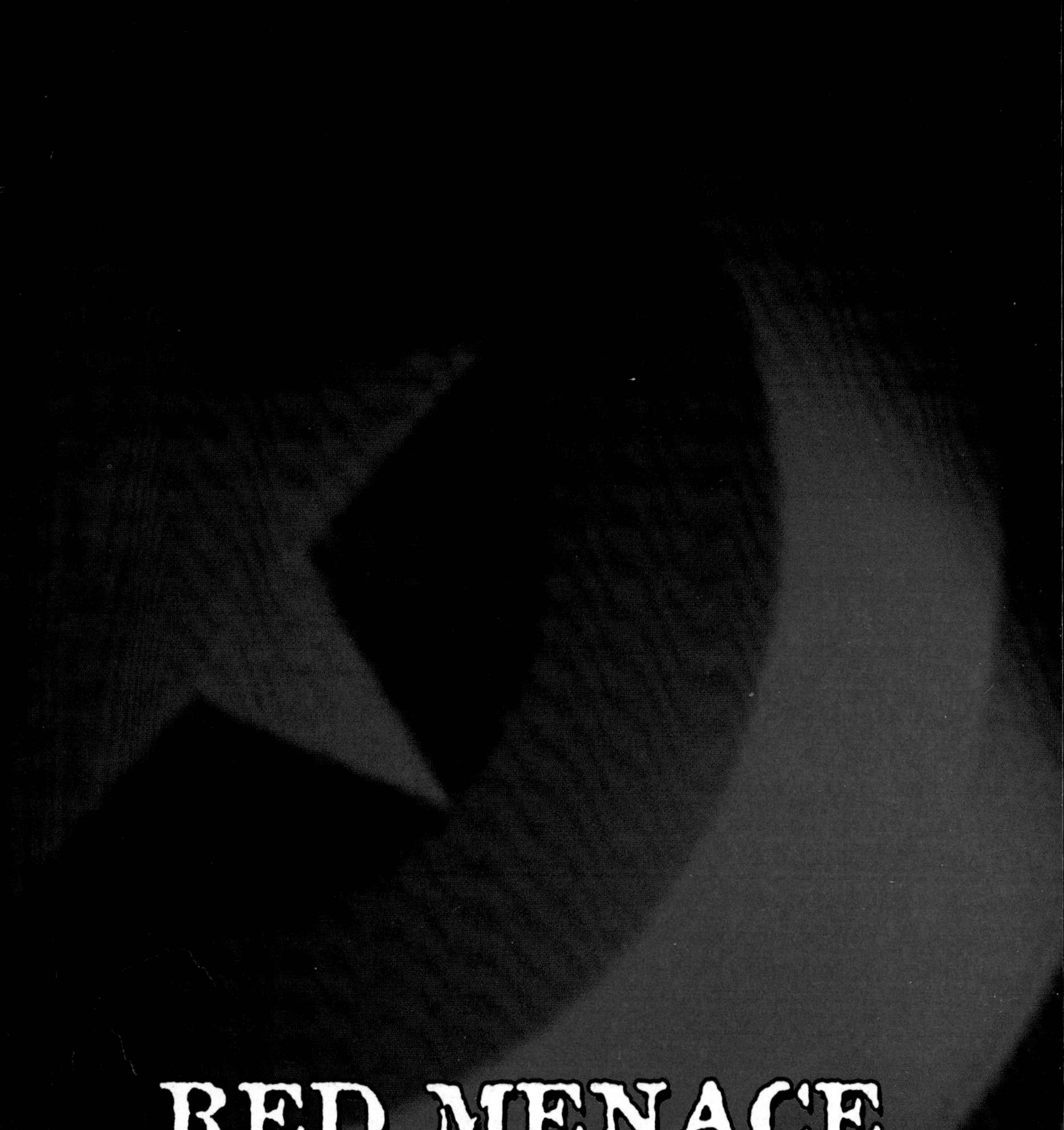

RED MENACE

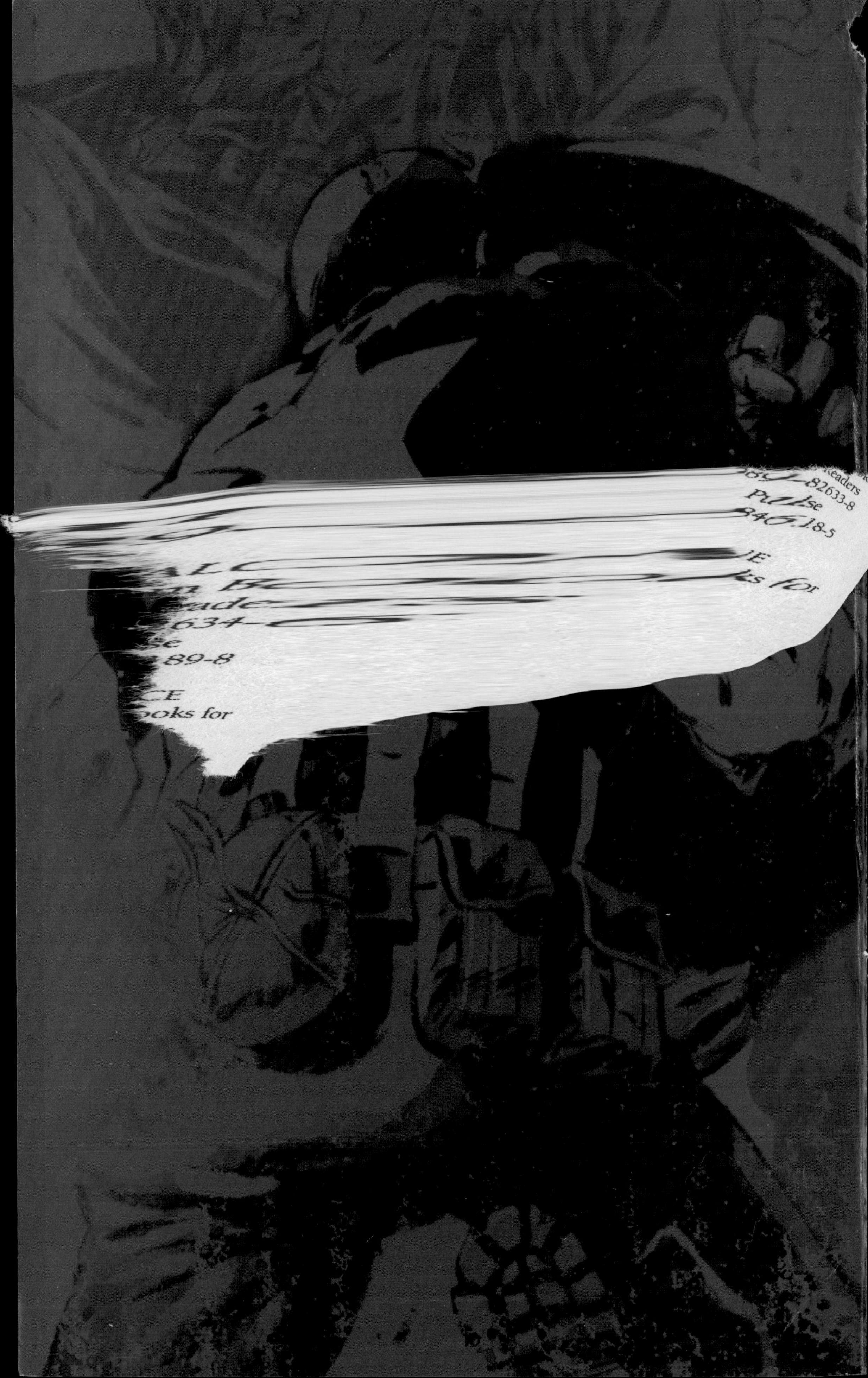

CAPTAIN AMERICA
RED MENACE

WRITER: Ed Brubaker
ART: Steve Epting
ADDITIONAL INKS (ISSUE #19): Mike Perkins
COLOR ART: Frank D'Armata
LETTERER: Virtual Calligraphy's
Joe Caramagna
ASSISTANT EDITORS: Molly Lazer &
Aubrey Sitterson
EDITOR: Tom Brevoort

Captain America created
by Joe Simon & Jack Kirby

COLLECTION EDITOR: Jennifer Grünwald
ASSISTANT EDITOR: Michael Short
ASSOCIATE EDITOR: Mark D. Beazley
SENIOR EDITOR, SPECIAL PROJECTS: Jeff Youngquist
VICE PRESIDENT OF SALES: David Gabriel
PRODUCTION: Jerron Quality Color
VICE PRESIDENT OF CREATIVE: Tom Marvelli

EDITOR IN CHIEF: Joe Quesada
PUBLISHER: Dan Buckley

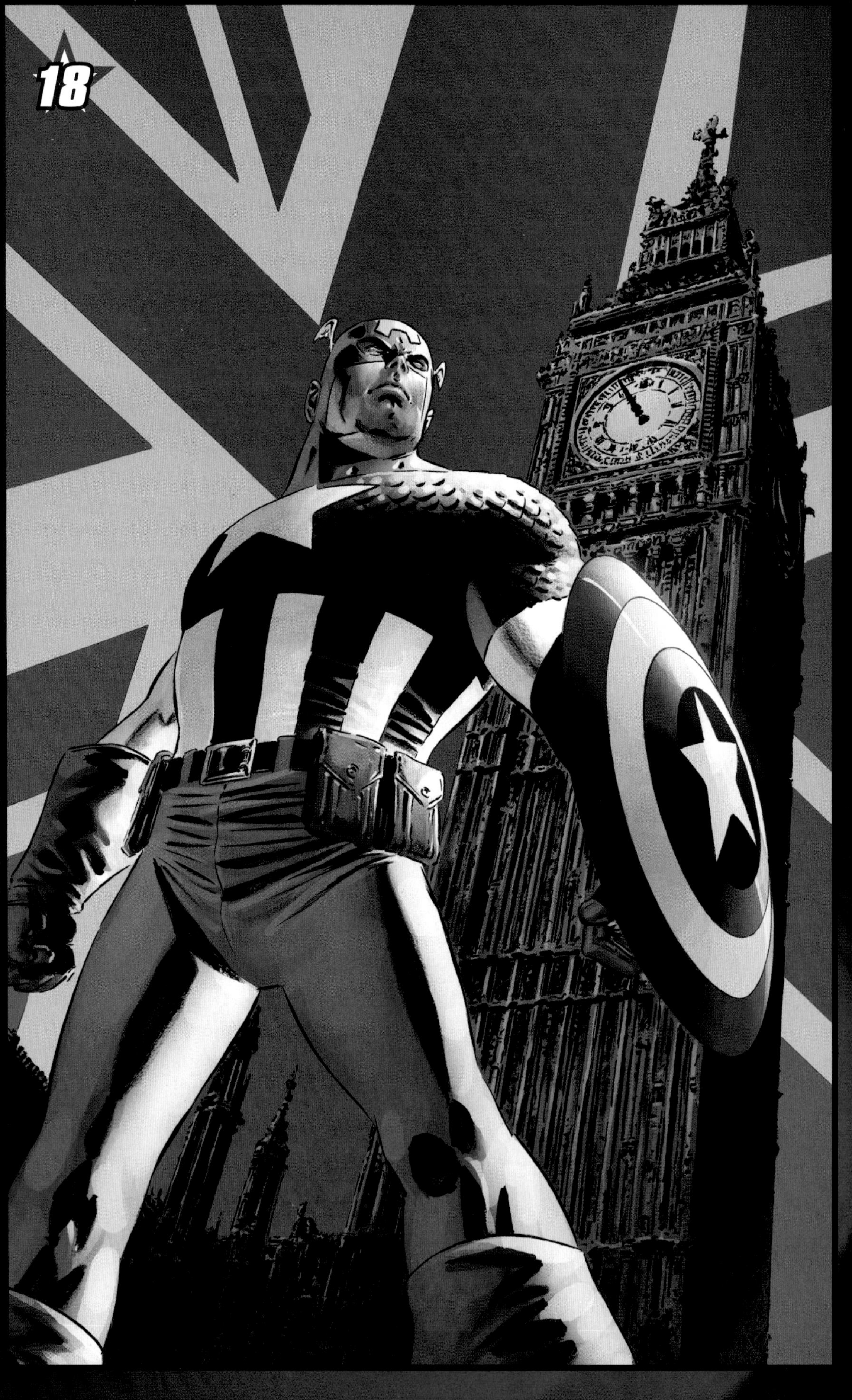
18

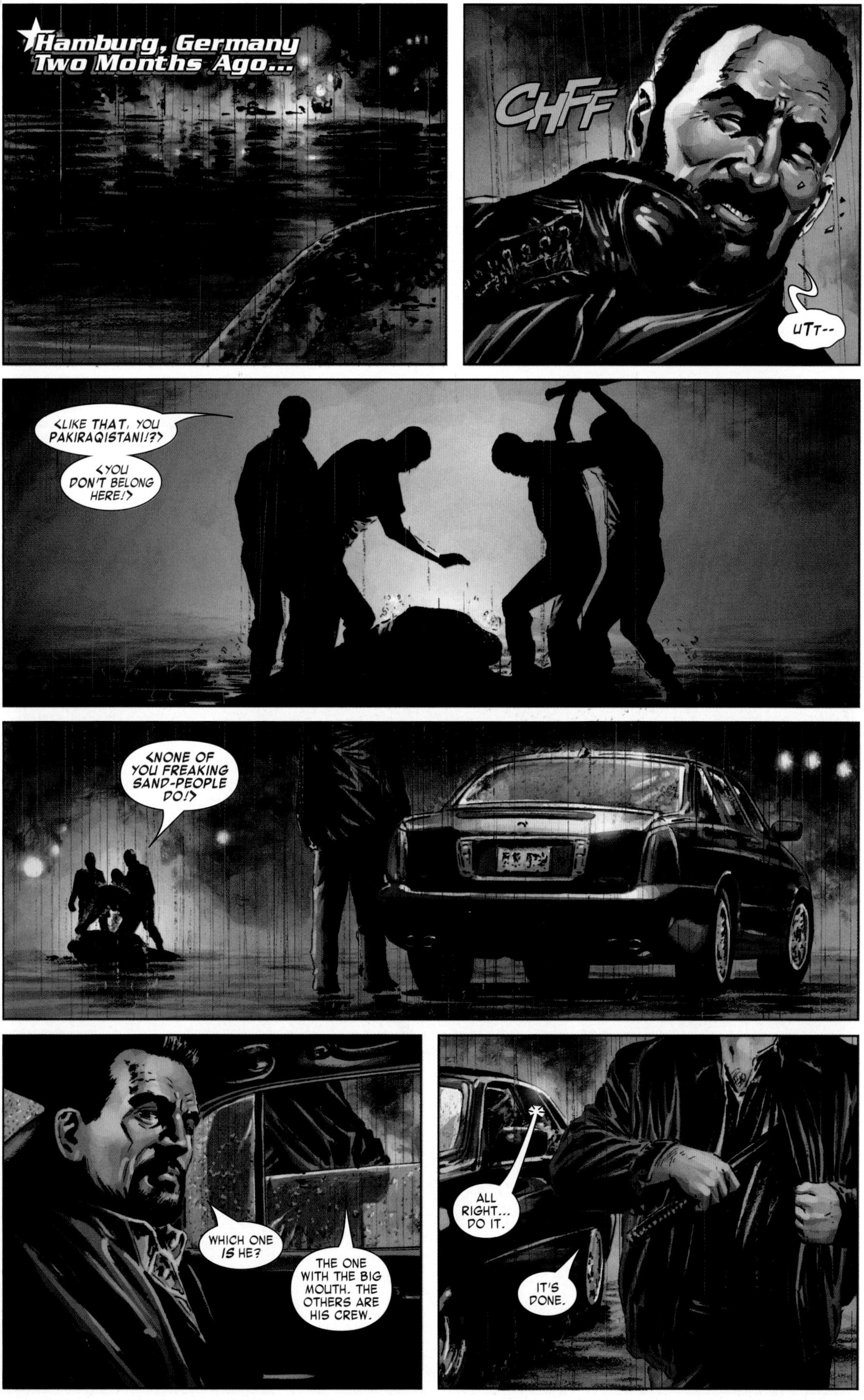
Hamburg, Germany
Two Months Ago...
CHFF
UTT--
<LIKE THAT, YOU PAKIRAQISTANI!?>
<YOU DON'T BELONG HERE!>
<NONE OF YOU FREAKING SAND-PEOPLE DO!>
WHICH ONE IS HE?
THE ONE WITH THE BIG MOUTH. THE OTHERS ARE HIS CREW.
ALL RIGHT... DO IT.
IT'S DONE.

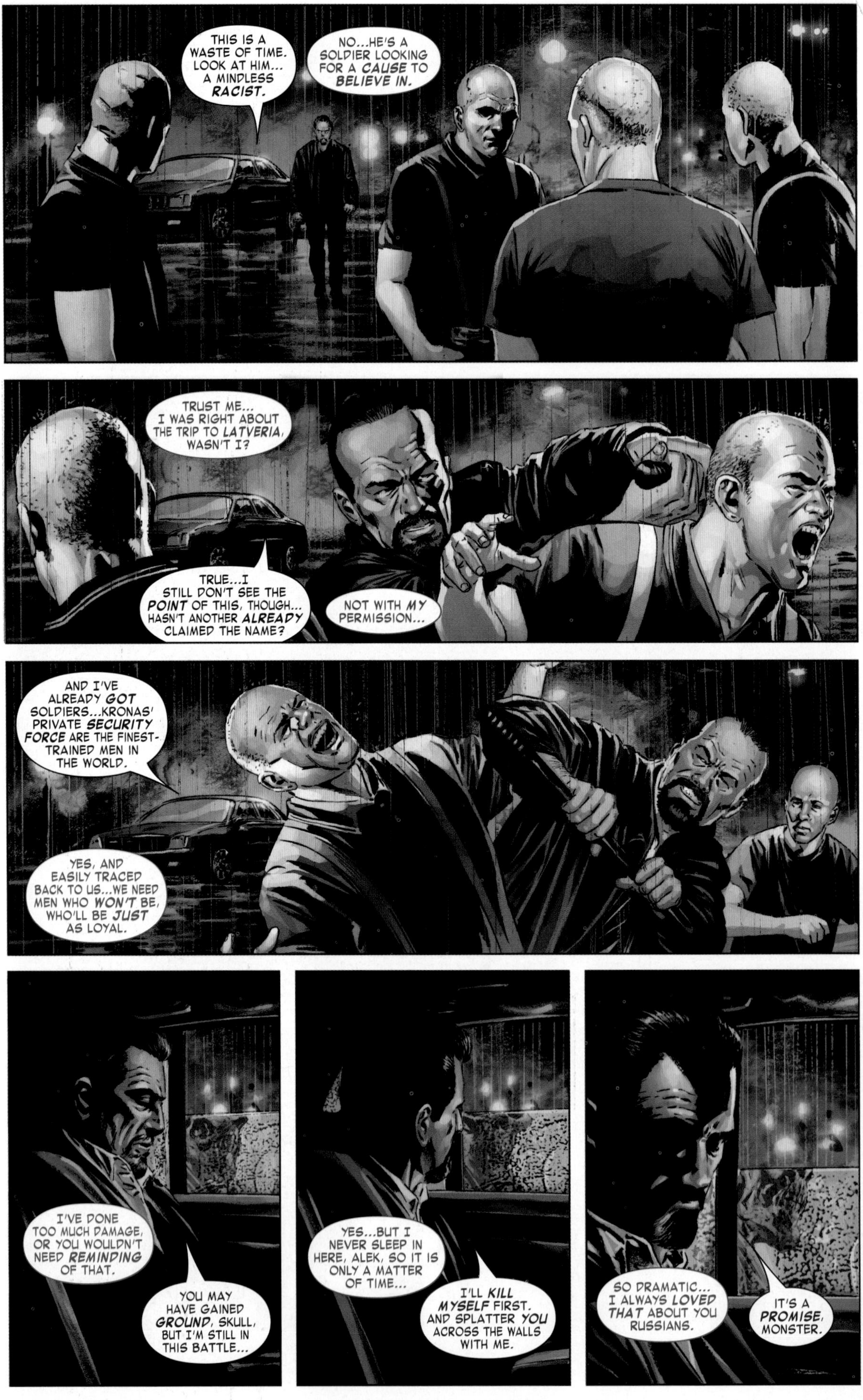
THIS IS A WASTE OF TIME. LOOK AT HIM... A MINDLESS RACIST.
NO...HE'S A SOLDIER LOOKING FOR A CAUSE TO BELIEVE IN.
TRUST ME... I WAS RIGHT ABOUT THE TRIP TO LATVERIA, WASN'T I?
TRUE...I STILL DON'T SEE THE POINT OF THIS, THOUGH... HASN'T ANOTHER ALREADY CLAIMED THE NAME?
NOT WITH MY PERMISSION...
AND I'VE ALREADY GOT SOLDIERS...KRONAS' PRIVATE SECURITY FORCE ARE THE FINEST-TRAINED MEN IN THE WORLD.
YES, AND EASILY TRACED BACK TO US...WE NEED MEN WHO WON'T BE, WHO'LL BE JUST AS LOYAL.
I'VE DONE TOO MUCH DAMAGE, OR YOU WOULDN'T NEED REMINDING OF THAT.
YOU MAY HAVE GAINED GROUND, SKULL, BUT I'M STILL IN THIS BATTLE...
YES...BUT I NEVER SLEEP IN HERE, ALEK, SO IT IS ONLY A MATTER OF TIME...
I'LL KILL MYSELF FIRST. AND SPLATTER YOU ACROSS THE WALLS WITH ME.
SO DRAMATIC... I ALWAYS LOVED THAT ABOUT YOU RUSSIANS.
IT'S A PROMISE, MONSTER.

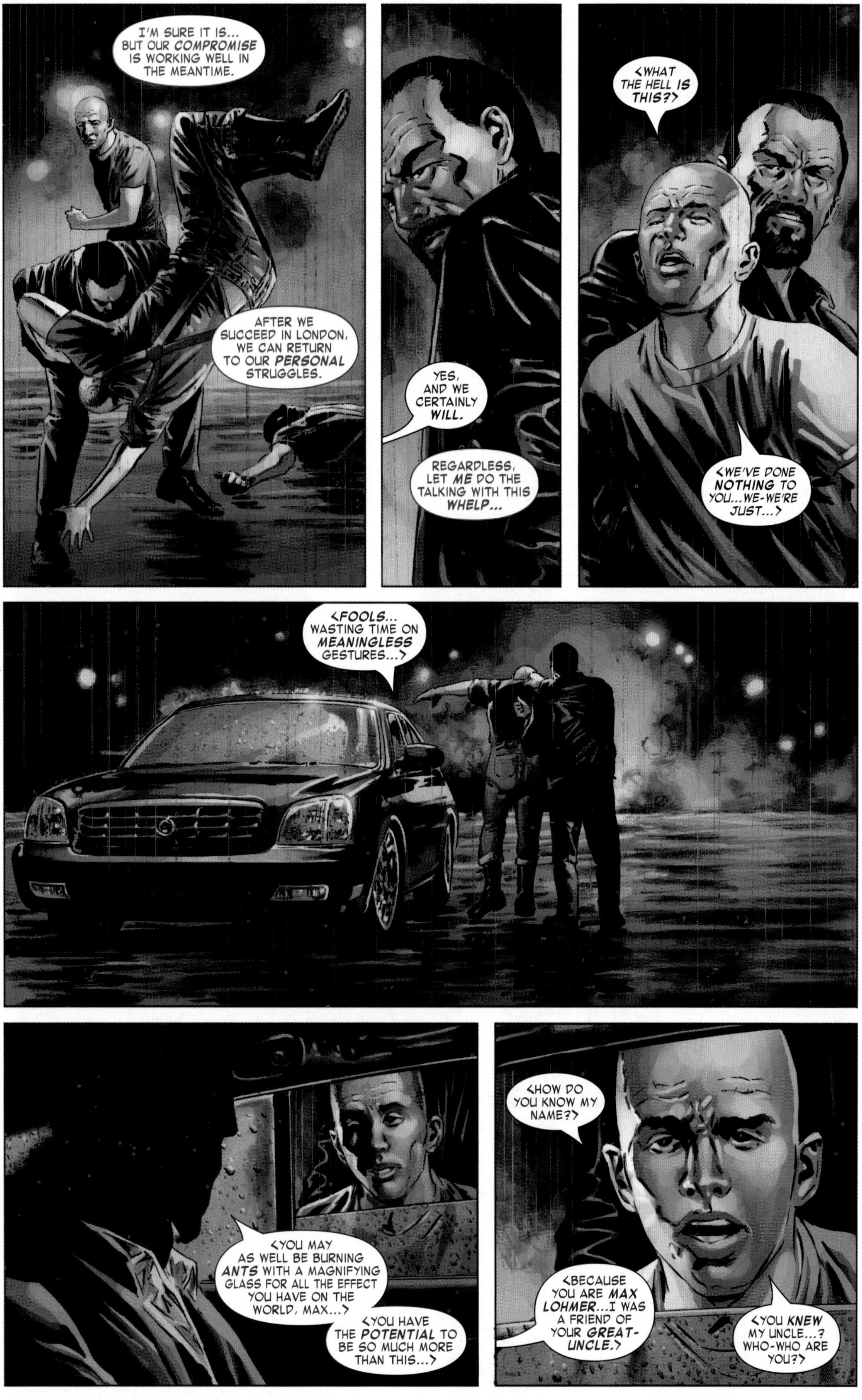
I'M SURE IT IS... BUT OUR COMPROMISE IS WORKING WELL IN THE MEANTIME.
AFTER WE SUCCEED IN LONDON, WE CAN RETURN TO OUR PERSONAL STRUGGLES.
YES, AND WE CERTAINLY WILL.
REGARDLESS, LET ME DO THE TALKING WITH THIS WHELP...
<WHAT THE HELL IS THIS?>
<WE'VE DONE NOTHING TO YOU...WE-WE'RE JUST...>
<FOOLS... WASTING TIME ON MEANINGLESS GESTURES...>
<YOU MAY AS WELL BE BURNING ANTS WITH A MAGNIFYING GLASS FOR ALL THE EFFECT YOU HAVE ON THE WORLD, MAX...>
<YOU HAVE THE POTENTIAL TO BE SO MUCH MORE THAN THIS...>
<HOW DO YOU KNOW MY NAME?>
<BECAUSE YOU ARE MAX LOHMER...I WAS A FRIEND OF YOUR GREAT-UNCLE.>
<YOU KNEW MY UNCLE...? WHO-WHO ARE YOU?>

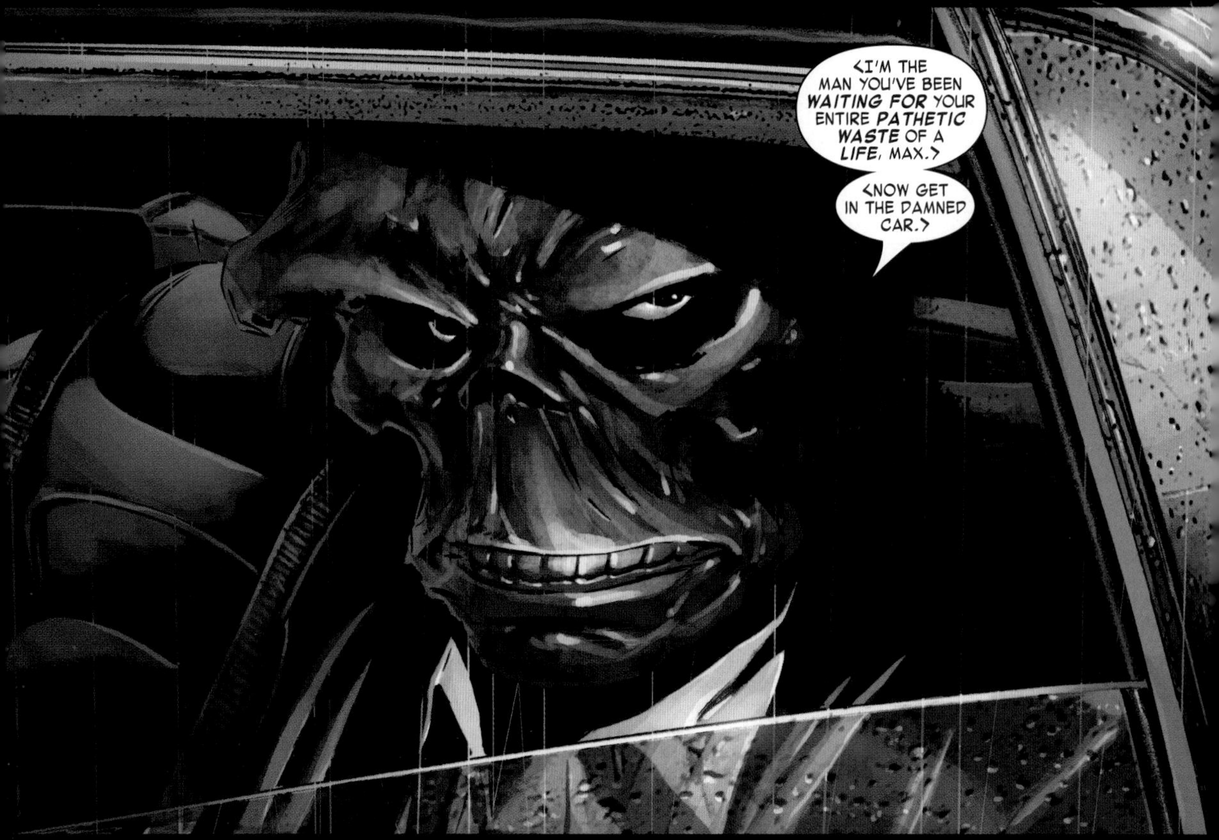
<I'M THE MAN YOU'VE BEEN WAITING FOR YOUR ENTIRE PATHETIC WASTE OF A LIFE, MAX.>
<NOW GET IN THE DAMNED CAR.>

Previously In Captain America...

Since the apparent death of the Red Skull, Cap's life has been a roller-coaster ride--from the reappearance of his WW2-era partner Bucky to a WMD going off on American soil, it's been a nightmarish trip. Now Cap is on a quest to track down his old partner, who he believes is gunning for the man who was until recently pulling his strings, ex-Soviet General Aleksander Lukin. But what no one yet knows is that the Red Skull is alive and well, inside the mind of General Lukin, where the two of them are waging a silent battle for control.

TWENTY-FIRST CENTURY BLITZ

PART ONE OF FOUR

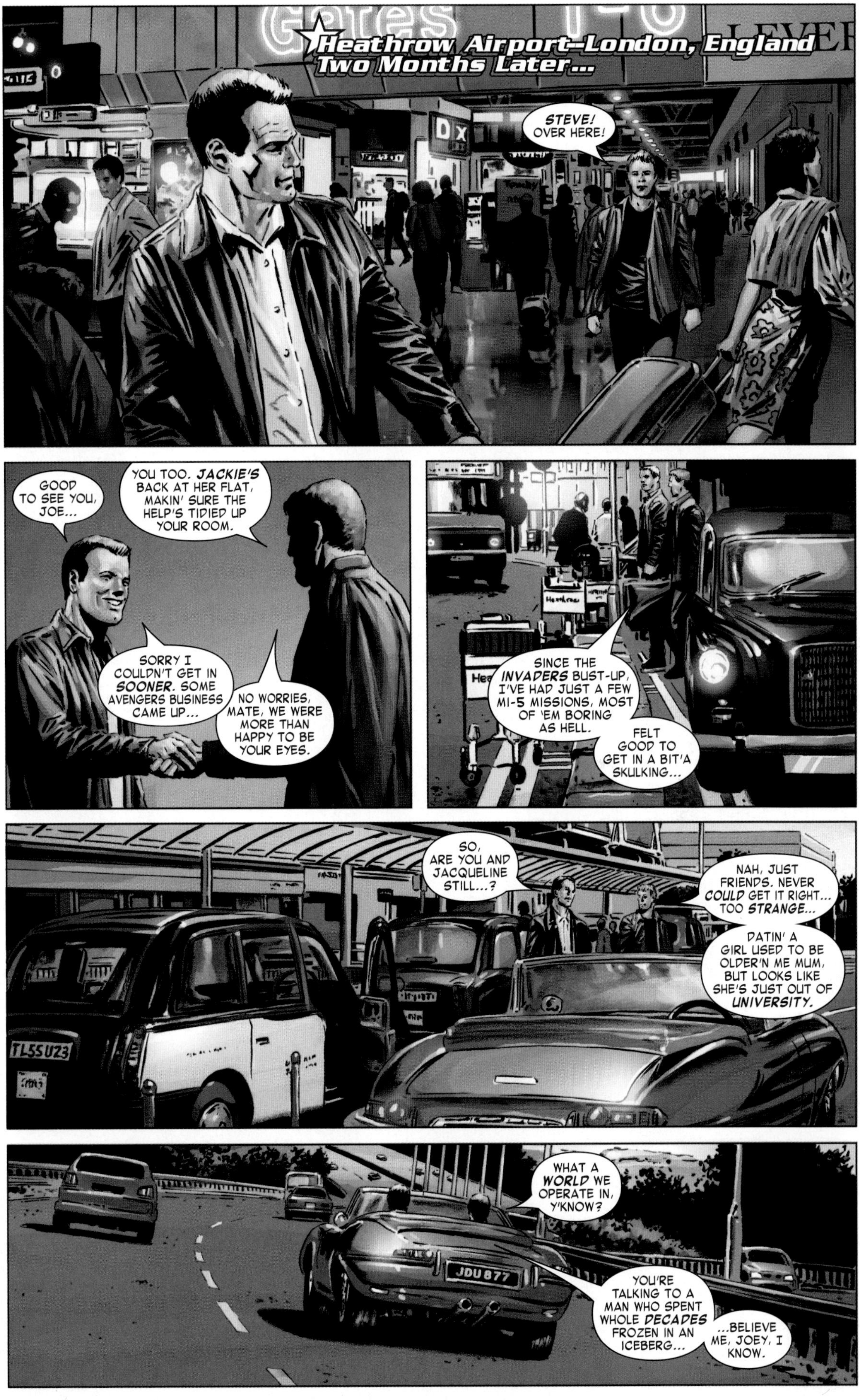
Heathrow Airport--London, England
Two Months Later...
STEVE! OVER HERE!
GOOD TO SEE YOU, JOE...
YOU TOO. JACKIE'S BACK AT HER FLAT, MAKIN' SURE THE HELP'S TIDIED UP YOUR ROOM.
SORRY I COULDN'T GET IN SOONER. SOME AVENGERS BUSINESS CAME UP...
NO WORRIES, MATE, WE WERE MORE THAN HAPPY TO BE YOUR EYES.
SINCE THE INVADERS BUST-UP, I'VE HAD JUST A FEW MI-5 MISSIONS, MOST OF 'EM BORING AS HELL.
FELT GOOD TO GET IN A BIT'A SKULKING...
SO, ARE YOU AND JACQUELINE STILL...?
NAH, JUST FRIENDS. NEVER COULD GET IT RIGHT... TOO STRANGE...
DATIN' A GIRL USED TO BE OLDER'N ME MUM, BUT LOOKS LIKE SHE'S JUST OUT OF UNIVERSITY.
WHAT A WORLD WE OPERATE IN, Y'KNOW?
YOU'RE TALKING TO A MAN WHO SPENT WHOLE DECADES FROZEN IN AN ICEBERG...
...BELIEVE ME, JOEY, I KNOW.

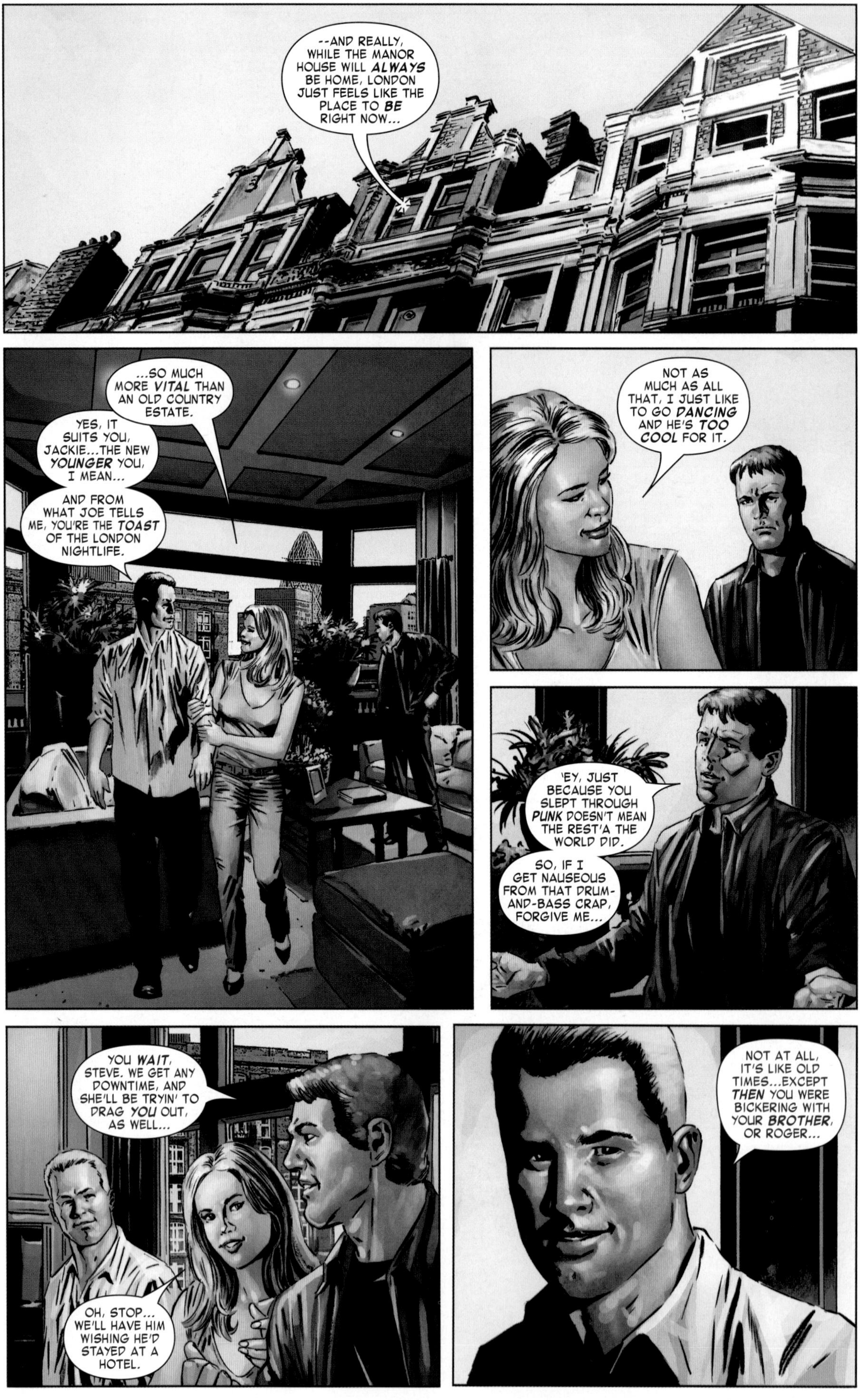
--AND REALLY, WHILE THE MANOR HOUSE WILL ALWAYS BE HOME, LONDON JUST FEELS LIKE THE PLACE TO BE RIGHT NOW...
...SO MUCH MORE VITAL THAN AN OLD COUNTRY ESTATE.
YES, IT SUITS YOU, JACKIE...THE NEW YOUNGER YOU, I MEAN...
AND FROM WHAT JOE TELLS ME, YOU'RE THE TOAST OF THE LONDON NIGHTLIFE.
NOT AS MUCH AS ALL THAT, I JUST LIKE TO GO DANCING AND HE'S TOO COOL FOR IT.
'EY, JUST BECAUSE YOU SLEPT THROUGH PUNK DOESN'T MEAN THE REST'A THE WORLD DID.
SO, IF I GET NAUSEOUS FROM THAT DRUM-AND-BASS CRAP, FORGIVE ME...
YOU WAIT, STEVE. WE GET ANY DOWNTIME, AND SHE'LL BE TRYIN' TO DRAG YOU OUT, AS WELL...
OH, STOP... WE'LL HAVE HIM WISHING HE'D STAYED AT A HOTEL.
NOT AT ALL, IT'S LIKE OLD TIMES...EXCEPT THEN YOU WERE BICKERING WITH YOUR BROTHER, OR ROGER...

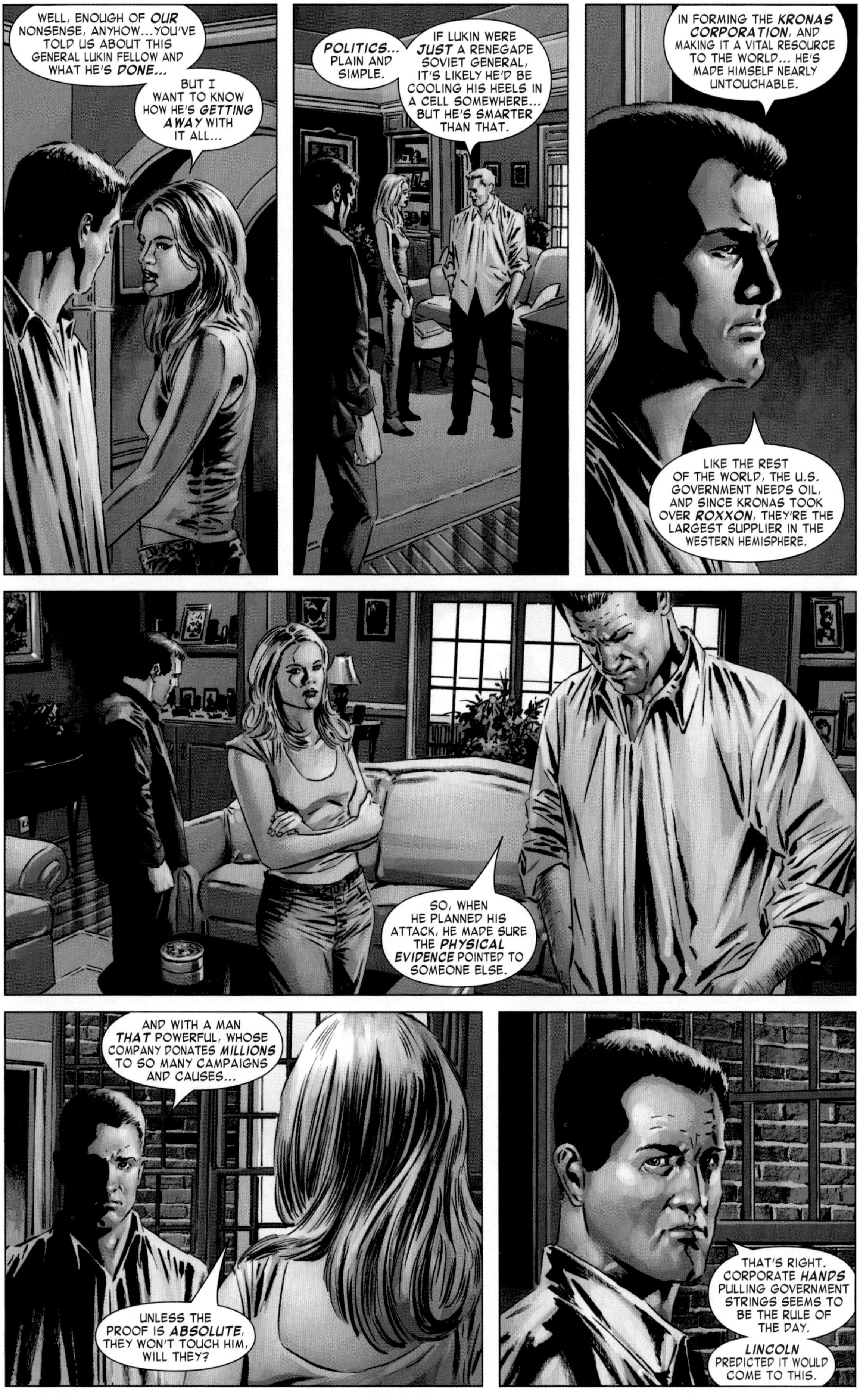
WELL, ENOUGH OF OUR NONSENSE, ANYHOW...YOU'VE TOLD US ABOUT THIS GENERAL LUKIN FELLOW AND WHAT HE'S DONE...
BUT I WANT TO KNOW HOW HE'S GETTING AWAY WITH IT ALL...
POLITICS... PLAIN AND SIMPLE.
IF LUKIN WERE JUST A RENEGADE SOVIET GENERAL, IT'S LIKELY HE'D BE COOLING HIS HEELS IN A CELL SOMEWHERE... BUT HE'S SMARTER THAN THAT.
IN FORMING THE KRONAS CORPORATION, AND MAKING IT A VITAL RESOURCE TO THE WORLD... HE'S MADE HIMSELF NEARLY UNTOUCHABLE.
LIKE THE REST OF THE WORLD, THE U.S. GOVERNMENT NEEDS OIL, AND SINCE KRONAS TOOK OVER ROXXON, THEY'RE THE LARGEST SUPPLIER IN THE WESTERN HEMISPHERE.
SO, WHEN HE PLANNED HIS ATTACK, HE MADE SURE THE PHYSICAL EVIDENCE POINTED TO SOMEONE ELSE.
AND WITH A MAN THAT POWERFUL, WHOSE COMPANY DONATES MILLIONS TO SO MANY CAMPAIGNS AND CAUSES...
UNLESS THE PROOF IS ABSOLUTE, THEY WON'T TOUCH HIM, WILL THEY?
THAT'S RIGHT. CORPORATE HANDS PULLING GOVERNMENT STRINGS SEEMS TO BE THE RULE OF THE DAY.
LINCOLN PREDICTED IT WOULD COME TO THIS.

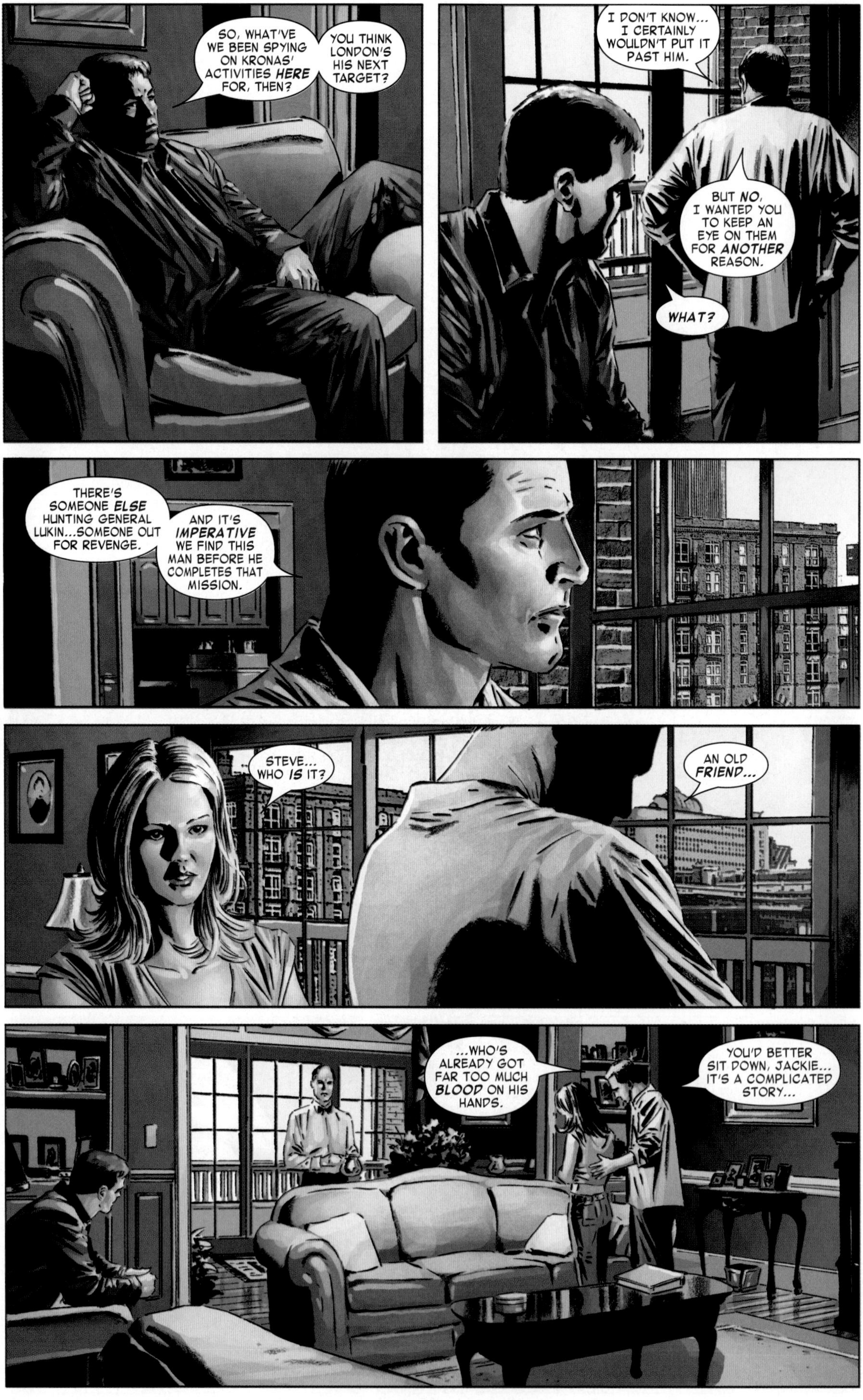
SO, WHAT'VE WE BEEN SPYING ON KRONAS' ACTIVITIES *HERE* FOR, THEN?
YOU THINK LONDON'S HIS NEXT TARGET?
I DON'T KNOW... I CERTAINLY WOULDN'T PUT IT PAST HIM.
BUT *NO*, I WANTED YOU TO KEEP AN EYE ON THEM FOR *ANOTHER* REASON.
WHAT?
THERE'S SOMEONE *ELSE* HUNTING GENERAL LUKIN...SOMEONE OUT FOR REVENGE.
AND IT'S *IMPERATIVE* WE FIND THIS MAN BEFORE HE COMPLETES THAT MISSION.
STEVE... WHO *IS* IT?
AN OLD *FRIEND*...
...WHO'S ALREADY GOT FAR TOO MUCH *BLOOD* ON HIS HANDS.
YOU'D BETTER SIT DOWN, JACKIE... IT'S A COMPLICATED STORY...

JUST THIS...

RIGHT. THANKS...

MONDAY MARCH 7 2005   thestale.com   TIM

GALA OPENING DRA
RECLUSIVE CEO TO LIME

International
Corp. Kronas'
London HQ
One

FATAL I-26 PILEUP

International
Corp. Kronas'
London HQ
Opens In
One Week

RE

ONE MORE WEEK, YOU SON OF A--

STOP! STOP HIM!

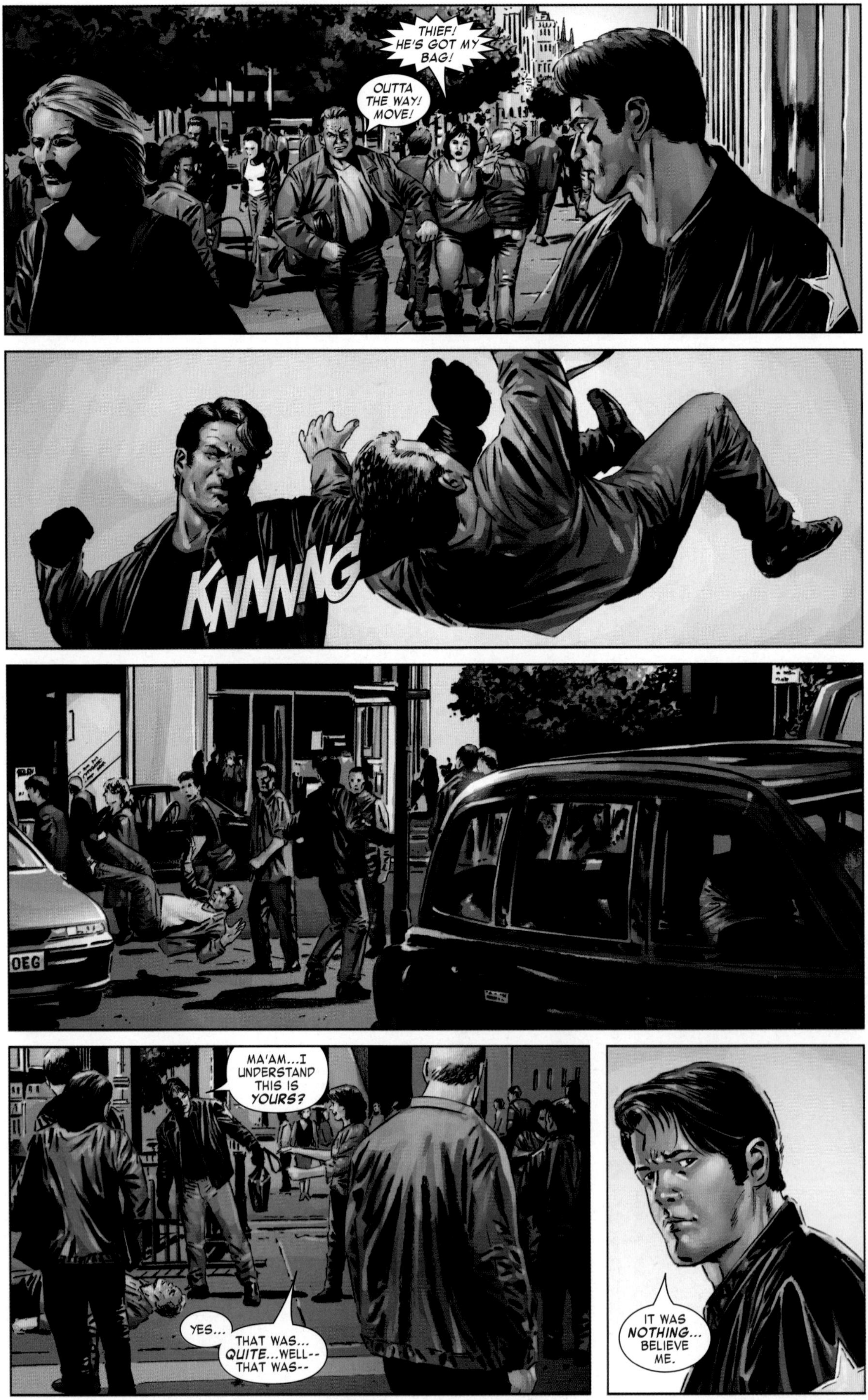
THIEF! HE'S GOT MY BAG!
OUTTA THE WAY! MOVE!
KNNNNG
MA'AM...I UNDERSTAND THIS IS *YOURS?*
YES...
THAT WAS... *QUITE*...WELL-- THAT WAS--
IT WAS *NOTHING*... BELIEVE ME.

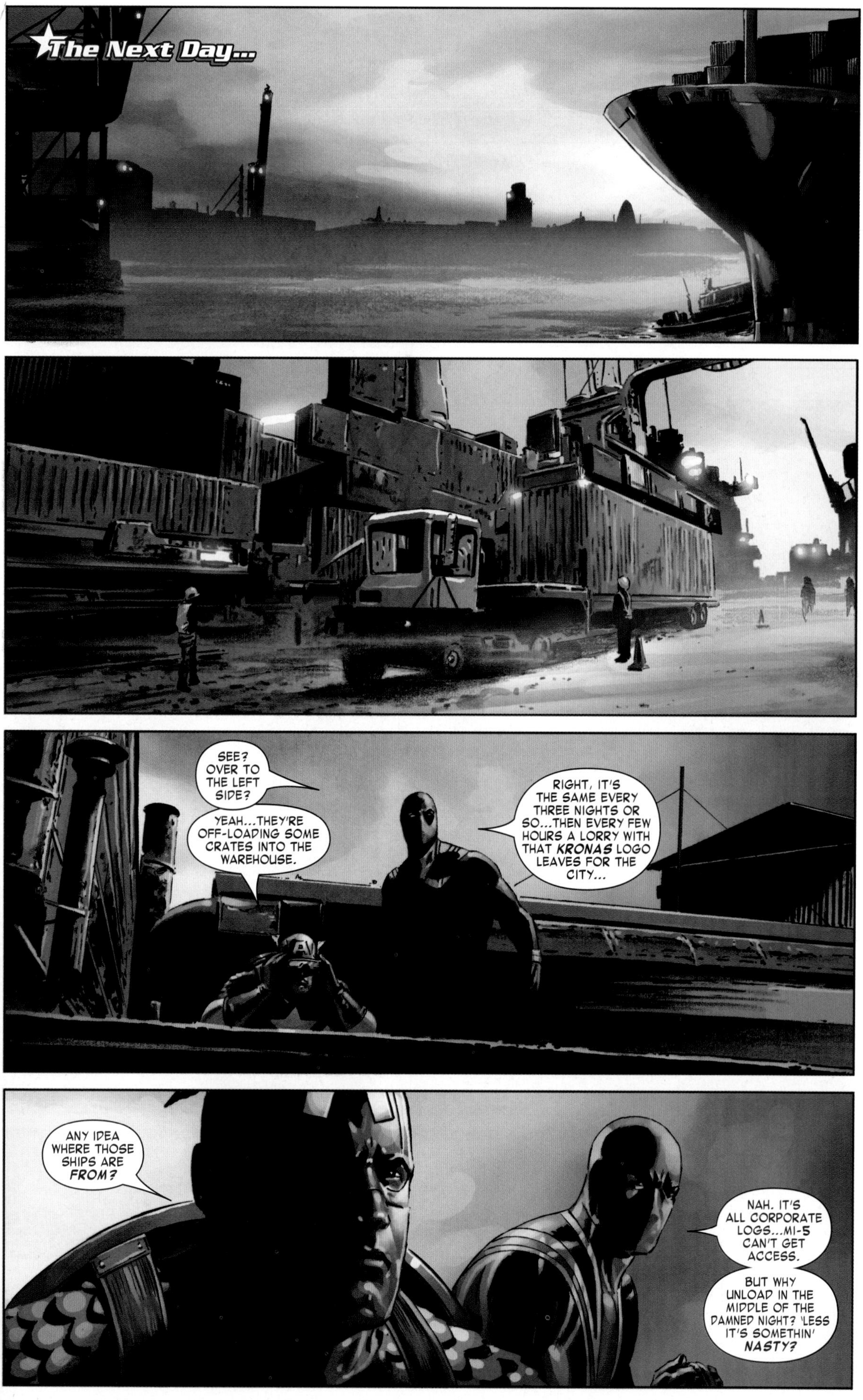
The Next Day...
SEE? OVER TO THE LEFT SIDE?
YEAH...THEY'RE OFF-LOADING SOME CRATES INTO THE WAREHOUSE.
RIGHT, IT'S THE SAME EVERY THREE NIGHTS OR SO...THEN EVERY FEW HOURS A LORRY WITH THAT KRONAS LOGO LEAVES FOR THE CITY...
ANY IDEA WHERE THOSE SHIPS ARE FROM?
NAH. IT'S ALL CORPORATE LOGS...MI-5 CAN'T GET ACCESS.
BUT WHY UNLOAD IN THE MIDDLE OF THE DAMNED NIGHT? 'LESS IT'S SOMETHIN' NASTY?

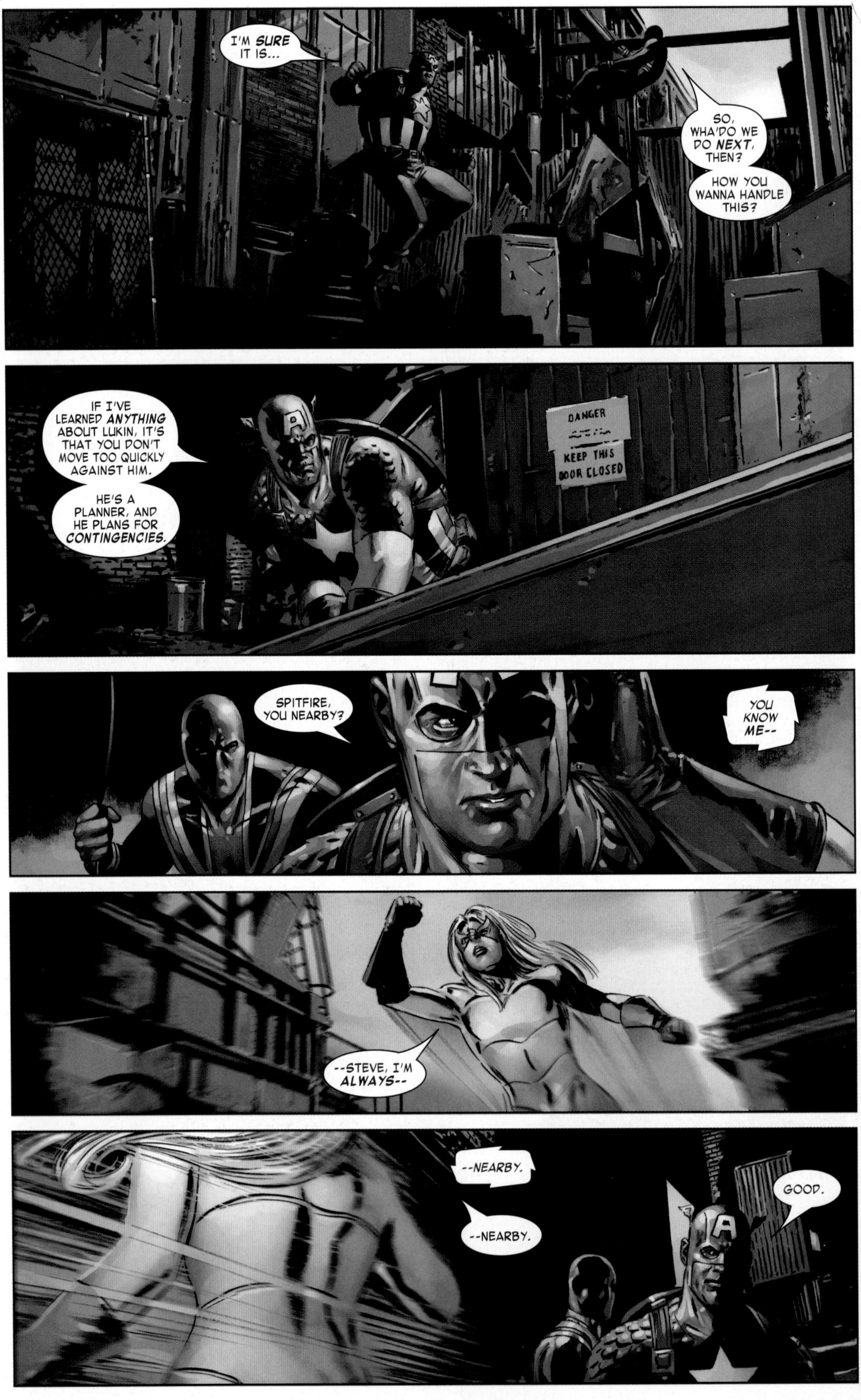
I'M SURE IT IS...
SO, WHA'DO WE DO NEXT, THEN?
HOW YOU WANNA HANDLE THIS?
IF I'VE LEARNED ANYTHING ABOUT LUKIN, IT'S THAT YOU DON'T MOVE TOO QUICKLY AGAINST HIM.
HE'S A PLANNER, AND HE PLANS FOR CONTINGENCIES.
DANGER
KEEP THIS DOOR CLOSED
SPITFIRE, YOU NEARBY?
YOU KNOW ME--
--STEVE, I'M ALWAYS--
--NEARBY.
--NEARBY.
GOOD.

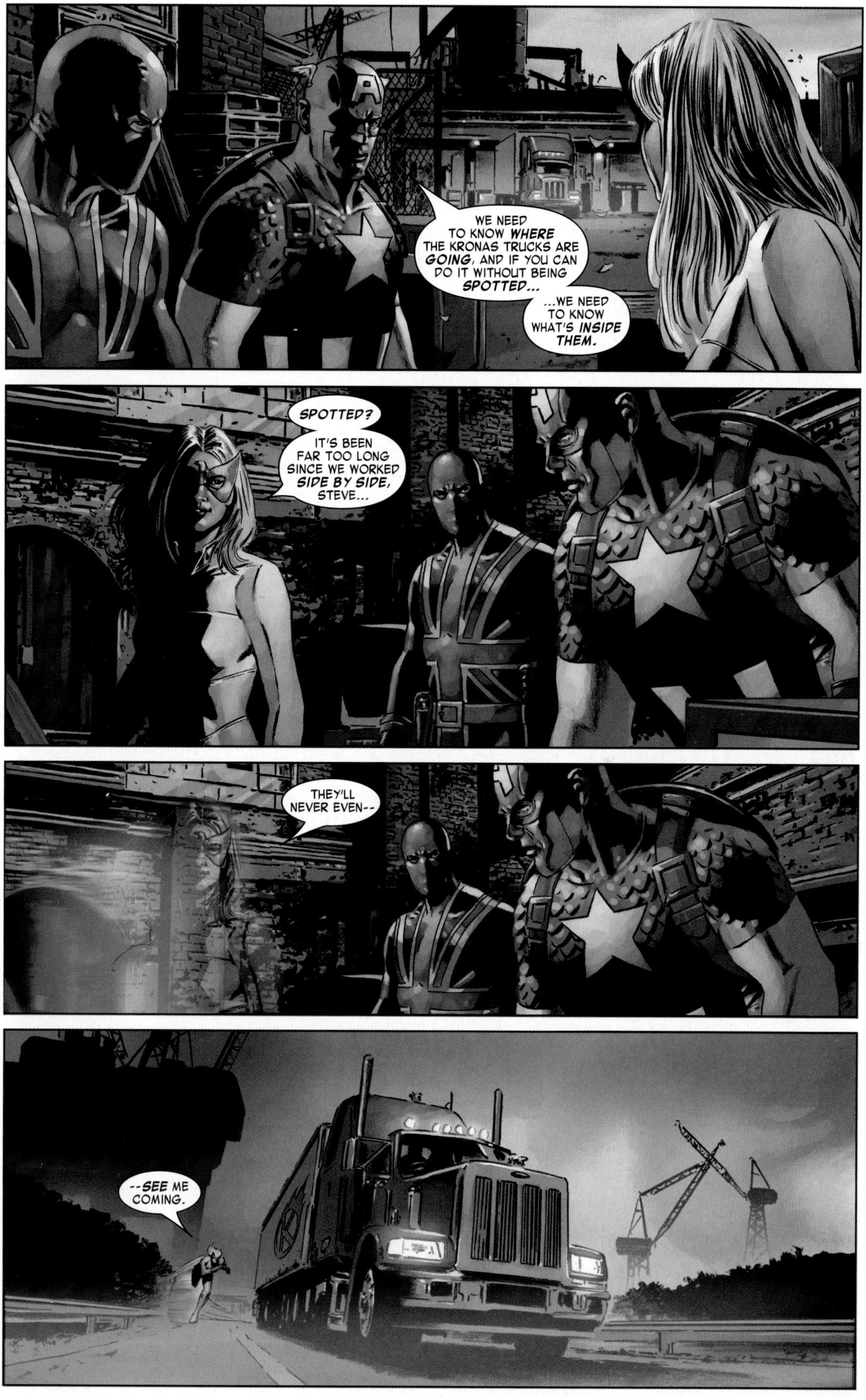
WE NEED TO KNOW WHERE THE KRONAS TRUCKS ARE GOING, AND IF YOU CAN DO IT WITHOUT BEING SPOTTED...
...WE NEED TO KNOW WHAT'S INSIDE THEM.
SPOTTED?
IT'S BEEN FAR TOO LONG SINCE WE WORKED SIDE BY SIDE, STEVE...
THEY'LL NEVER EVEN--
--SEE ME COMING.

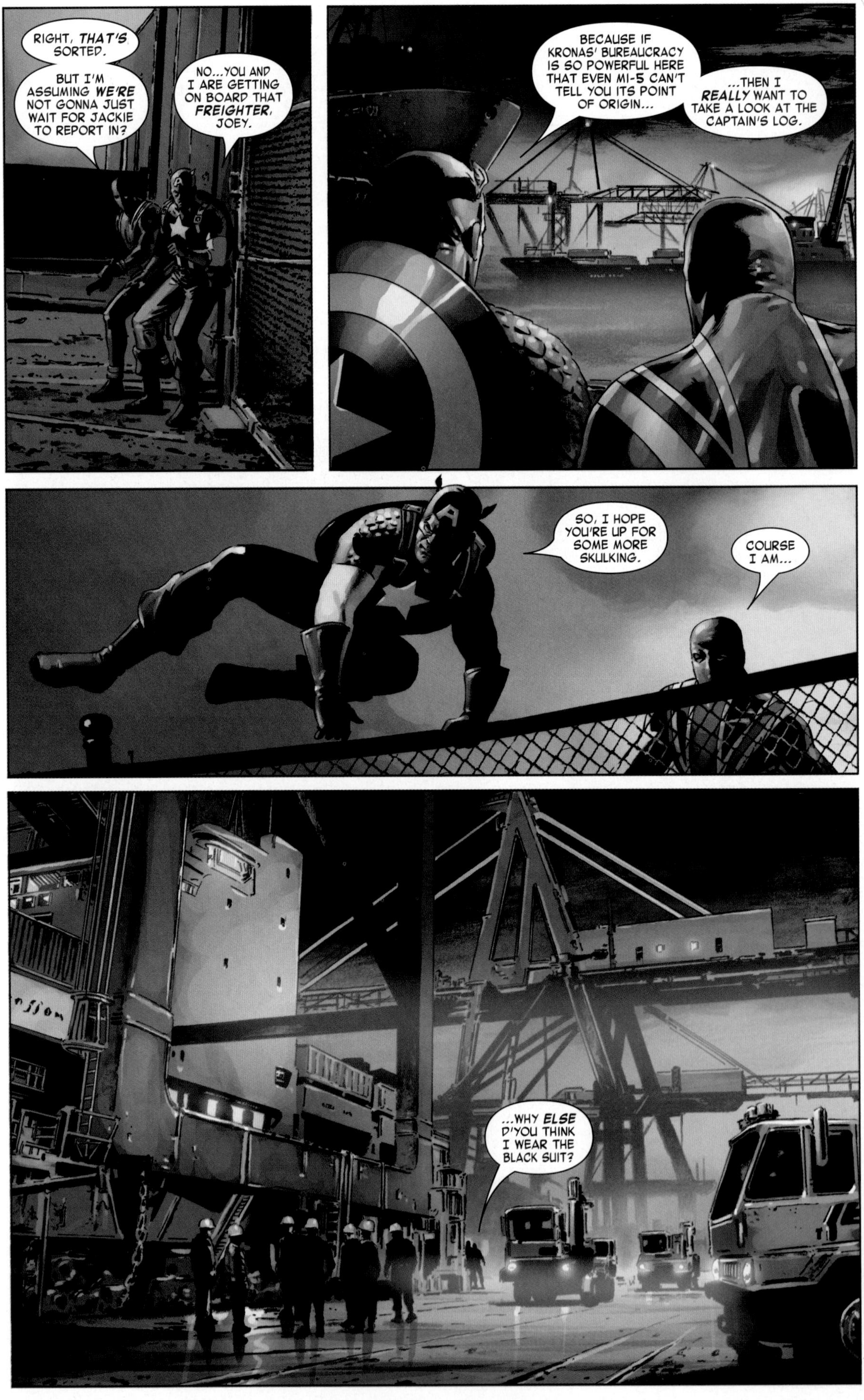
RIGHT, THAT'S SORTED.
BUT I'M ASSUMING WE'RE NOT GONNA JUST WAIT FOR JACKIE TO REPORT IN?
NO...YOU AND I ARE GETTING ON BOARD THAT FREIGHTER, JOEY.
BECAUSE IF KRONAS' BUREAUCRACY IS SO POWERFUL HERE THAT EVEN MI-5 CAN'T TELL YOU ITS POINT OF ORIGIN...
...THEN I REALLY WANT TO TAKE A LOOK AT THE CAPTAIN'S LOG.
SO, I HOPE YOU'RE UP FOR SOME MORE SKULKING.
COURSE I AM...
...WHY ELSE D'YOU THINK I WEAR THE BLACK SUIT?

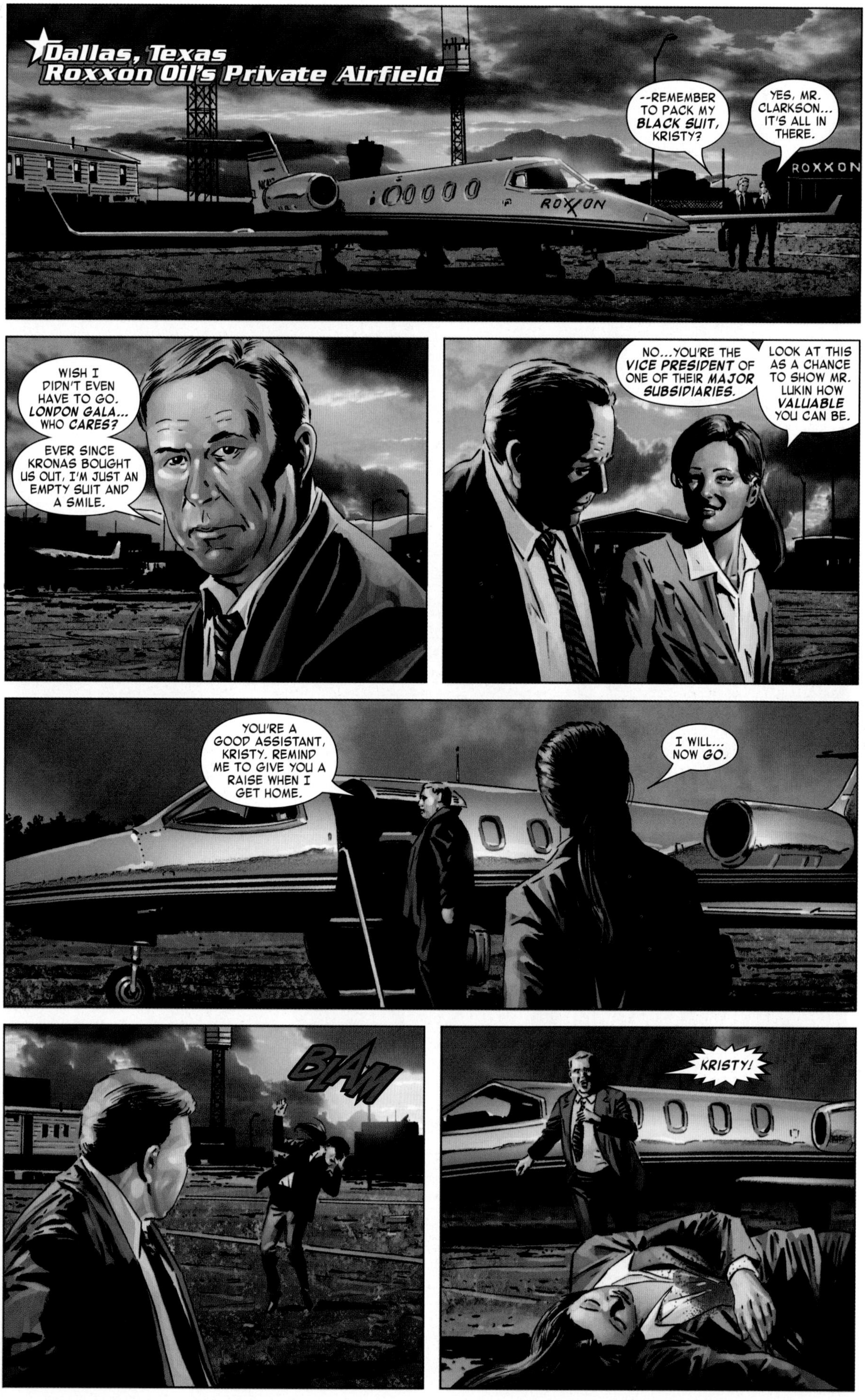
Dallas, Texas
Roxxon Oil's Private Airfield
--REMEMBER TO PACK MY BLACK SUIT, KRISTY?
YES, MR. CLARKSON... IT'S ALL IN THERE.
ROXXON
ROXXON
WISH I DIDN'T EVEN HAVE TO GO. LONDON GALA... WHO CARES?
EVER SINCE KRONAS BOUGHT US OUT, I'M JUST AN EMPTY SUIT AND A SMILE.
NO...YOU'RE THE VICE PRESIDENT OF ONE OF THEIR MAJOR SUBSIDIARIES.
LOOK AT THIS AS A CHANCE TO SHOW MR. LUKIN HOW VALUABLE YOU CAN BE.
YOU'RE A GOOD ASSISTANT, KRISTY. REMIND ME TO GIVE YOU A RAISE WHEN I GET HOME.
I WILL... NOW GO.
BLAM
KRISTY!

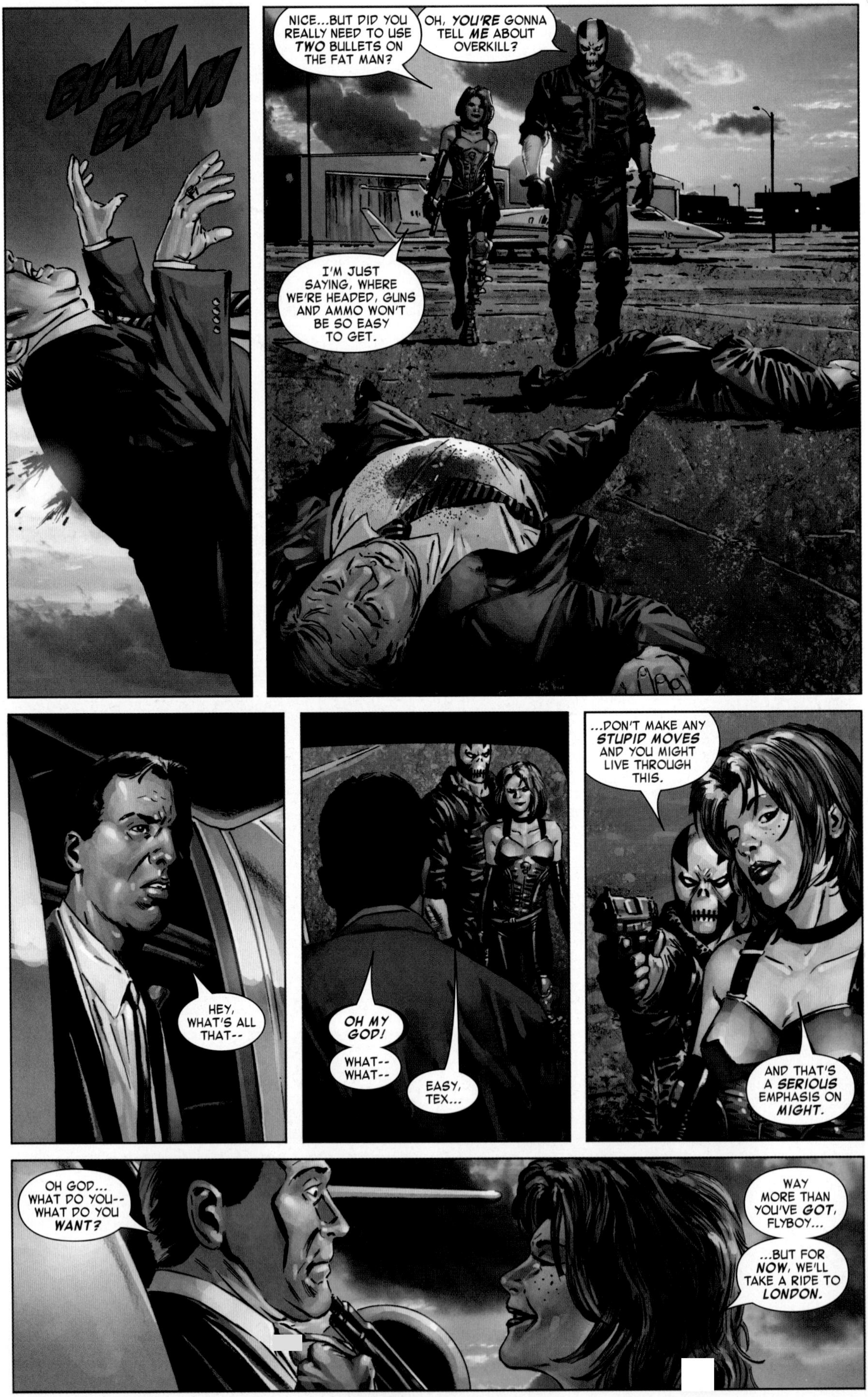
BLAM BLAM
NICE...BUT DID YOU REALLY NEED TO USE TWO BULLETS ON THE FAT MAN?
OH, YOU'RE GONNA TELL ME ABOUT OVERKILL?
I'M JUST SAYING, WHERE WE'RE HEADED, GUNS AND AMMO WON'T BE SO EASY TO GET.
HEY, WHAT'S ALL THAT--
OH MY GOD!
WHAT-- WHAT--
EASY, TEX...
...DON'T MAKE ANY STUPID MOVES AND YOU MIGHT LIVE THROUGH THIS.
AND THAT'S A SERIOUS EMPHASIS ON MIGHT.
OH GOD... WHAT DO YOU-- WHAT DO YOU WANT?
WAY MORE THAN YOU'VE GOT, FLYBOY...
...BUT FOR NOW, WE'LL TAKE A RIDE TO LONDON.

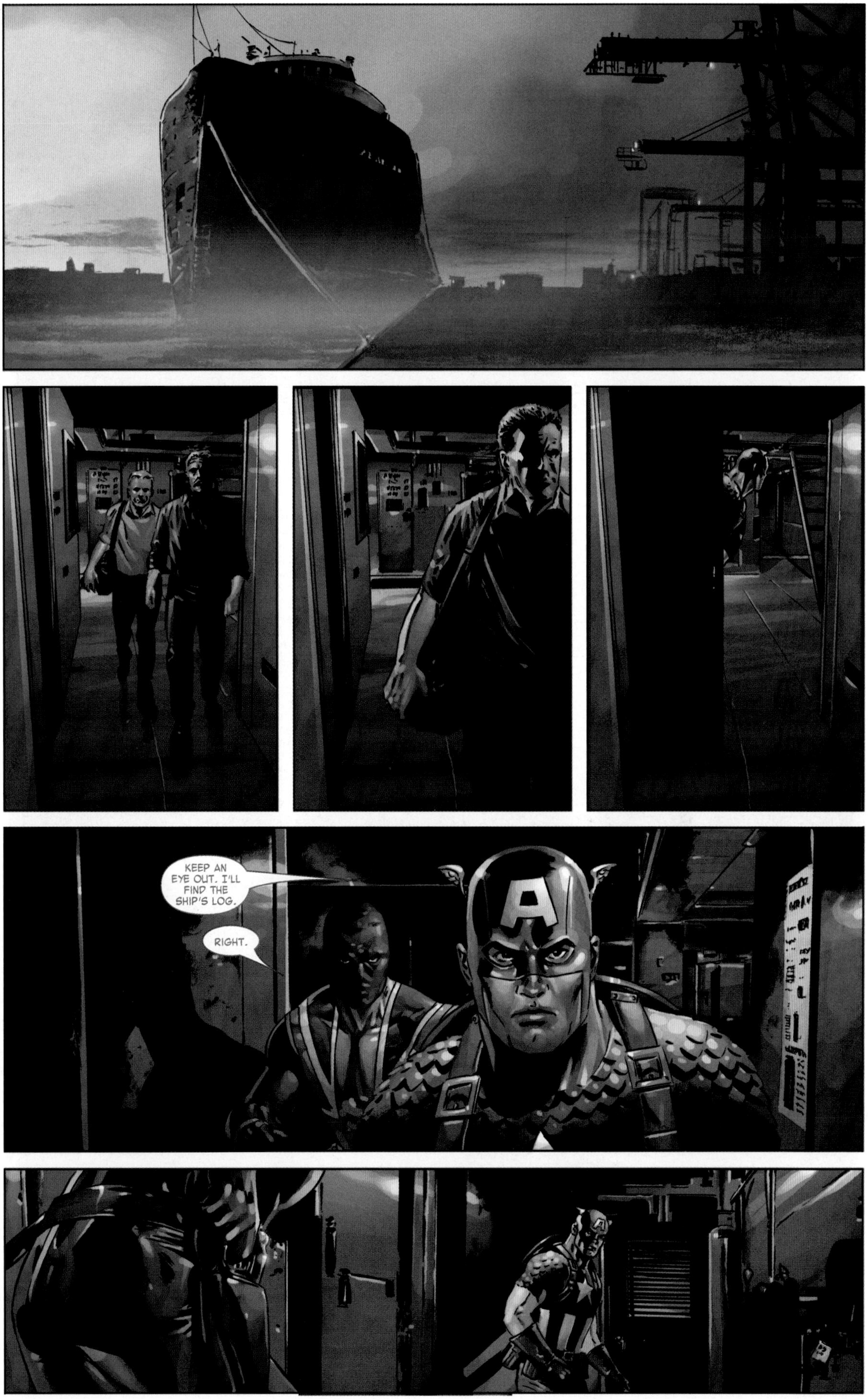
KEEP AN EYE OUT. I'LL FIND THE SHIP'S LOG.
RIGHT.

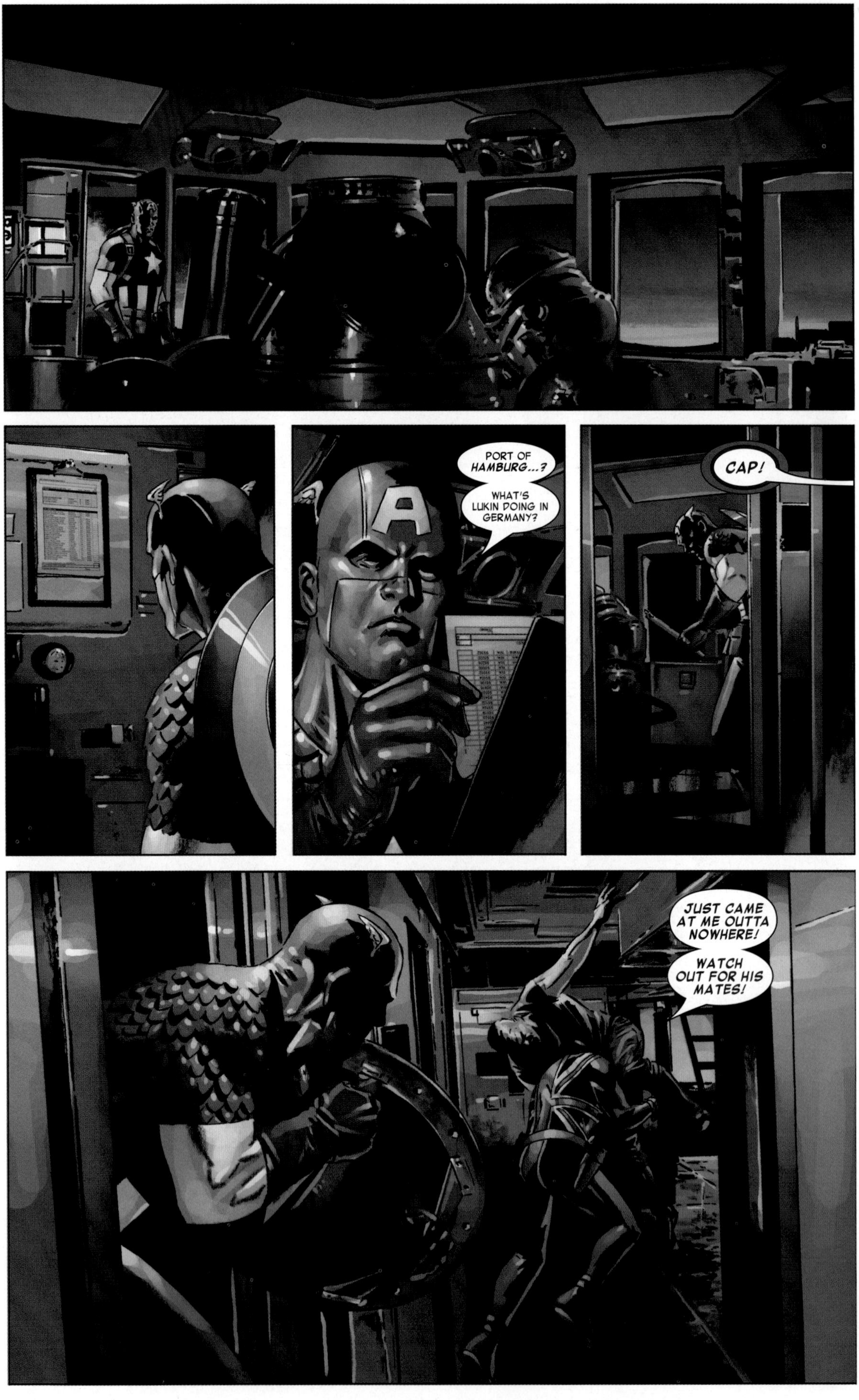
PORT OF HAMBURG...?
WHAT'S LUKIN DOING IN GERMANY?
CAP!
JUST CAME AT ME OUTTA NOWHERE!
WATCH OUT FOR HIS MATES!

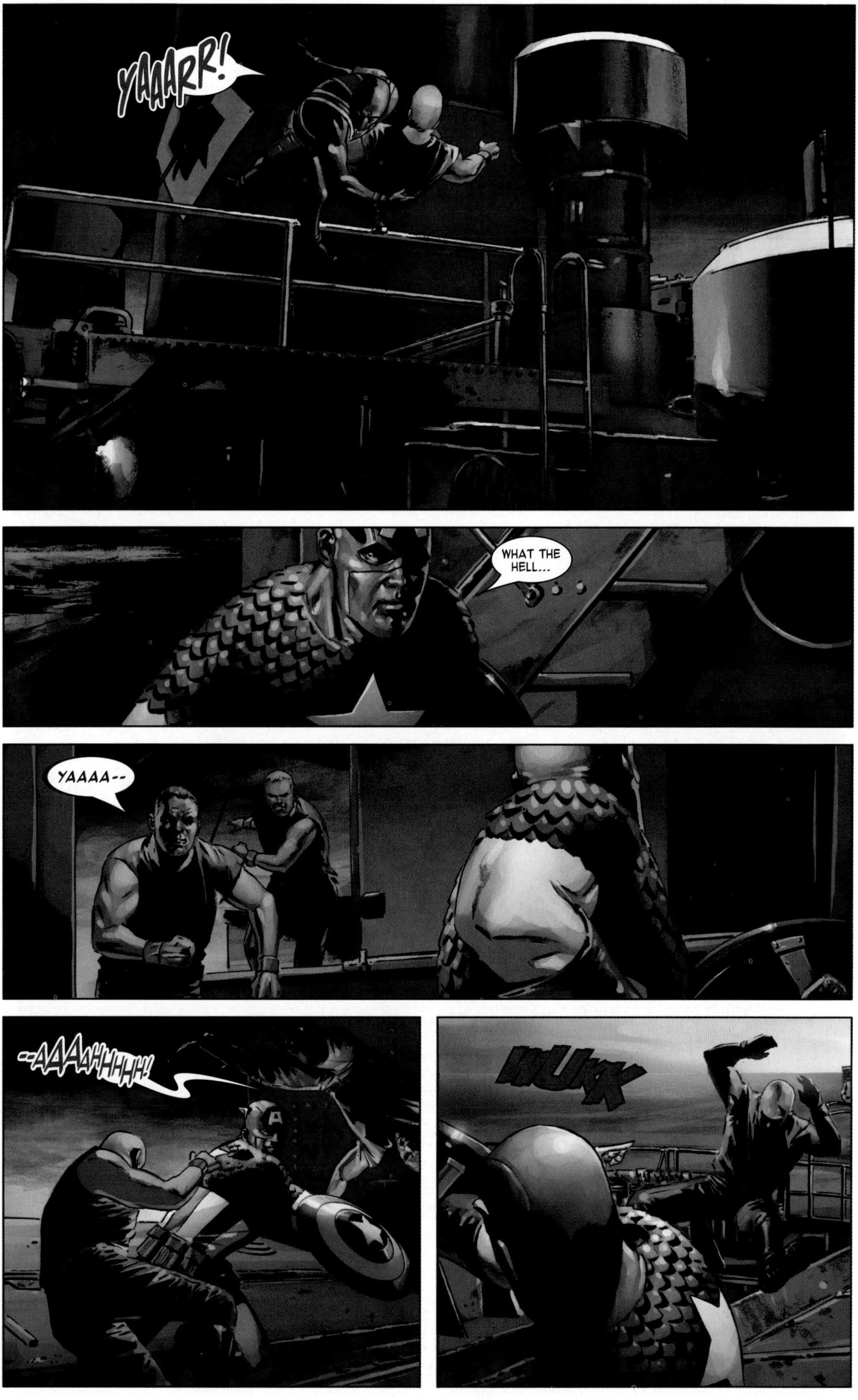
YAAARR!
WHAT THE HELL...
YAAAA--
--AAAAHHHH!
HUKK

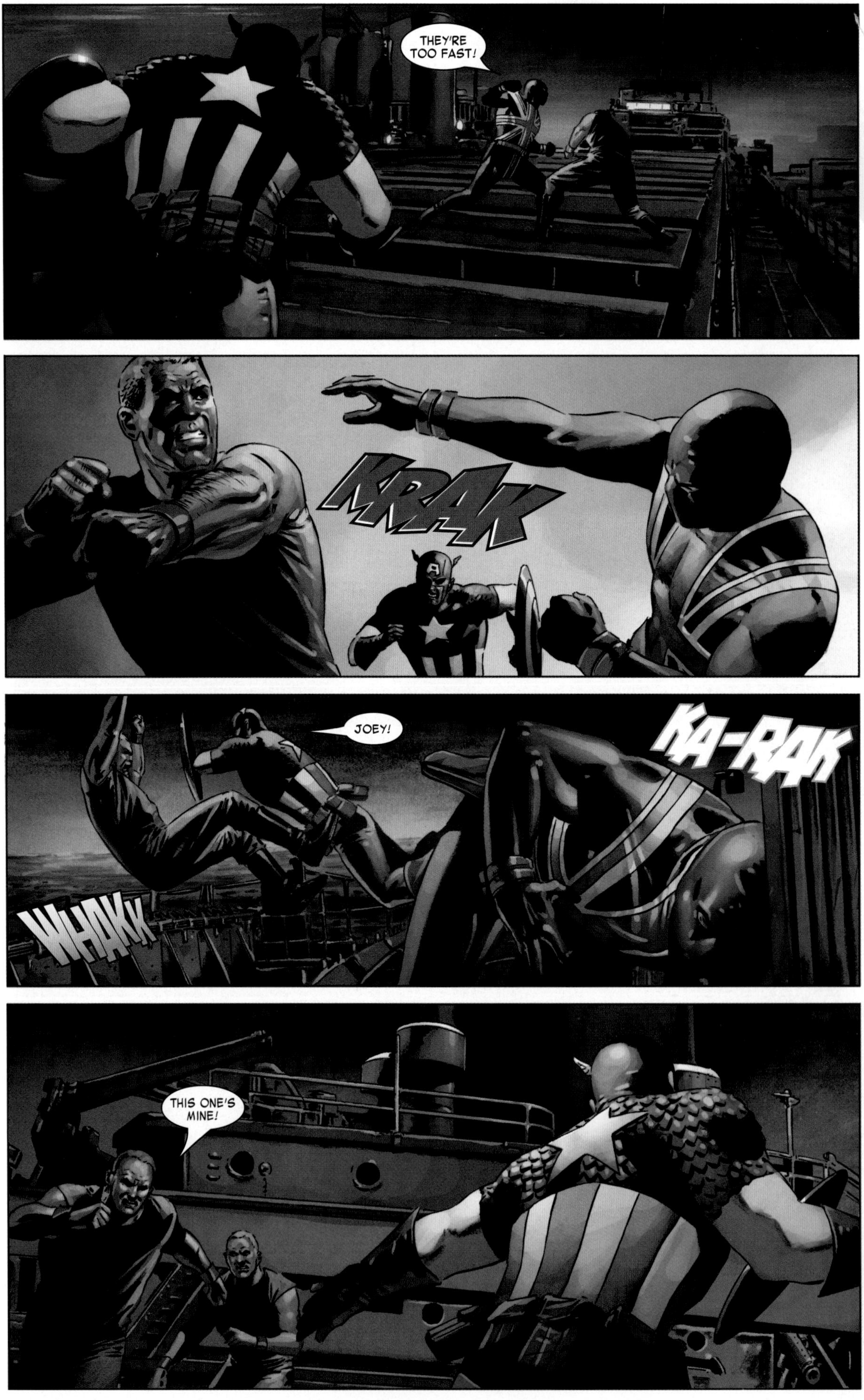
THEY'RE TOO FAST!
KRAK
JOEY!
KA-RAK
WHAKK
THIS ONE'S MINE!

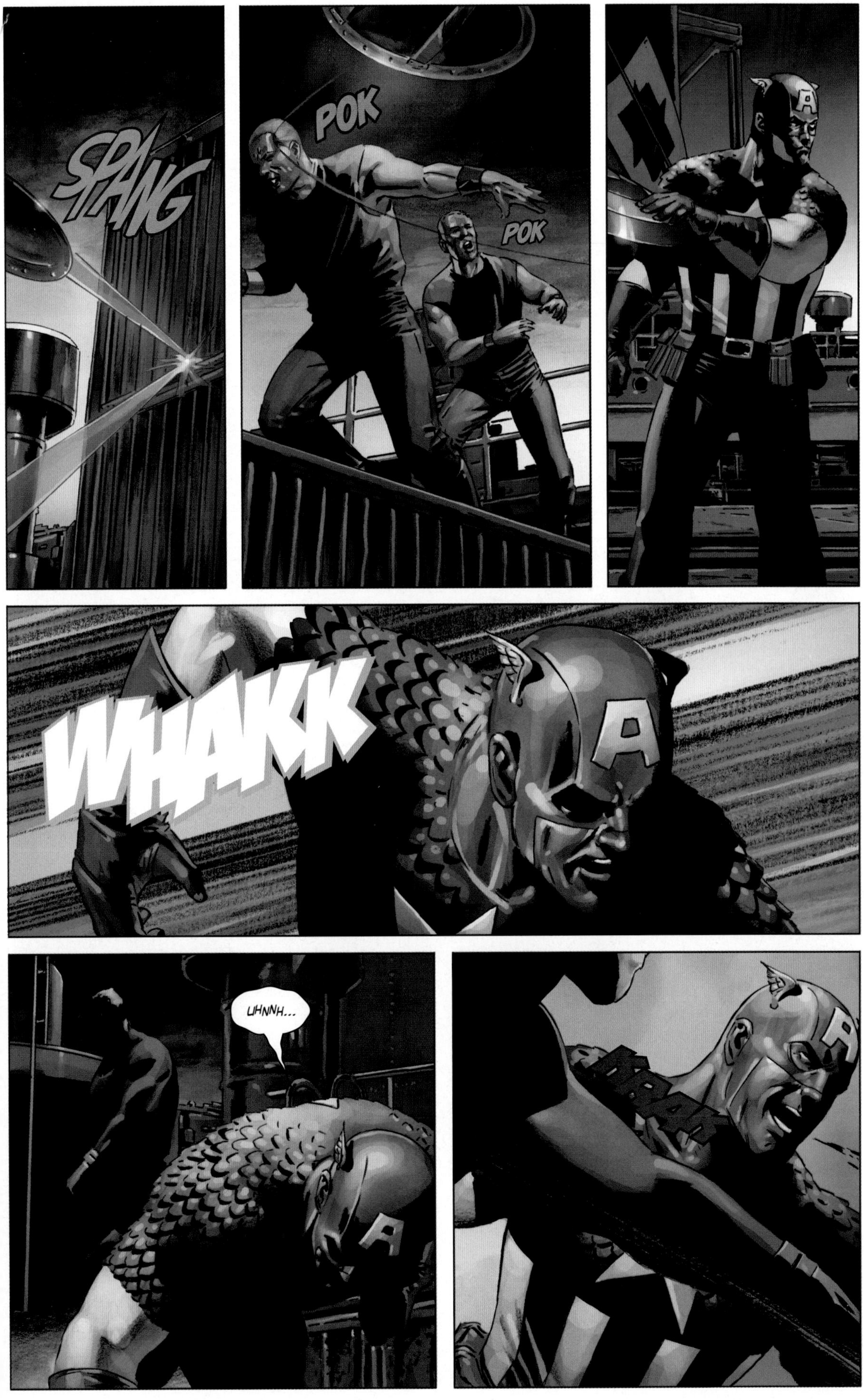
SPANG
POK
POK
WHAKK
UHNNH...
KRAK

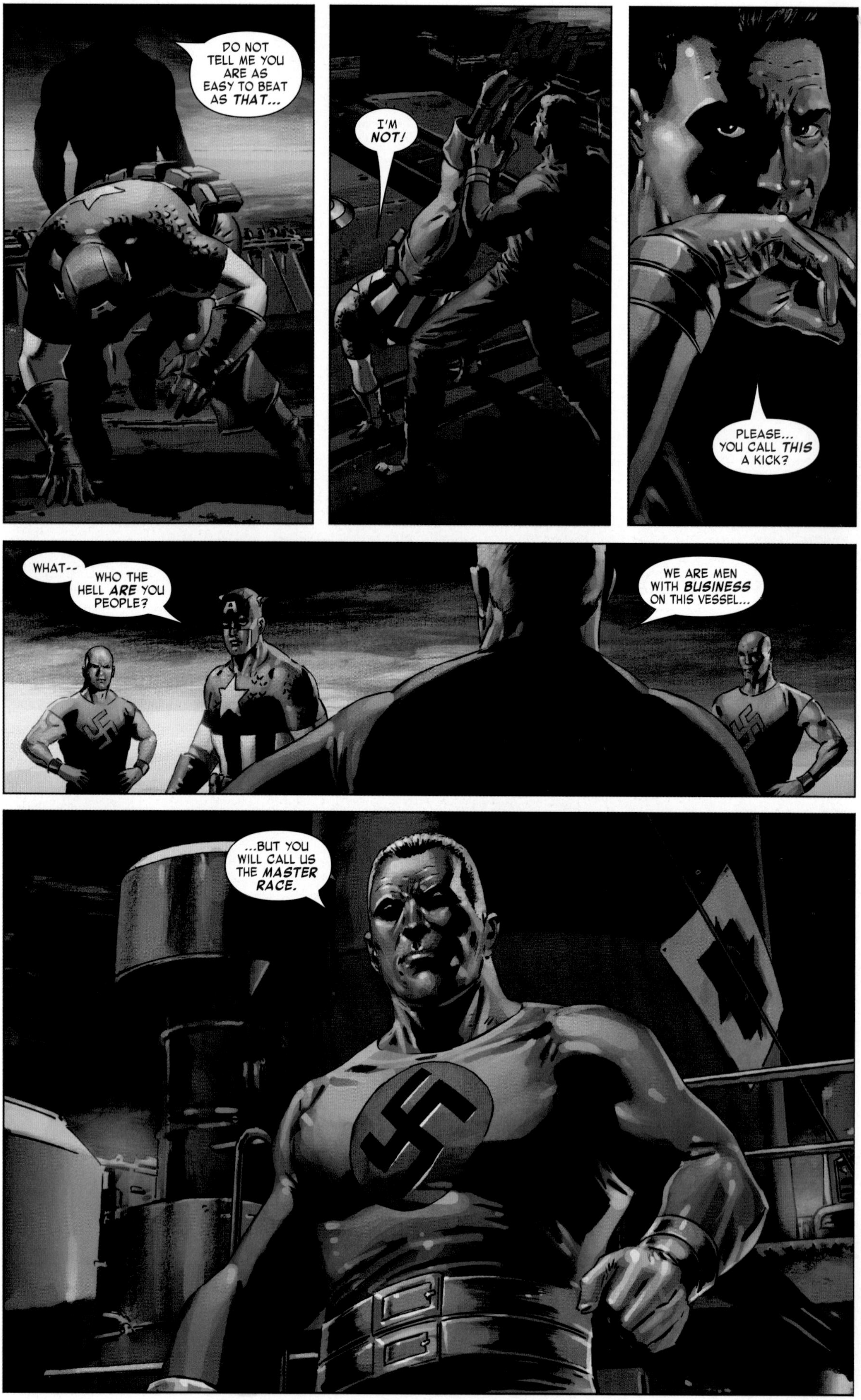
DO NOT TELL ME YOU ARE AS EASY TO BEAT AS *THAT...*
I'M *NOT!*
PLEASE... YOU CALL *THIS* A KICK?
WHAT--
WHO THE HELL *ARE* YOU PEOPLE?
WE ARE MEN WITH *BUSINESS* ON THIS VESSEL...
...BUT YOU WILL CALL US THE *MASTER RACE.*

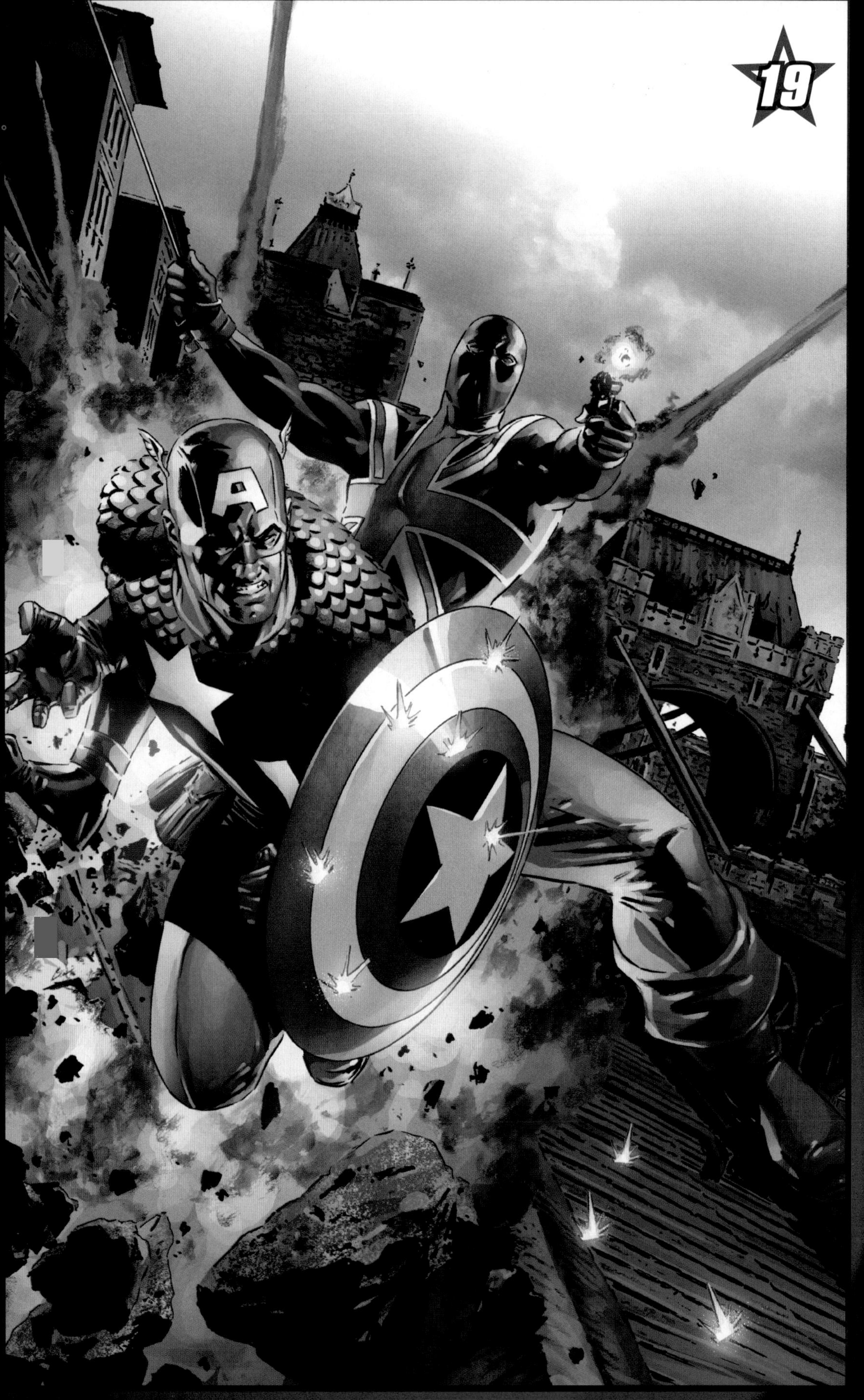
19

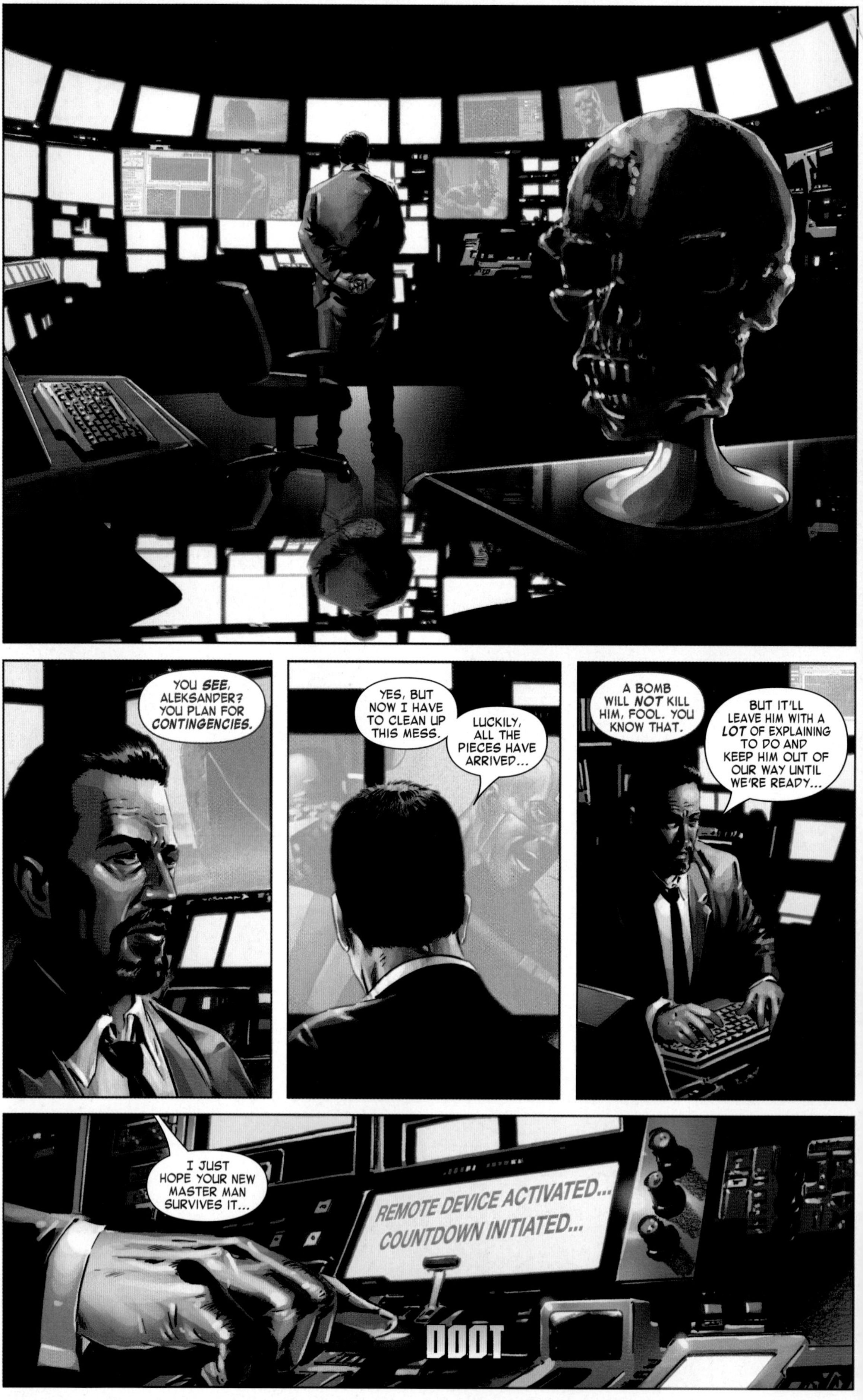

YOU SEE, ALEKSANDER? YOU PLAN FOR CONTINGENCIES.
YES, BUT NOW I HAVE TO CLEAN UP THIS MESS.
LUCKILY, ALL THE PIECES HAVE ARRIVED...
A BOMB WILL NOT KILL HIM, FOOL. YOU KNOW THAT.
BUT IT'LL LEAVE HIM WITH A LOT OF EXPLAINING TO DO AND KEEP HIM OUT OF OUR WAY UNTIL WE'RE READY...
I JUST HOPE YOUR NEW MASTER MAN SURVIVES IT...
REMOTE DEVICE ACTIVATED... COUNTDOWN INITIATED...
DOOT

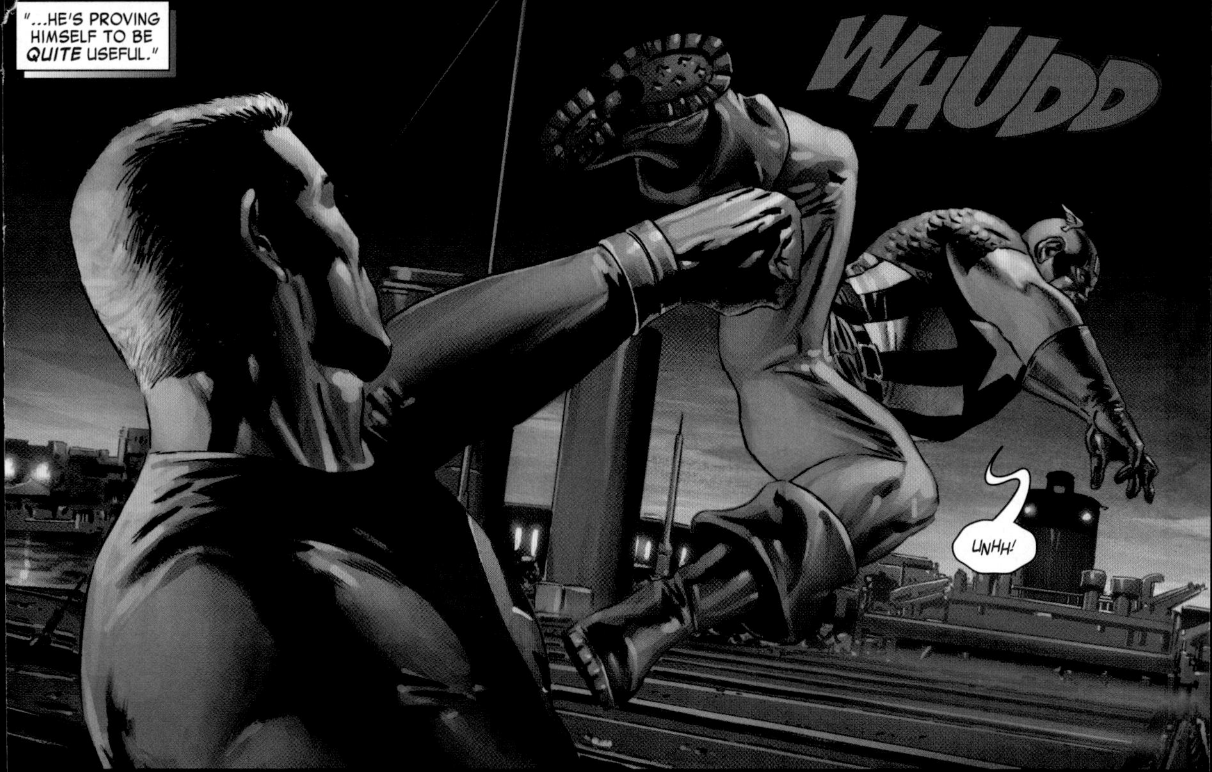
"...HE'S PROVING HIMSELF TO BE QUITE USEFUL."
WHUDD
UNHH!

TWENTY-FIRST CENTURY BLITZ

PART TWO OF FOUR

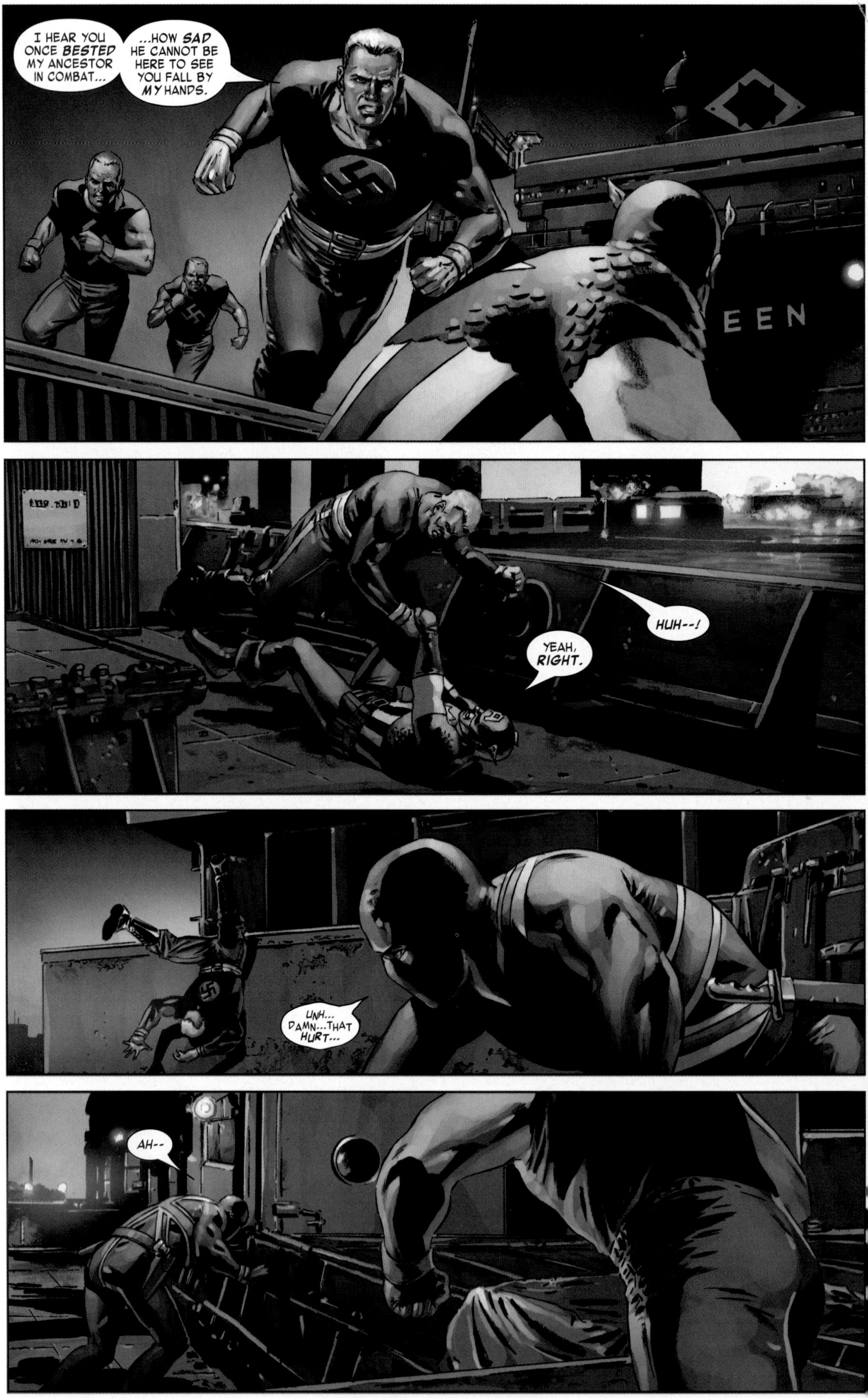
I HEAR YOU ONCE BESTED MY ANCESTOR IN COMBAT...
...HOW SAD HE CANNOT BE HERE TO SEE YOU FALL BY MY HANDS.
EEN
HUH--!
YEAH, RIGHT.
UNH... DAMN...THAT HURT...
AH--

OW...NOW THAT'S JUST NOT--

--RIGHT?

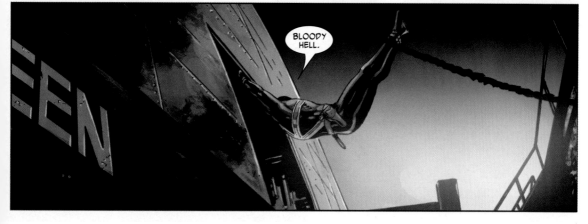

BLOODY HELL.

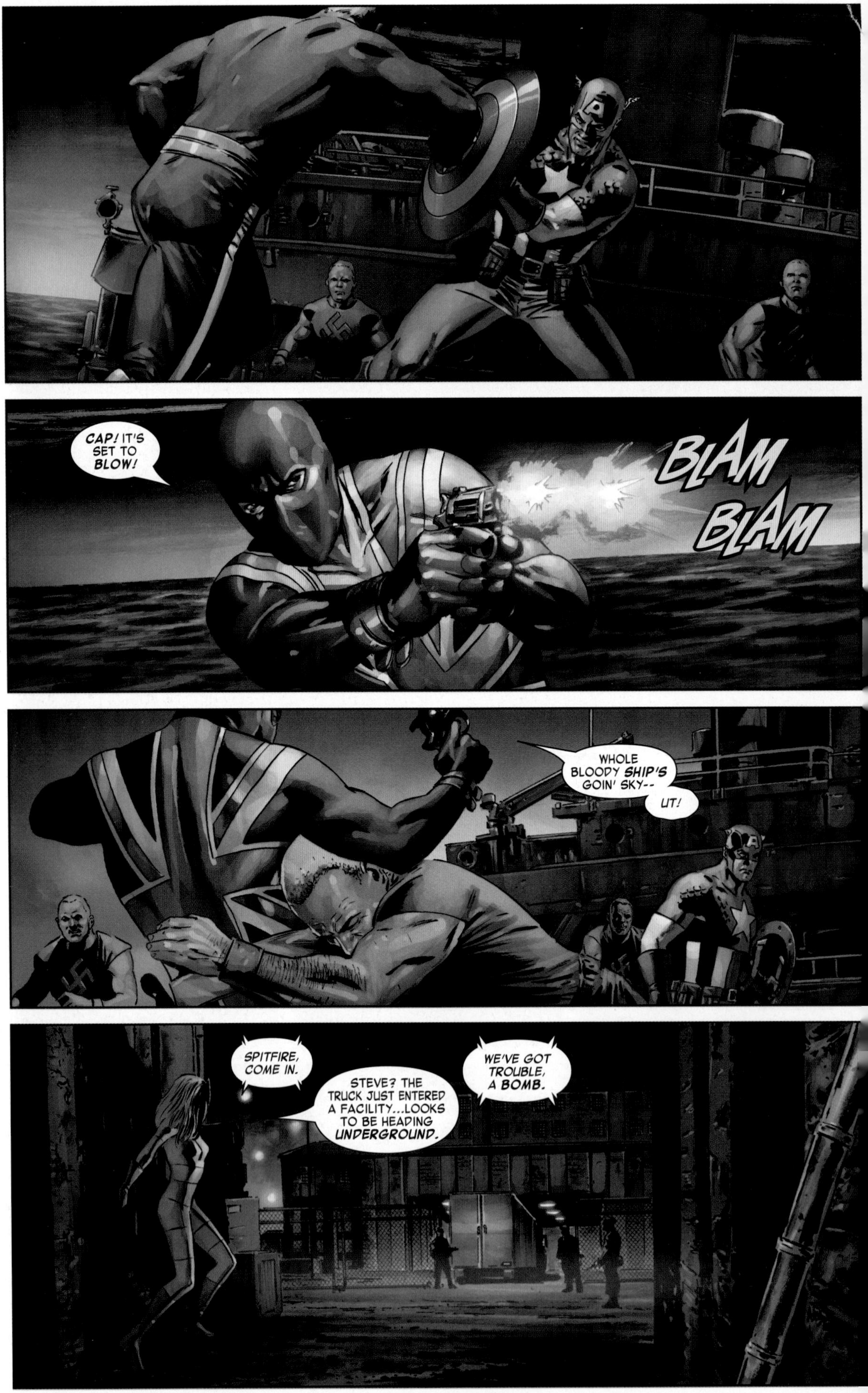
CAP! IT'S SET TO BLOW!
BLAM
BLAM
WHOLE BLOODY SHIP'S GOIN' SKY--
--UT!
SPITFIRE, COME IN.
STEVE? THE TRUCK JUST ENTERED A FACILITY...LOOKS TO BE HEADING UNDERGROUND.
WE'VE GOT TROUBLE, A BOMB.

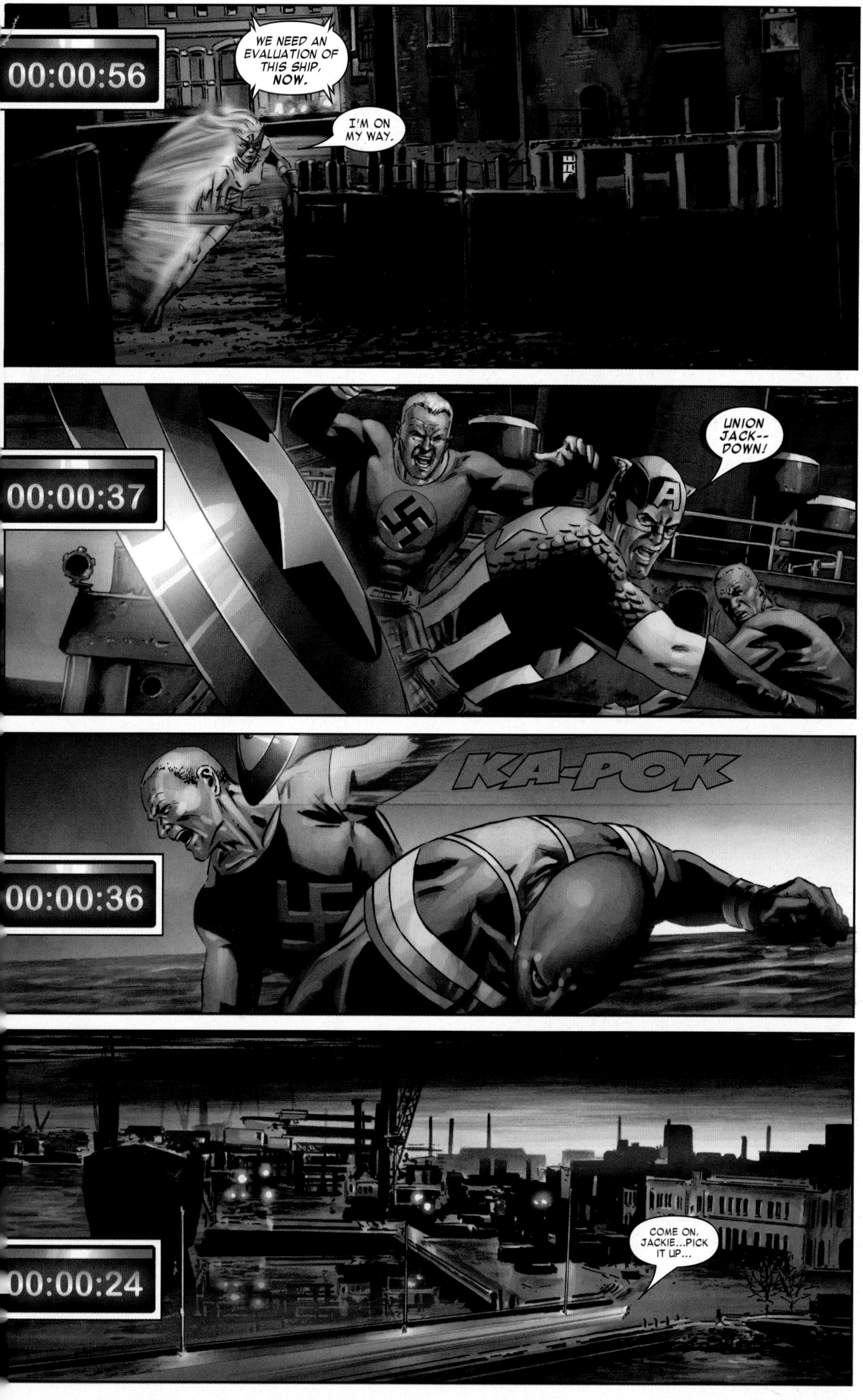
00:00:56
WE NEED AN EVALUATION OF THIS SHIP, NOW.
I'M ON MY WAY.
00:00:37
UNION JACK-- DOWN!
KA-POK
00:00:36
00:00:24
COME ON, JACKIE...PICK IT UP...

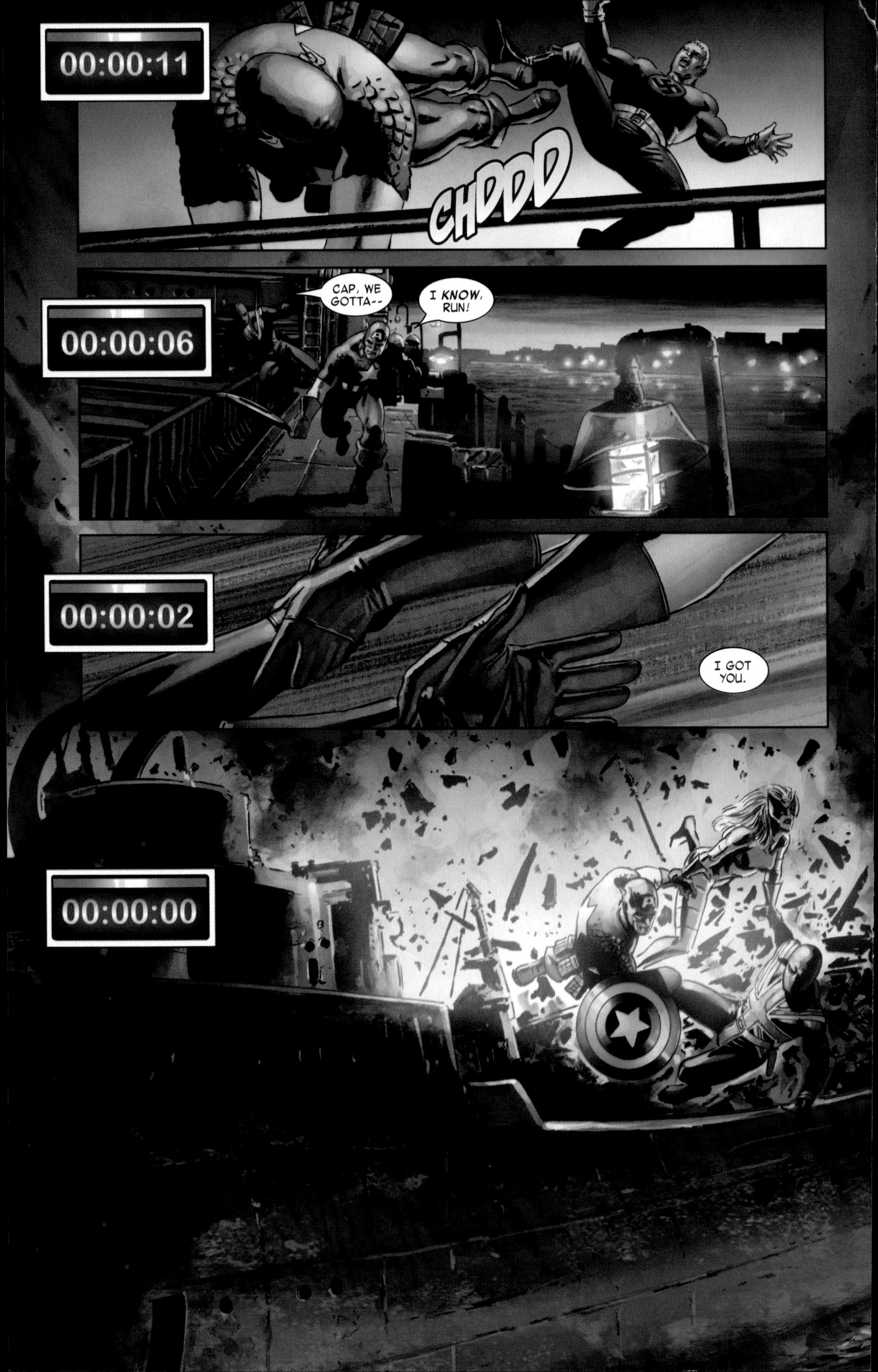
00:00:11
CHDDD
00:00:06
CAP, WE GOTTA--
I KNOW, RUN!
00:00:02
I GOT YOU.
00:00:00

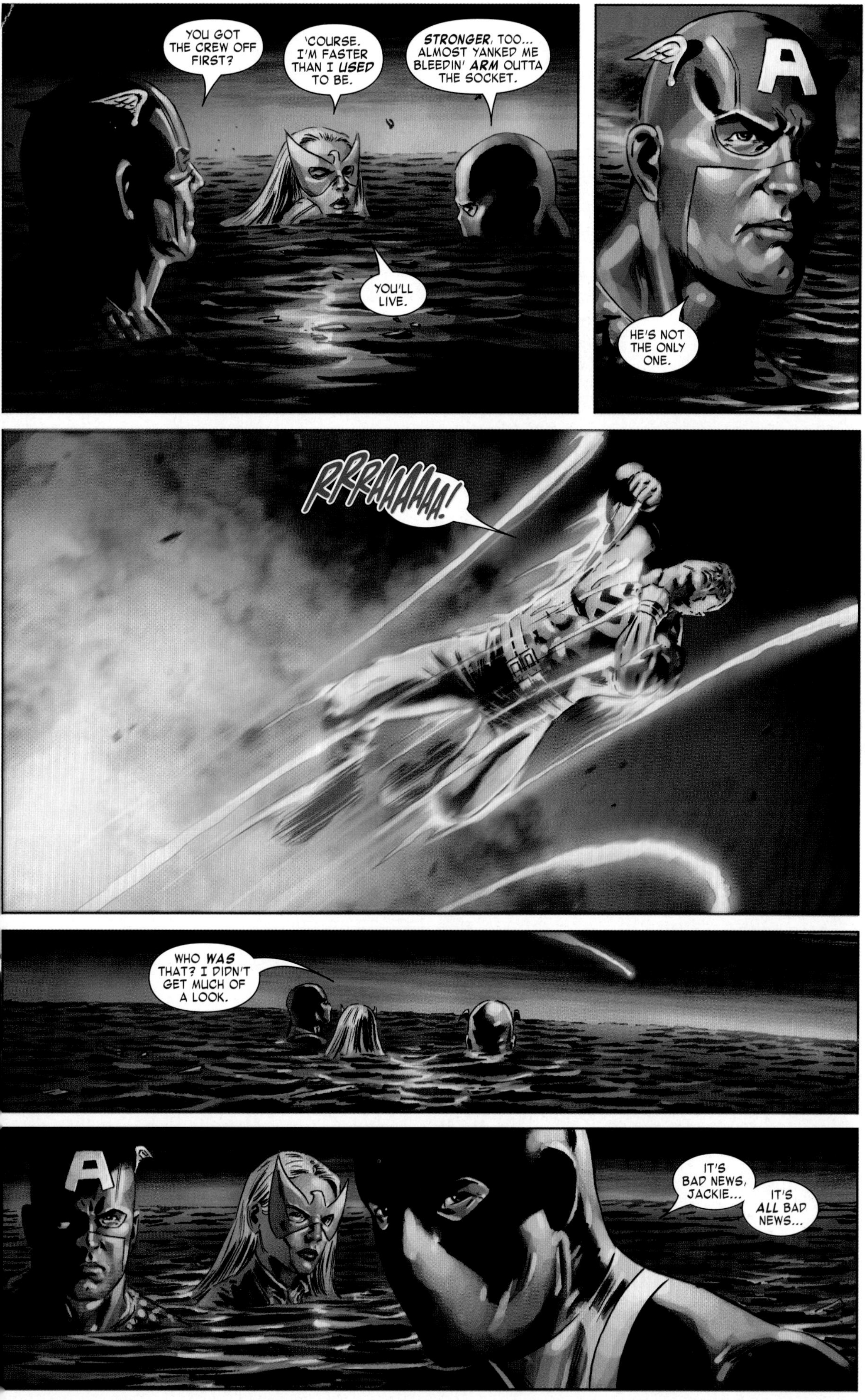
YOU GOT THE CREW OFF FIRST?
'COURSE. I'M FASTER THAN I USED TO BE.
STRONGER, TOO... ALMOST YANKED ME BLEEDIN' ARM OUTTA THE SOCKET.
YOU'LL LIVE.
HE'S NOT THE ONLY ONE.
RRRAAAAAAA!
WHO WAS THAT? I DIDN'T GET MUCH OF A LOOK.
IT'S BAD NEWS, JACKIE...
IT'S ALL BAD NEWS...

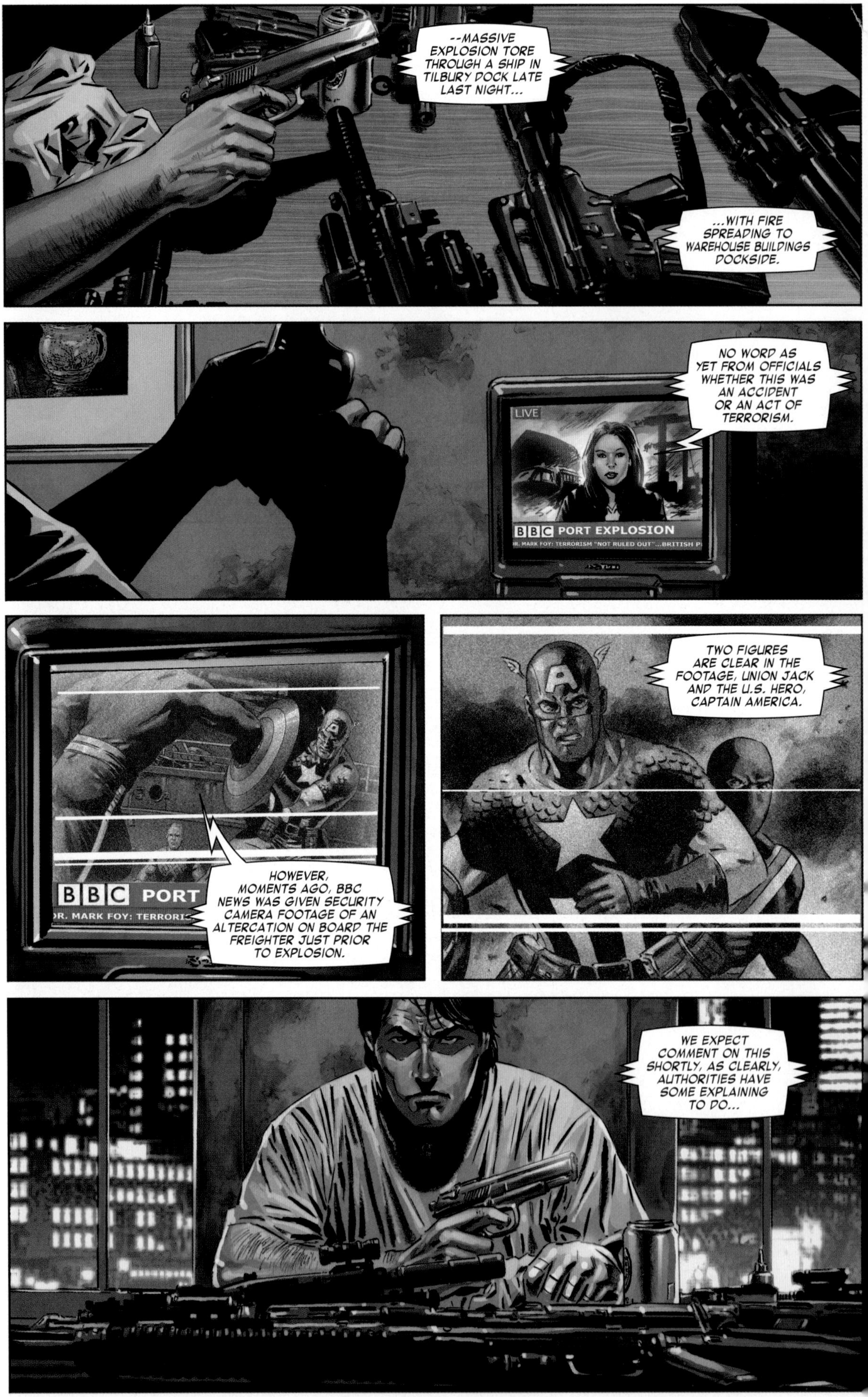
--MASSIVE EXPLOSION TORE THROUGH A SHIP IN TILBURY DOCK LATE LAST NIGHT...
...WITH FIRE SPREADING TO WAREHOUSE BUILDINGS DOCKSIDE.
LIVE
BBC PORT EXPLOSION
DR. MARK FOY: TERRORISM "NOT RULED OUT"...BRITISH P
NO WORD AS YET FROM OFFICIALS WHETHER THIS WAS AN ACCIDENT OR AN ACT OF TERRORISM.
BBC PORT
DR. MARK FOY: TERRORI
HOWEVER, MOMENTS AGO, BBC NEWS WAS GIVEN SECURITY CAMERA FOOTAGE OF AN ALTERCATION ON BOARD THE FREIGHTER JUST PRIOR TO EXPLOSION.
TWO FIGURES ARE CLEAR IN THE FOOTAGE, UNION JACK AND THE U.S. HERO, CAPTAIN AMERICA.
WE EXPECT COMMENT ON THIS SHORTLY, AS CLEARLY, AUTHORITIES HAVE SOME EXPLAINING TO DO...

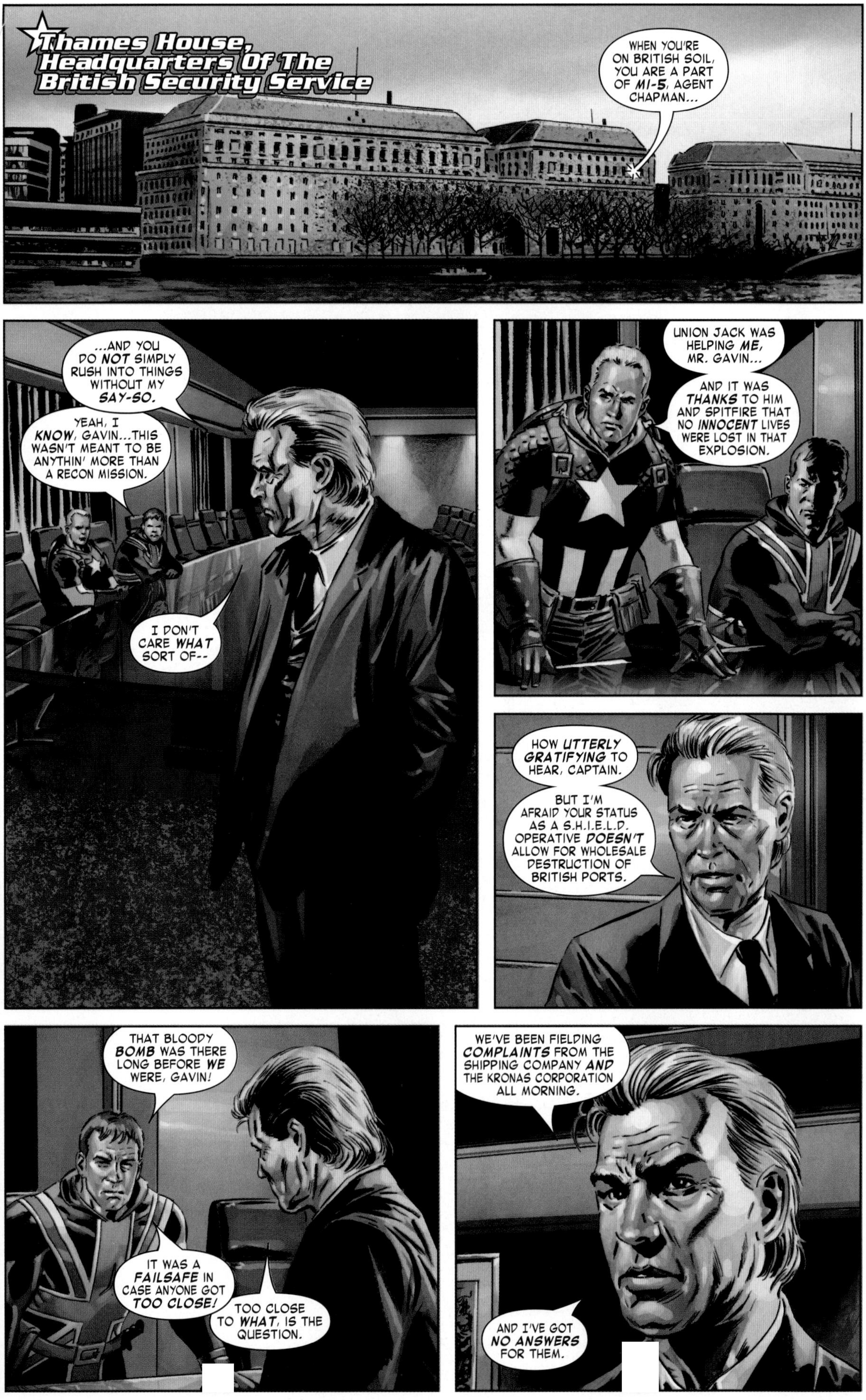
Thames House, Headquarters Of The British Security Service
WHEN YOU'RE ON BRITISH SOIL, YOU ARE A PART OF MI-5, AGENT CHAPMAN...
...AND YOU DO NOT SIMPLY RUSH INTO THINGS WITHOUT MY SAY-SO.
YEAH, I KNOW, GAVIN...THIS WASN'T MEANT TO BE ANYTHIN' MORE THAN A RECON MISSION.
I DON'T CARE WHAT SORT OF--
UNION JACK WAS HELPING ME, MR. GAVIN...
AND IT WAS THANKS TO HIM AND SPITFIRE THAT NO INNOCENT LIVES WERE LOST IN THAT EXPLOSION.
HOW UTTERLY GRATIFYING TO HEAR, CAPTAIN.
BUT I'M AFRAID YOUR STATUS AS A S.H.I.E.L.D. OPERATIVE DOESN'T ALLOW FOR WHOLESALE DESTRUCTION OF BRITISH PORTS.
THAT BLOODY BOMB WAS THERE LONG BEFORE WE WERE, GAVIN!
IT WAS A FAILSAFE IN CASE ANYONE GOT TOO CLOSE!
TOO CLOSE TO WHAT, IS THE QUESTION.
WE'VE BEEN FIELDING COMPLAINTS FROM THE SHIPPING COMPANY AND THE KRONAS CORPORATION ALL MORNING.
AND I'VE GOT NO ANSWERS FOR THEM.

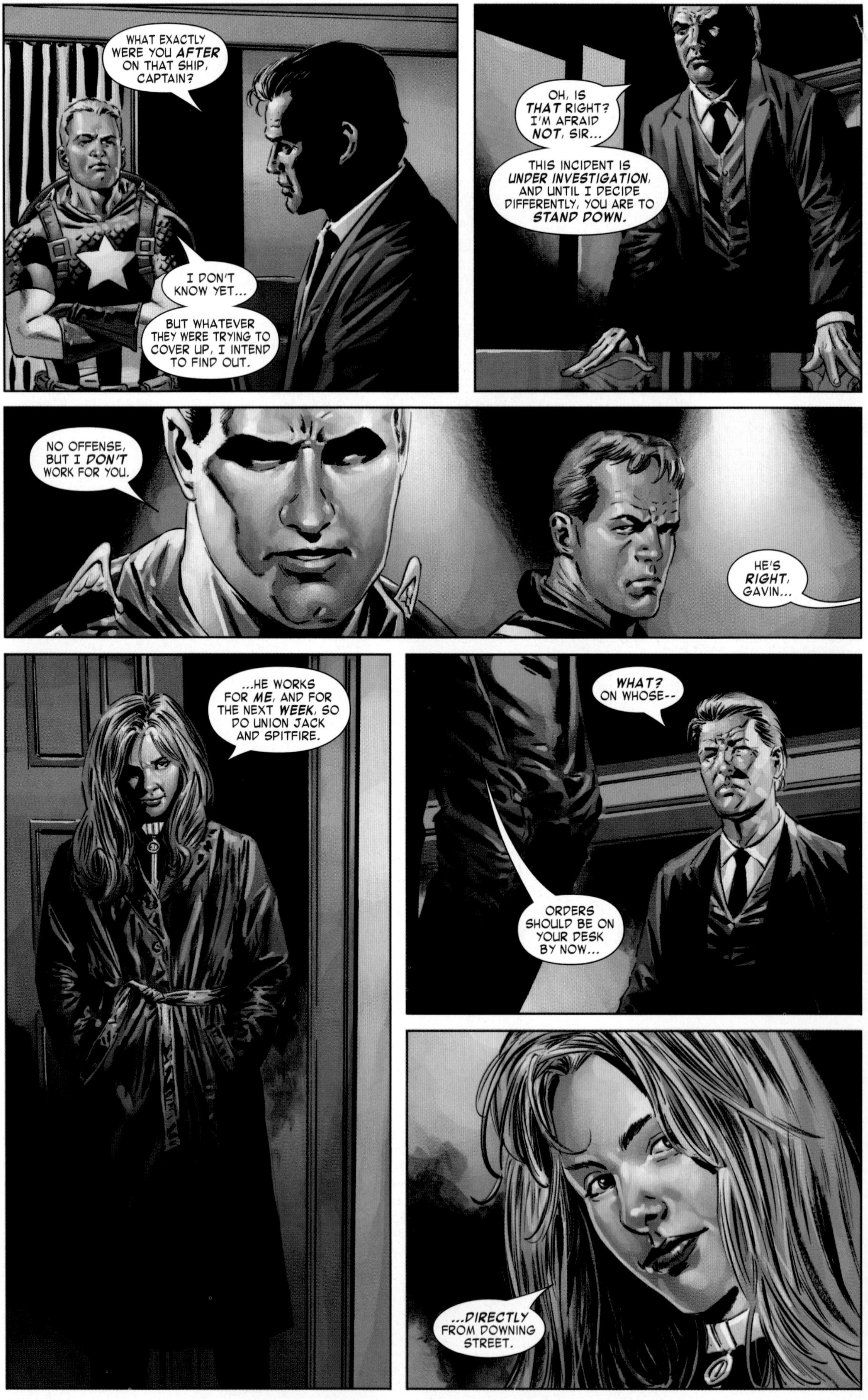
WHAT EXACTLY WERE YOU AFTER ON THAT SHIP, CAPTAIN?
I DON'T KNOW YET...
BUT WHATEVER THEY WERE TRYING TO COVER UP, I INTEND TO FIND OUT.
OH, IS THAT RIGHT? I'M AFRAID NOT, SIR...
THIS INCIDENT IS UNDER INVESTIGATION, AND UNTIL I DECIDE DIFFERENTLY, YOU ARE TO STAND DOWN.
NO OFFENSE, BUT I DON'T WORK FOR YOU.
HE'S RIGHT, GAVIN...
...HE WORKS FOR ME, AND FOR THE NEXT WEEK, SO DO UNION JACK AND SPITFIRE.
WHAT? ON WHOSE--
ORDERS SHOULD BE ON YOUR DESK BY NOW...
...DIRECTLY FROM DOWNING STREET.

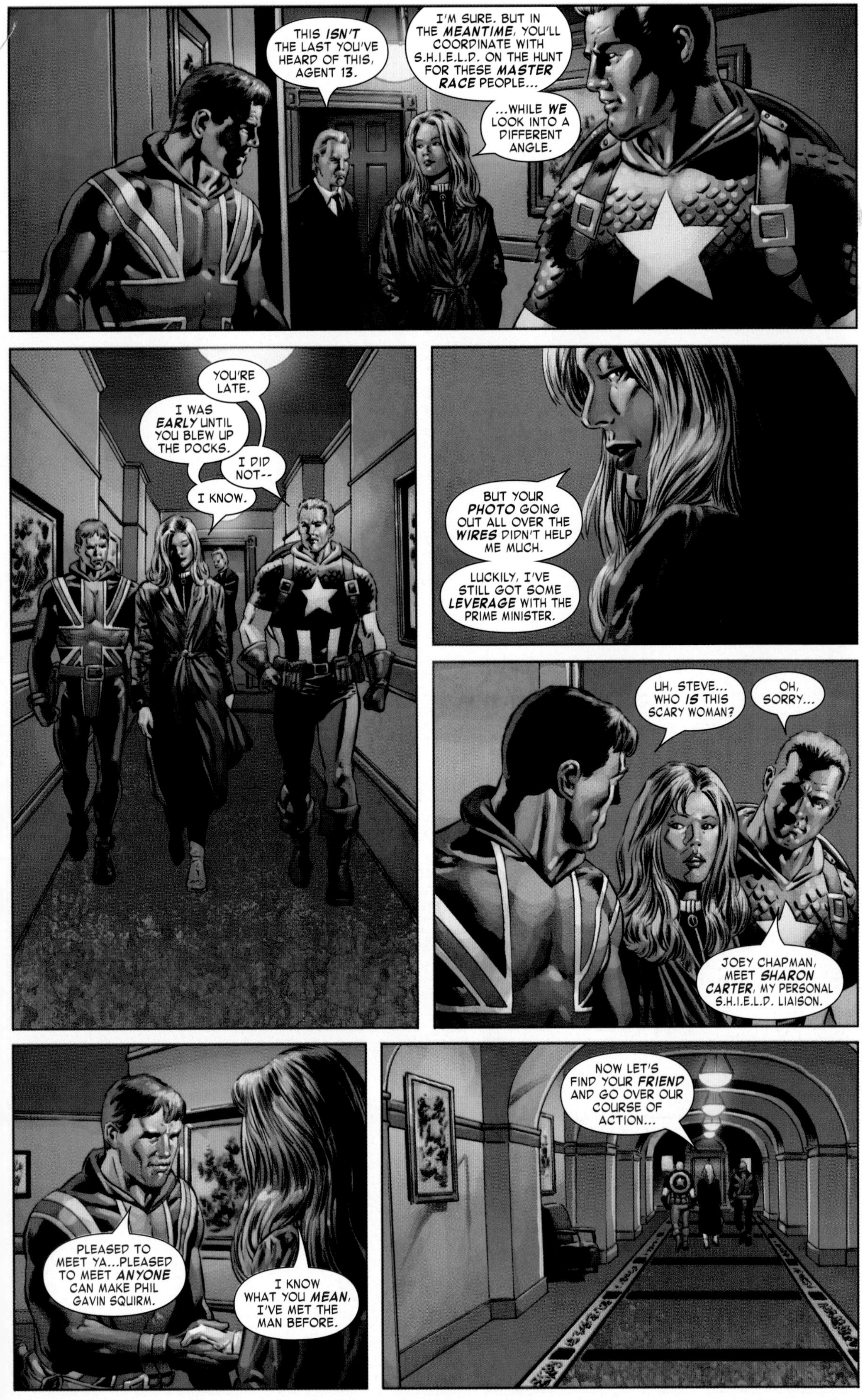
THIS ISN'T THE LAST YOU'VE HEARD OF THIS, AGENT 13.
I'M SURE. BUT IN THE MEANTIME, YOU'LL COORDINATE WITH S.H.I.E.L.D. ON THE HUNT FOR THESE MASTER RACE PEOPLE...
...WHILE WE LOOK INTO A DIFFERENT ANGLE.
YOU'RE LATE.
I WAS EARLY UNTIL YOU BLEW UP THE DOCKS.
I DID NOT--
I KNOW.
BUT YOUR PHOTO GOING OUT ALL OVER THE WIRES DIDN'T HELP ME MUCH.
LUCKILY, I'VE STILL GOT SOME LEVERAGE WITH THE PRIME MINISTER.
UH, STEVE... WHO IS THIS SCARY WOMAN?
OH, SORRY...
JOEY CHAPMAN, MEET SHARON CARTER, MY PERSONAL S.H.I.E.L.D. LIAISON.
PLEASED TO MEET YA...PLEASED TO MEET ANYONE CAN MAKE PHIL GAVIN SQUIRM.
I KNOW WHAT YOU MEAN, I'VE MET THE MAN BEFORE.
NOW LET'S FIND YOUR FRIEND AND GO OVER OUR COURSE OF ACTION...

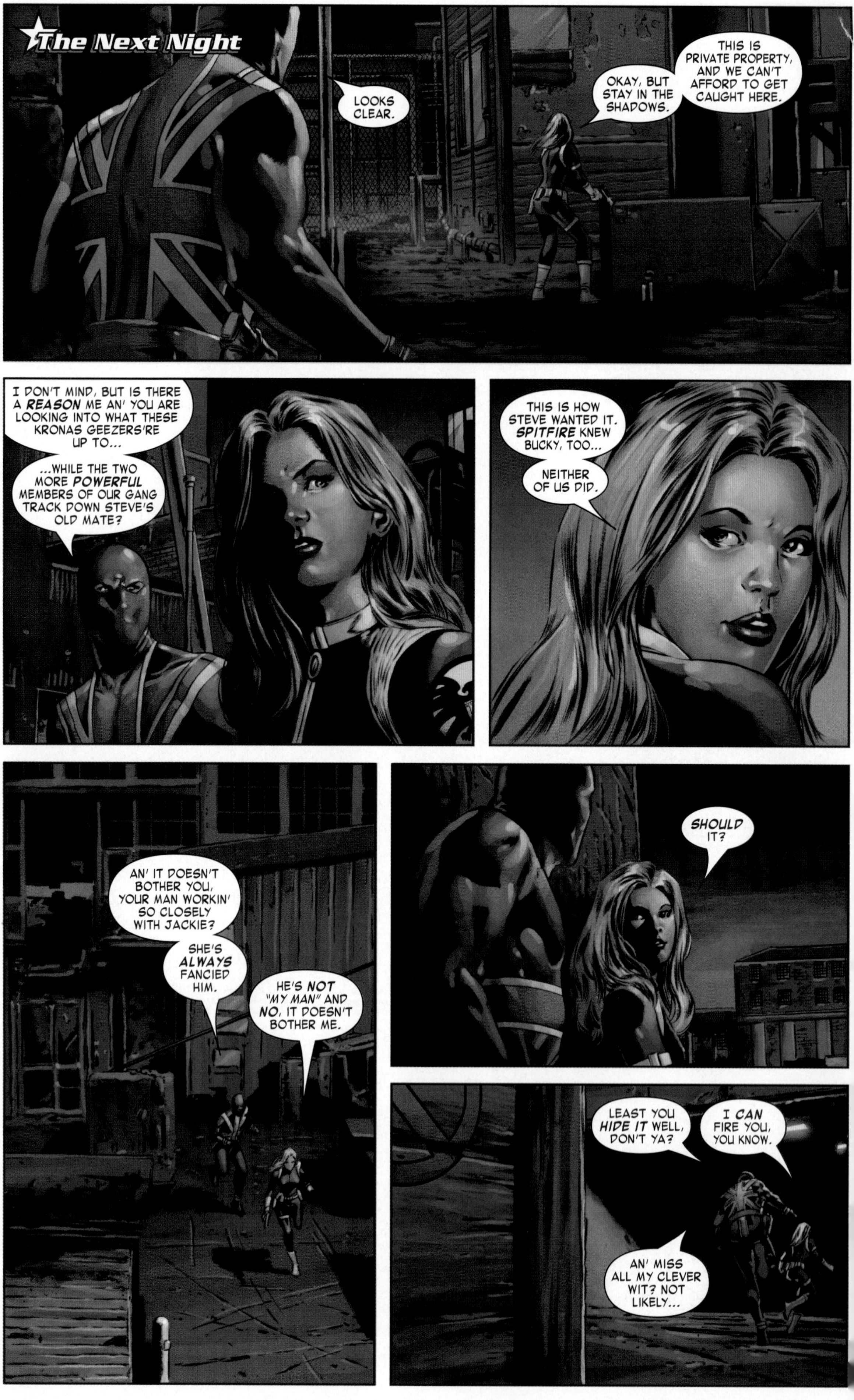
The Next Night
LOOKS CLEAR.
OKAY, BUT STAY IN THE SHADOWS.
THIS IS PRIVATE PROPERTY, AND WE CAN'T AFFORD TO GET CAUGHT HERE.
I DON'T MIND, BUT IS THERE A REASON ME AN' YOU ARE LOOKING INTO WHAT THESE KRONAS GEEZERS'RE UP TO...
...WHILE THE TWO MORE POWERFUL MEMBERS OF OUR GANG TRACK DOWN STEVE'S OLD MATE?
THIS IS HOW STEVE WANTED IT. SPITFIRE KNEW BUCKY, TOO...
NEITHER OF US DID.
AN' IT DOESN'T BOTHER YOU, YOUR MAN WORKIN' SO CLOSELY WITH JACKIE?
SHE'S ALWAYS FANCIED HIM.
HE'S NOT "MY MAN" AND NO, IT DOESN'T BOTHER ME.
SHOULD IT?
LEAST YOU HIDE IT WELL, DON'T YA?
I CAN FIRE YOU, YOU KNOW.
AN' MISS ALL MY CLEVER WIT? NOT LIKELY...

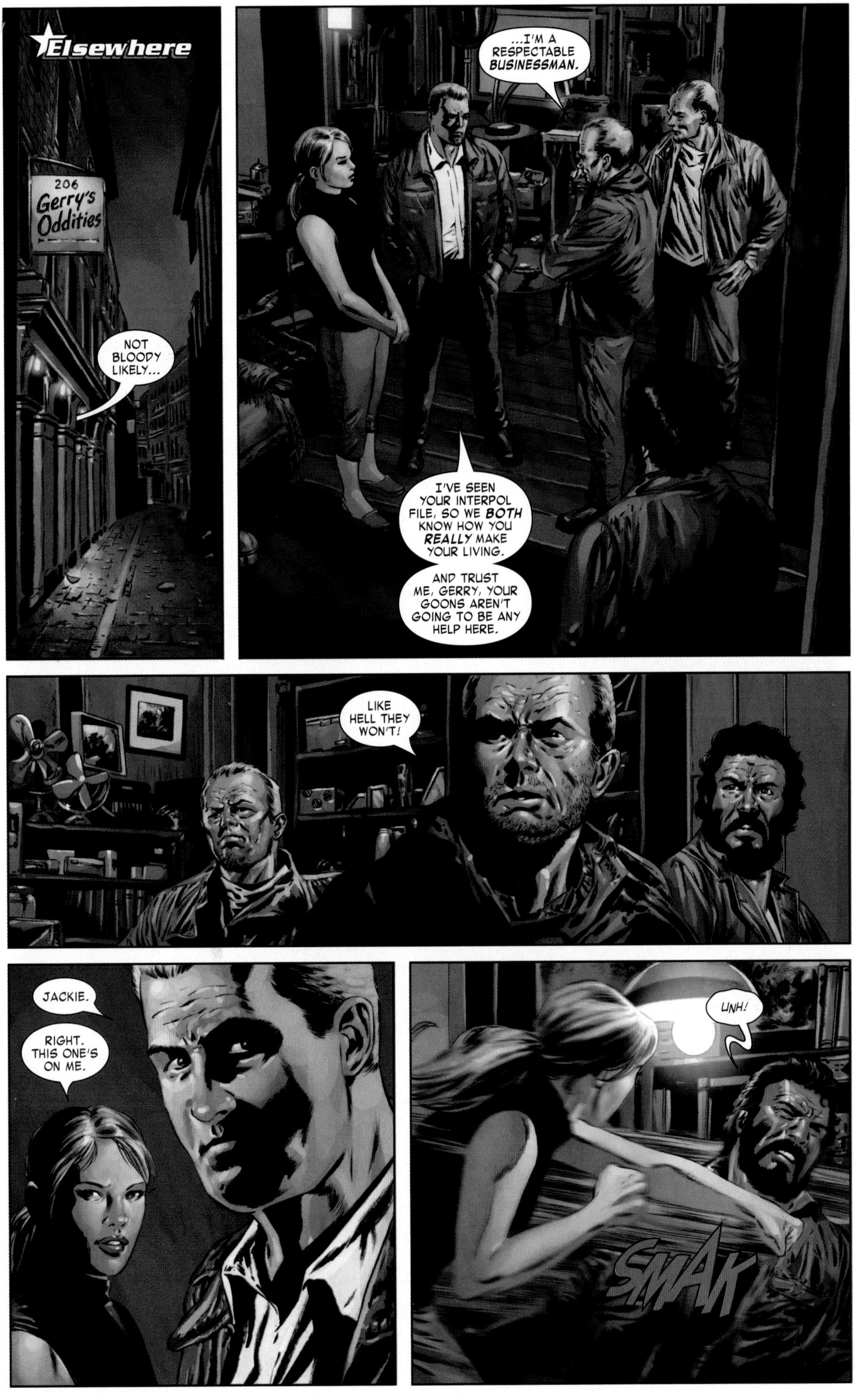
Elsewhere
206 Gerry's Oddities
NOT BLOODY LIKELY...
...I'M A RESPECTABLE BUSINESSMAN.
I'VE SEEN YOUR INTERPOL FILE, SO WE BOTH KNOW HOW YOU REALLY MAKE YOUR LIVING.
AND TRUST ME, GERRY, YOUR GOONS AREN'T GOING TO BE ANY HELP HERE.
LIKE HELL THEY WON'T!
JACKIE.
RIGHT. THIS ONE'S ON ME.
UNH!
SMAK

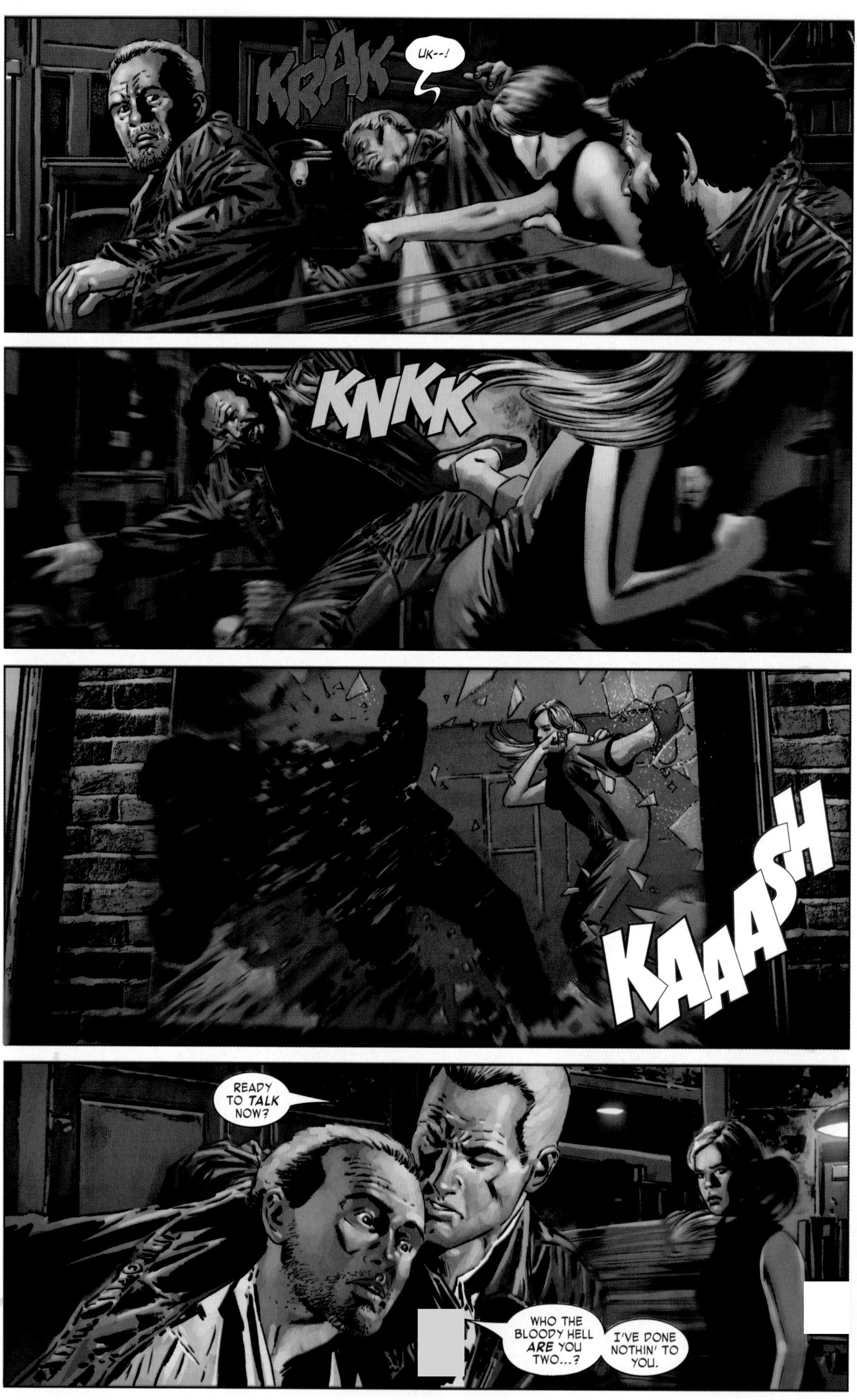
KRAK
UK--!
KNKK
KAAASH
READY TO *TALK* NOW?
WHO THE BLOODY HELL *ARE* YOU TWO...?
I'VE DONE NOTHIN' TO YOU.

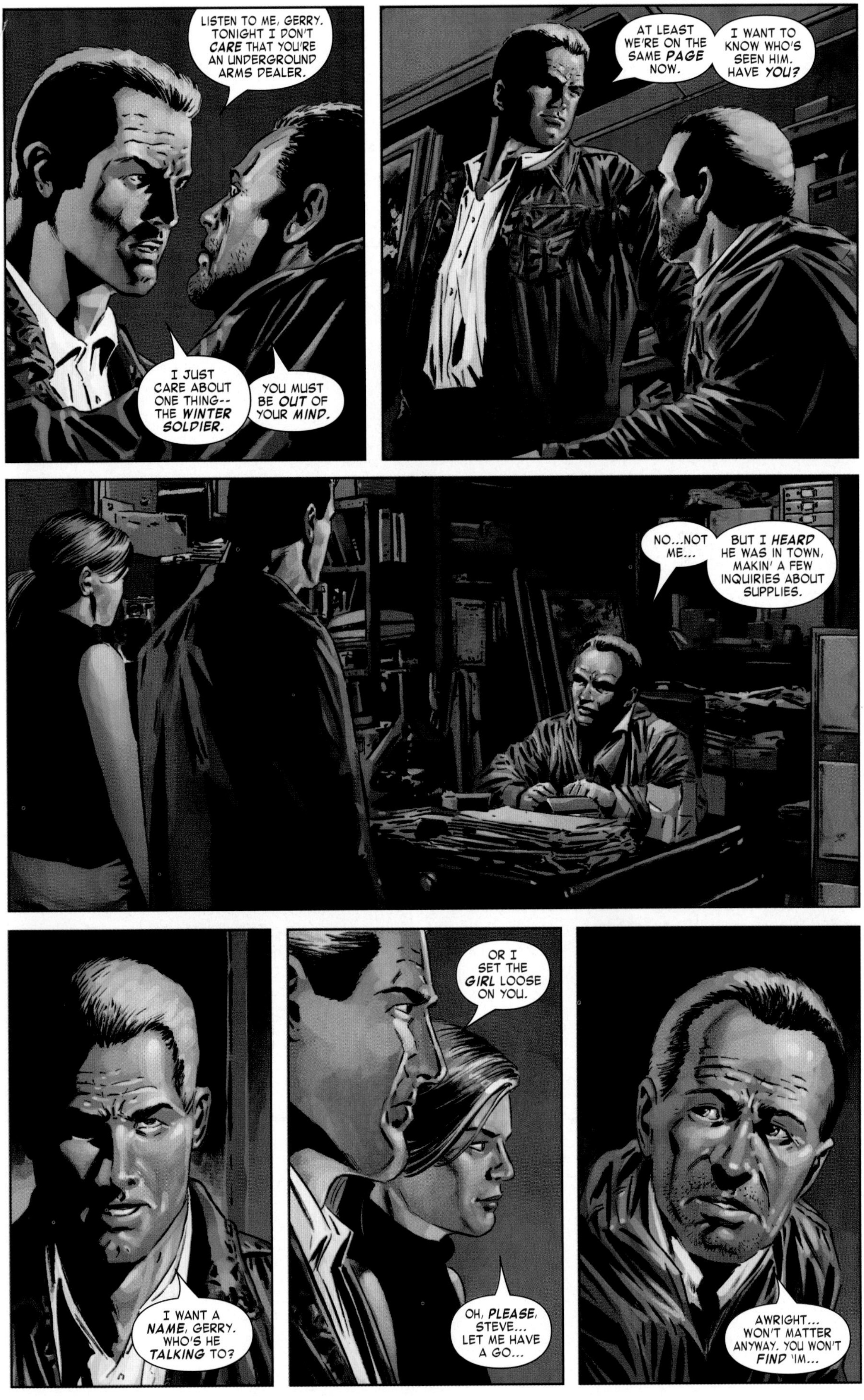
LISTEN TO ME, GERRY. TONIGHT I DON'T CARE THAT YOU'RE AN UNDERGROUND ARMS DEALER.
I JUST CARE ABOUT ONE THING-- THE WINTER SOLDIER.
YOU MUST BE OUT OF YOUR MIND.
AT LEAST WE'RE ON THE SAME PAGE NOW.
I WANT TO KNOW WHO'S SEEN HIM. HAVE YOU?
NO...NOT ME...
BUT I HEARD HE WAS IN TOWN, MAKIN' A FEW INQUIRIES ABOUT SUPPLIES.
I WANT A NAME, GERRY. WHO'S HE TALKING TO?
OR I SET THE GIRL LOOSE ON YOU.
OH, PLEASE, STEVE... LET ME HAVE A GO...
AWRIGHT... WON'T MATTER ANYWAY. YOU WON'T FIND 'IM...

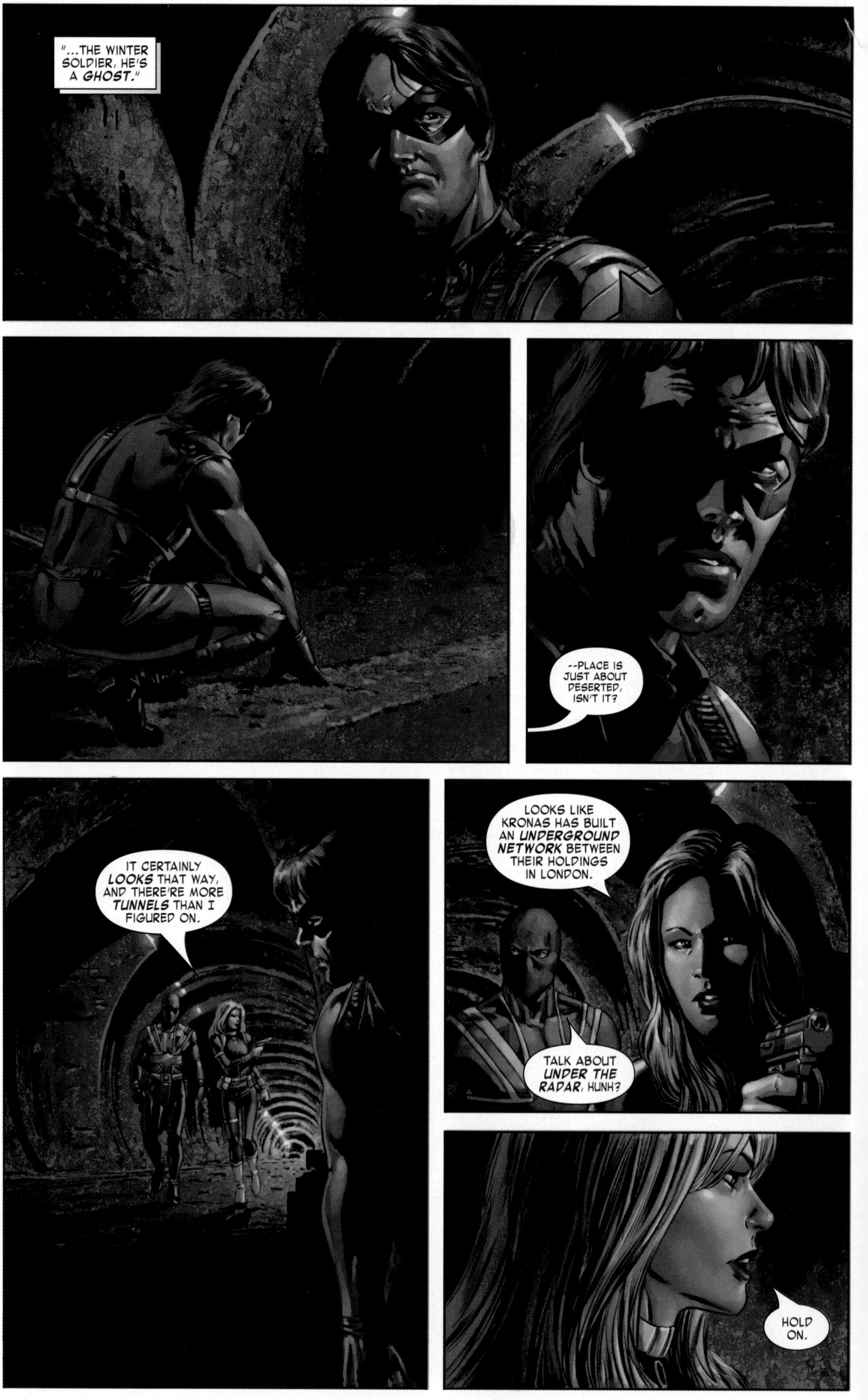
"...THE WINTER SOLDIER, HE'S A GHOST."
--PLACE IS JUST ABOUT DESERTED, ISN'T IT?
IT CERTAINLY LOOKS THAT WAY, AND THERE'RE MORE TUNNELS THAN I FIGURED ON.
LOOKS LIKE KRONAS HAS BUILT AN UNDERGROUND NETWORK BETWEEN THEIR HOLDINGS IN LONDON.
TALK ABOUT UNDER THE RADAR, HUNH?
HOLD ON.

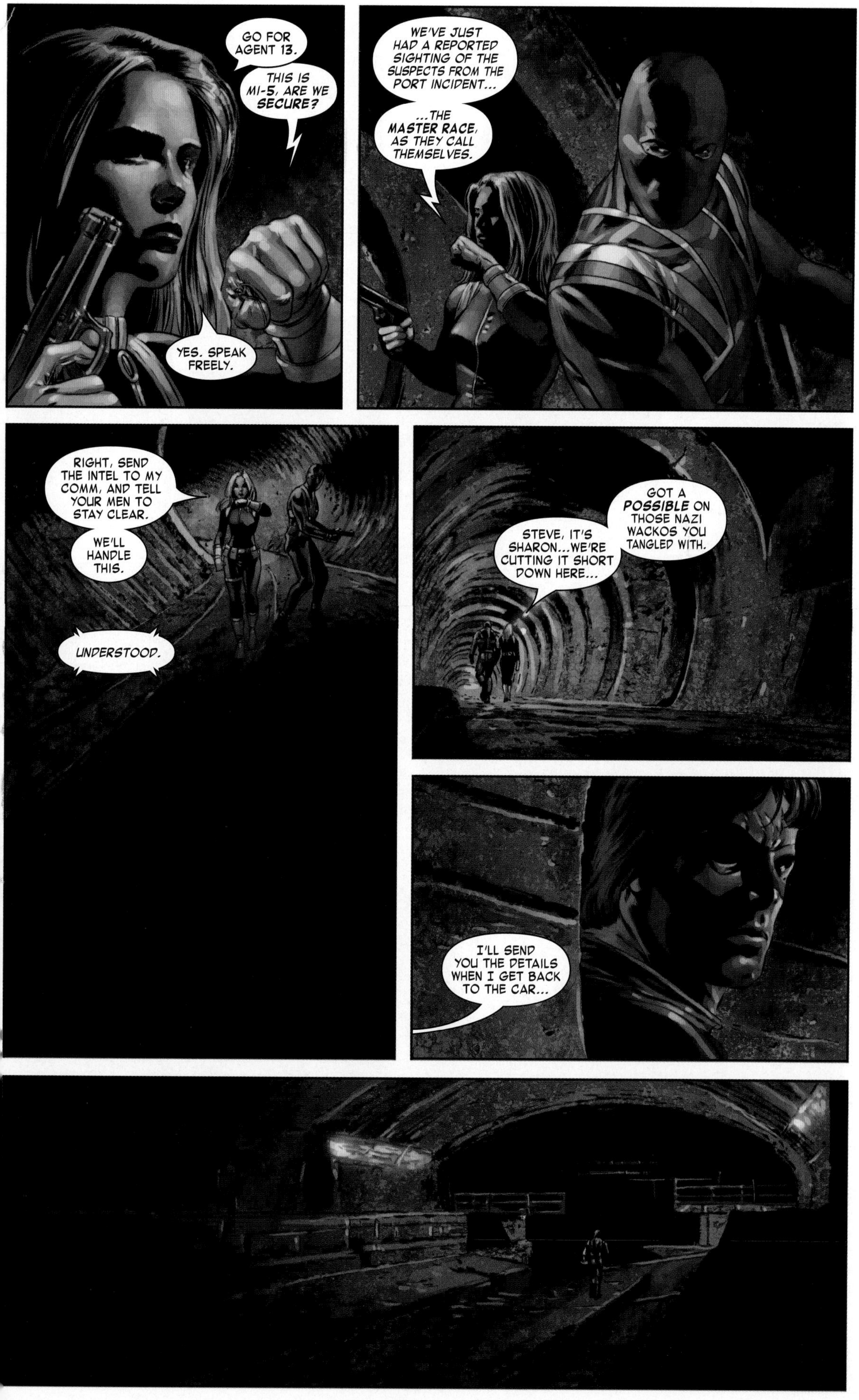
GO FOR AGENT 13.
THIS IS MI-5, ARE WE SECURE?
YES. SPEAK FREELY.
WE'VE JUST HAD A REPORTED SIGHTING OF THE SUSPECTS FROM THE PORT INCIDENT...
...THE MASTER RACE, AS THEY CALL THEMSELVES.
RIGHT, SEND THE INTEL TO MY COMM, AND TELL YOUR MEN TO STAY CLEAR.
WE'LL HANDLE THIS.
UNDERSTOOD.
STEVE, IT'S SHARON...WE'RE CUTTING IT SHORT DOWN HERE...
GOT A POSSIBLE ON THOSE NAZI WACKOS YOU TANGLED WITH.
I'LL SEND YOU THE DETAILS WHEN I GET BACK TO THE CAR...

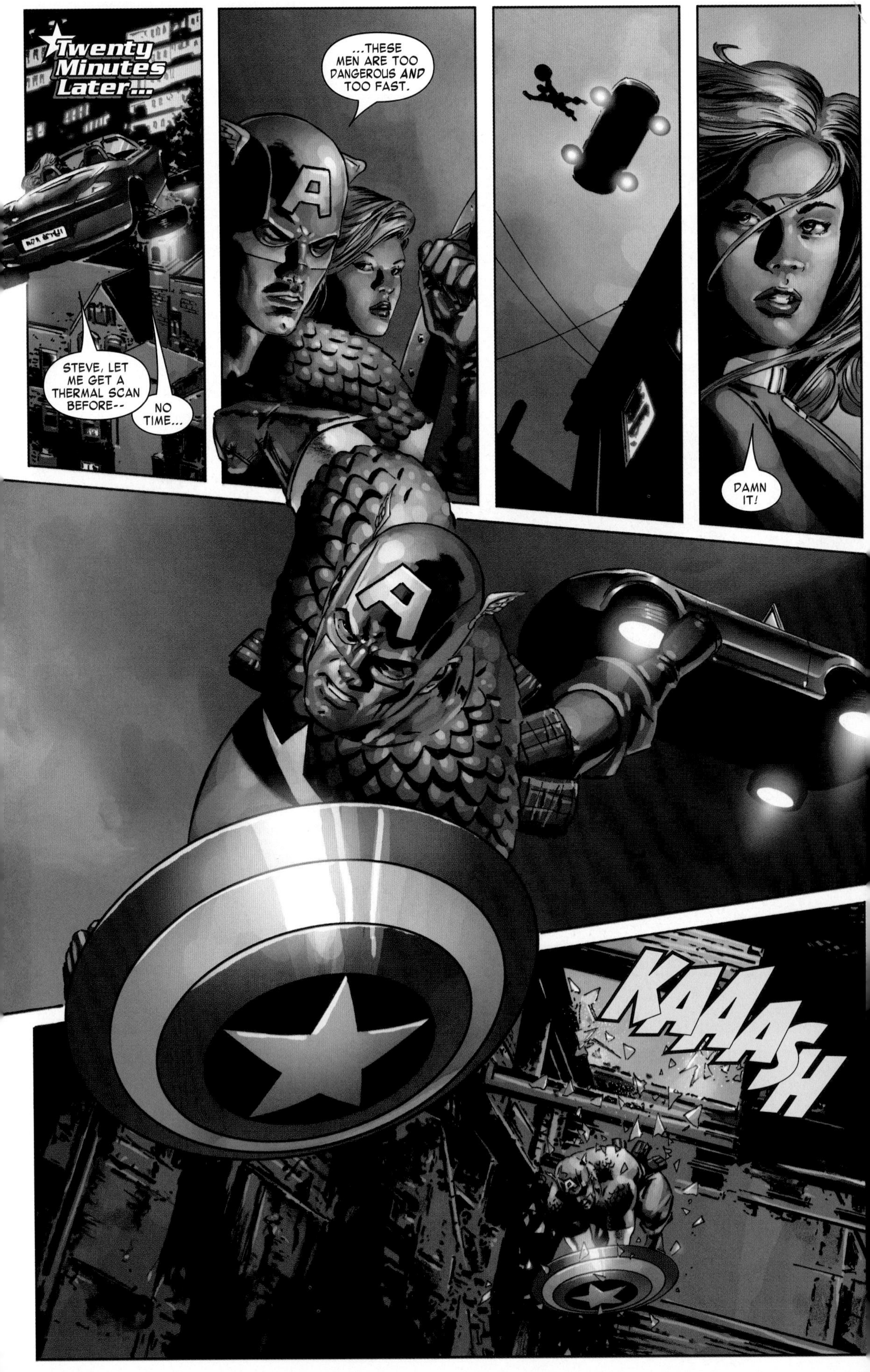
Twenty Minutes Later...
STEVE, LET ME GET A THERMAL SCAN BEFORE--
NO TIME...
...THESE MEN ARE TOO DANGEROUS AND TOO FAST.
DAMN IT!
KAAASH

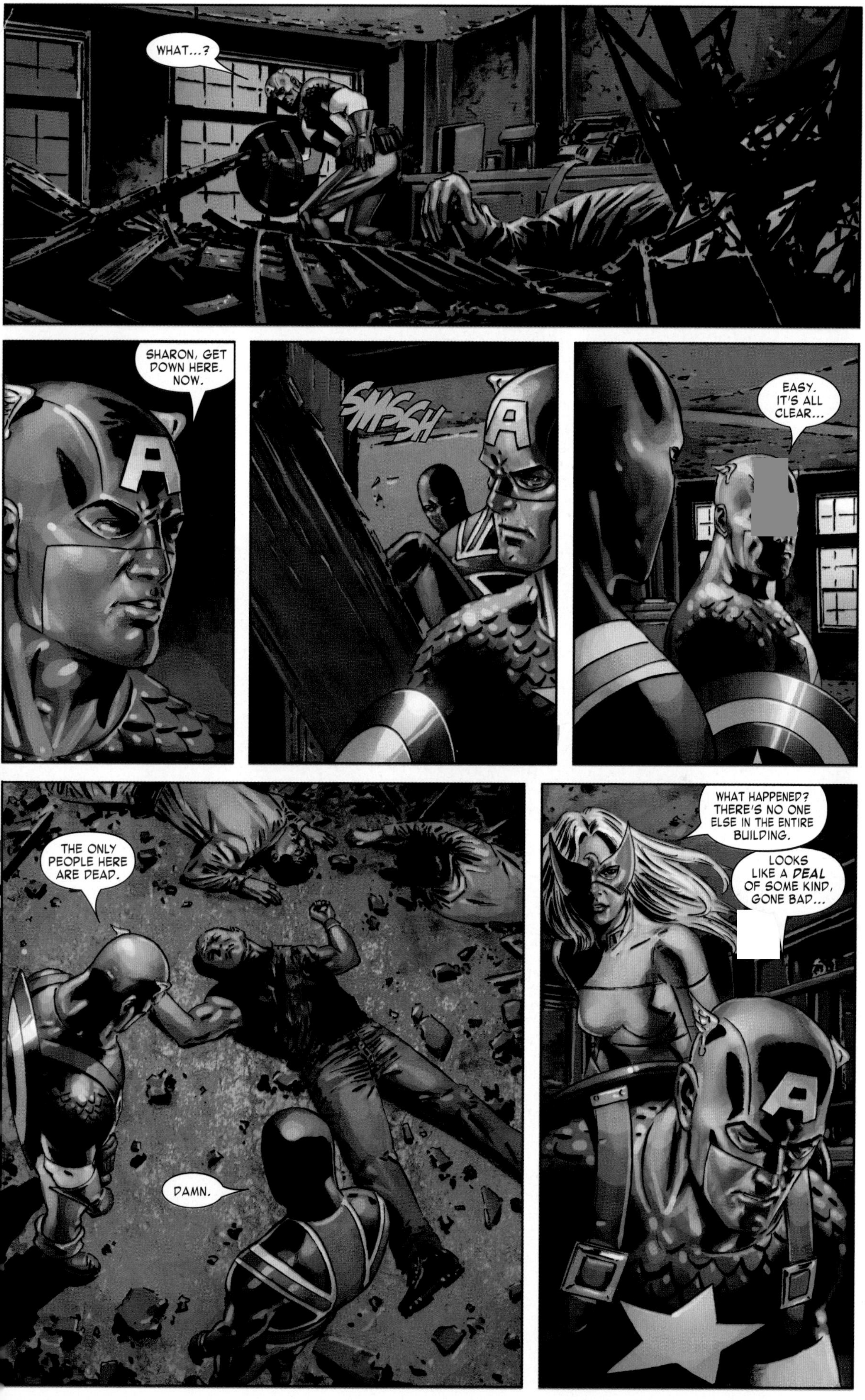
WHAT...?
SHARON, GET DOWN HERE. NOW.
SMSSH
EASY. IT'S ALL CLEAR...
THE ONLY PEOPLE HERE ARE DEAD.
DAMN.
WHAT HAPPENED? THERE'S NO ONE ELSE IN THE ENTIRE BUILDING.
LOOKS LIKE A *DEAL* OF SOME KIND, GONE BAD...

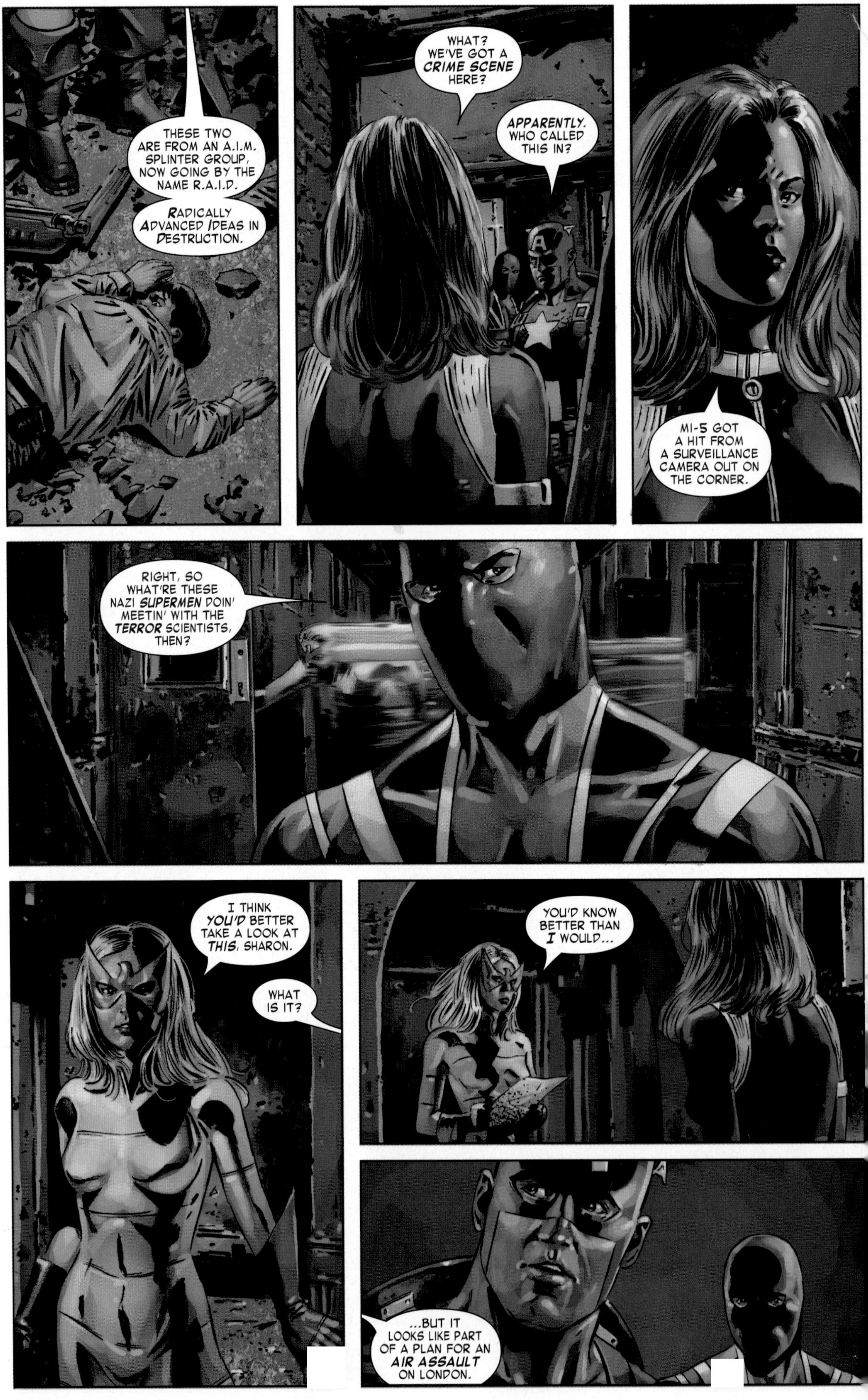

THESE TWO ARE FROM AN A.I.M. SPLINTER GROUP, NOW GOING BY THE NAME R.A.I.D.
RADICALLY ADVANCED IDEAS IN DESTRUCTION.
WHAT? WE'VE GOT A CRIME SCENE HERE?
APPARENTLY. WHO CALLED THIS IN?
MI-5 GOT A HIT FROM A SURVEILLANCE CAMERA OUT ON THE CORNER.
RIGHT, SO WHAT'RE THESE NAZI SUPERMEN DOIN' MEETIN' WITH THE TERROR SCIENTISTS, THEN?
I THINK YOU'D BETTER TAKE A LOOK AT THIS, SHARON.
WHAT IS IT?
YOU'D KNOW BETTER THAN I WOULD...
...BUT IT LOOKS LIKE PART OF A PLAN FOR AN AIR ASSAULT ON LONDON.

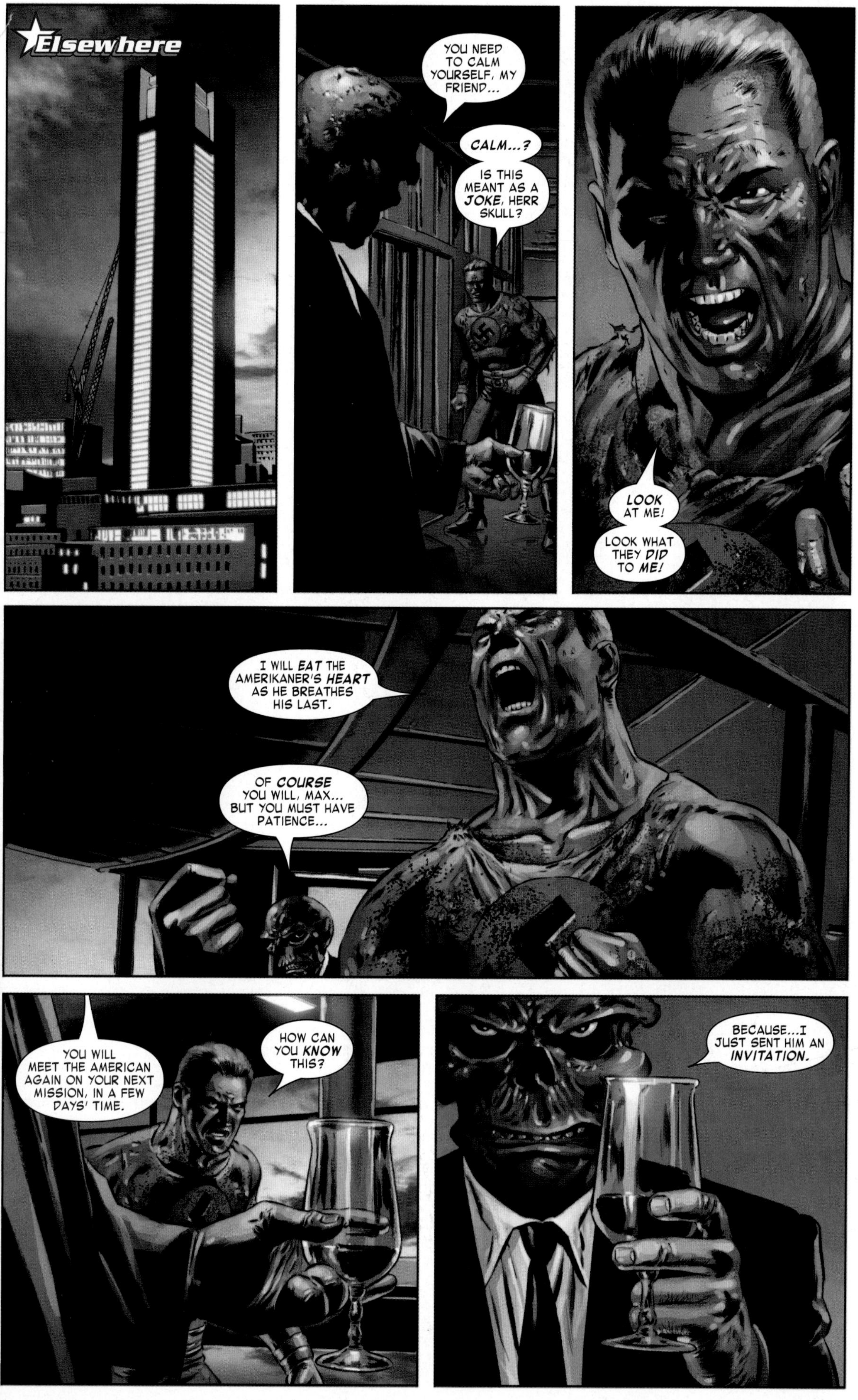
Elsewhere
YOU NEED TO CALM YOURSELF, MY FRIEND...
CALM...?
IS THIS MEANT AS A JOKE, HERR SKULL?
LOOK AT ME!
LOOK WHAT THEY DID TO ME!
I WILL EAT THE AMERIKANER'S HEART AS HE BREATHES HIS LAST.
OF COURSE YOU WILL, MAX... BUT YOU MUST HAVE PATIENCE...
YOU WILL MEET THE AMERICAN AGAIN ON YOUR NEXT MISSION, IN A FEW DAYS' TIME.
HOW CAN YOU KNOW THIS?
BECAUSE...I JUST SENT HIM AN INVITATION.

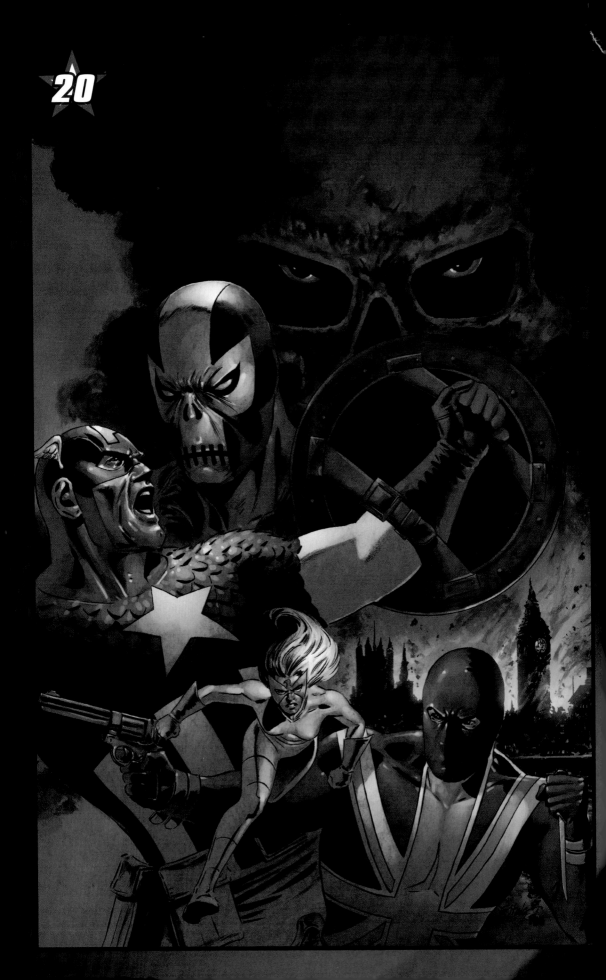

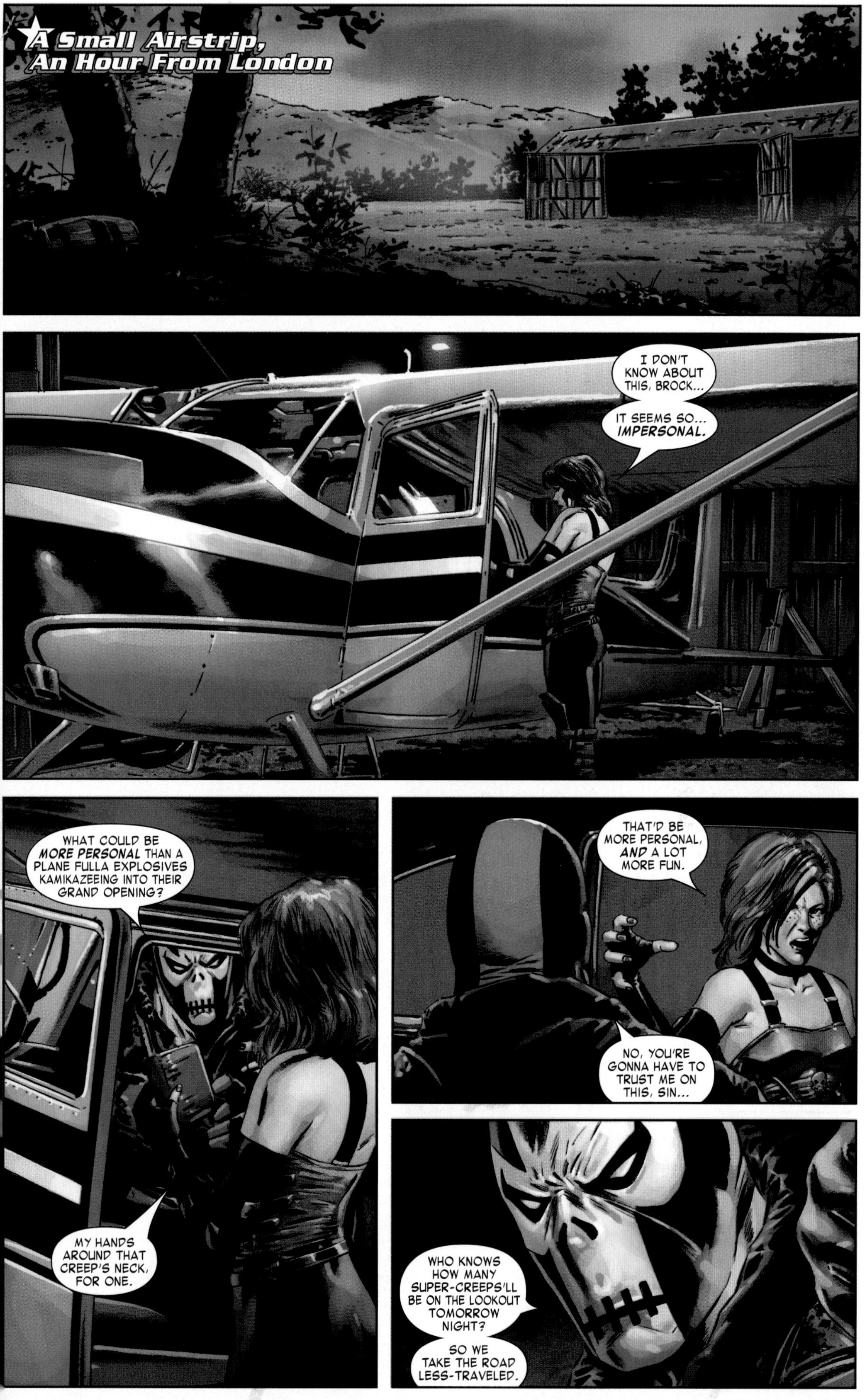
A Small Airstrip, An Hour From London
I DON'T KNOW ABOUT THIS, BROCK...
IT SEEMS SO... IMPERSONAL.
WHAT COULD BE MORE PERSONAL THAN A PLANE FULLA EXPLOSIVES KAMIKAZEEING INTO THEIR GRAND OPENING?
MY HANDS AROUND THAT CREEP'S NECK, FOR ONE.
THAT'D BE MORE PERSONAL, AND A LOT MORE FUN.
NO, YOU'RE GONNA HAVE TO TRUST ME ON THIS, SIN...
WHO KNOWS HOW MANY SUPER-CREEPS'LL BE ON THE LOOKOUT TOMORROW NIGHT?
SO WE TAKE THE ROAD LESS-TRAVELED.

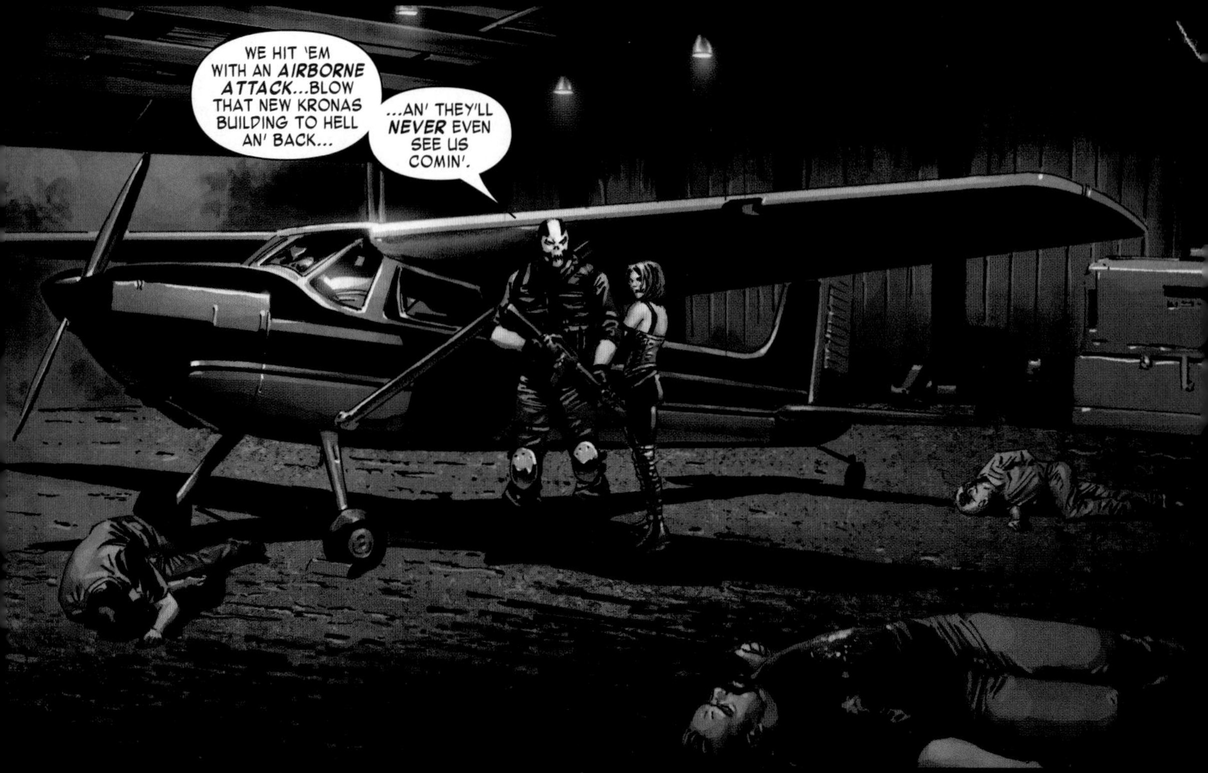
WE HIT 'EM WITH AN AIRBORNE ATTACK...BLOW THAT NEW KRONAS BUILDING TO HELL AN' BACK...
...AN' THEY'LL NEVER EVEN SEE US COMIN'.

TWENTY-FIRST CENTURY BLITZ

PART THREE OF FOUR

SO, AERIAL ATTACKS ON LONDON... WHAT'VE WE FIGURED OUT SO FAR?

THAT GAVIN AT MI-5 IS A TWIT.

OOH... YOU'RE PICKING UP U.K. SLANG. I LIKE IT.

BUT YOU'RE *RIGHT* ABOUT GAVIN.

THOUGH, HONESTLY, WHAT'S HE GOING TO DO?

HALT ALL AIR-TRAFFIC IN THE LONDON AREA.

BASED ON A HALF-BURNED *PLAN* THAT CAN'T BE CONFIRMED THROUGH *ANY* INTELLIGENCE SOURCE...

...AND WHICH HAD NO *DATE* FOR THE ATTACK ON IT?

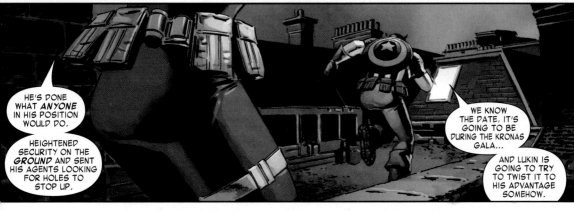

HE'S DONE WHAT *ANYONE* IN HIS POSITION WOULD DO.

HEIGHTENED SECURITY ON THE *GROUND* AND SENT HIS AGENTS LOOKING FOR HOLES TO STOP UP.

WE KNOW THE DATE, IT'S GOING TO BE DURING THE KRONAS GALA...

...AND LUKIN IS GOING TO TRY TO TWIST IT TO HIS ADVANTAGE SOMEHOW.

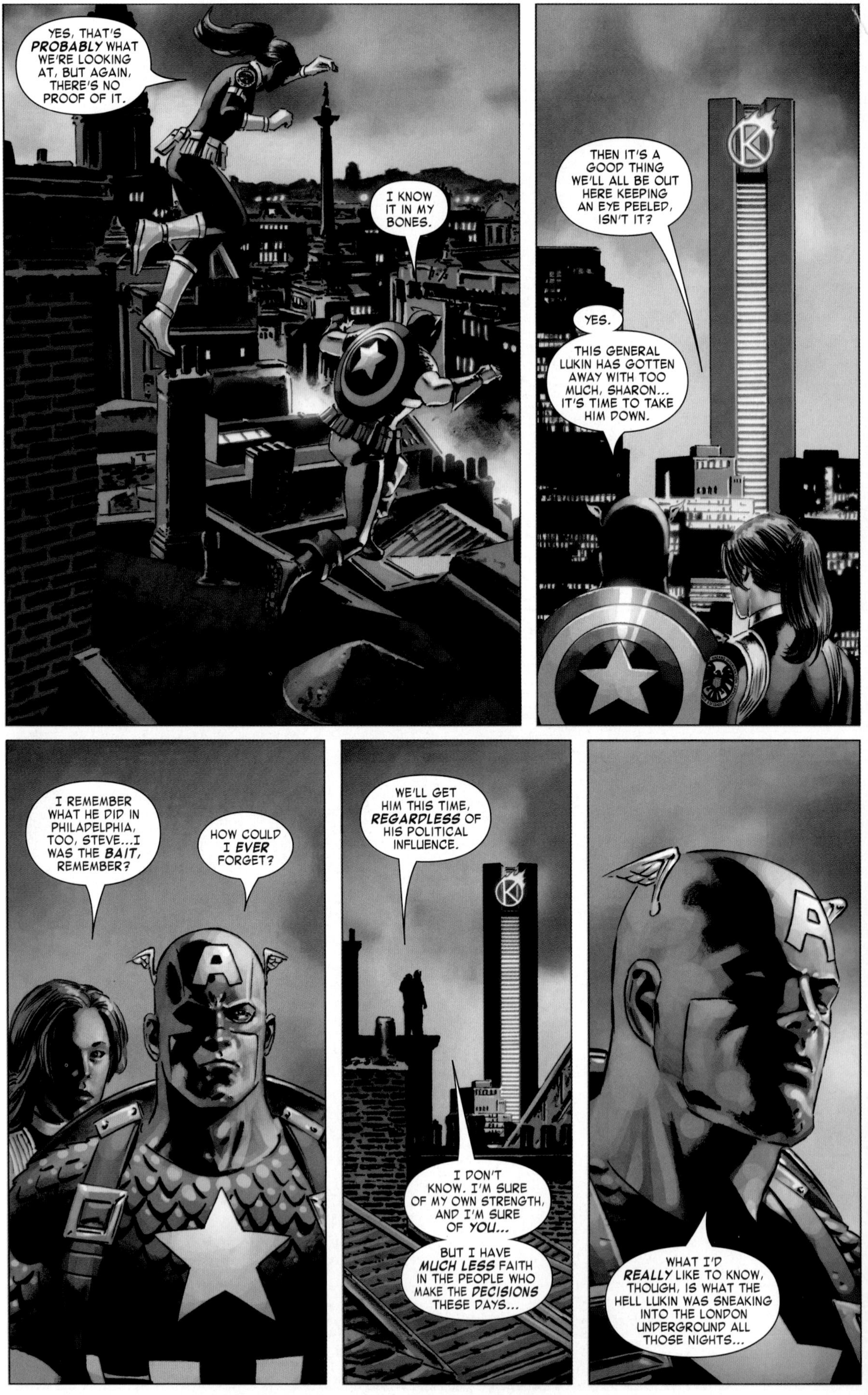
YES, THAT'S PROBABLY WHAT WE'RE LOOKING AT, BUT AGAIN, THERE'S NO PROOF OF IT.
I KNOW IT IN MY BONES.
THEN IT'S A GOOD THING WE'LL ALL BE OUT HERE KEEPING AN EYE PEELED, ISN'T IT?
YES.
THIS GENERAL LUKIN HAS GOTTEN AWAY WITH TOO MUCH, SHARON... IT'S TIME TO TAKE HIM DOWN.
I REMEMBER WHAT HE DID IN PHILADELPHIA, TOO, STEVE...I WAS THE BAIT, REMEMBER?
HOW COULD I EVER FORGET?
WE'LL GET HIM THIS TIME, REGARDLESS OF HIS POLITICAL INFLUENCE.
I DON'T KNOW. I'M SURE OF MY OWN STRENGTH, AND I'M SURE OF YOU...
BUT I HAVE MUCH LESS FAITH IN THE PEOPLE WHO MAKE THE DECISIONS THESE DAYS...
WHAT I'D REALLY LIKE TO KNOW, THOUGH, IS WHAT THE HELL LUKIN WAS SNEAKING INTO THE LONDON UNDERGROUND ALL THOSE NIGHTS...

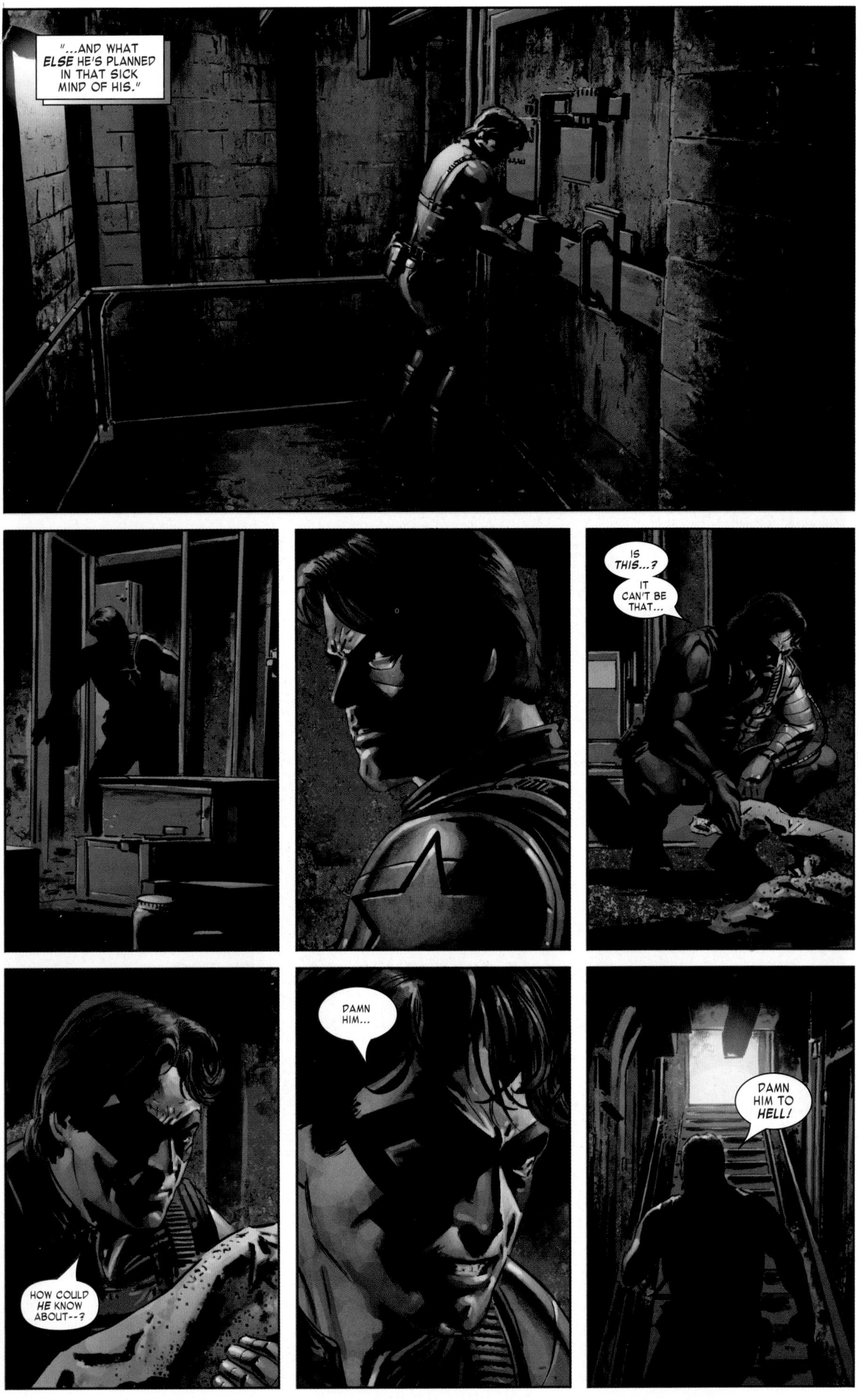
"...AND WHAT ELSE HE'S PLANNED IN THAT SICK MIND OF HIS."
IS THIS...?
IT CAN'T BE THAT...
HOW COULD HE KNOW ABOUT--?
DAMN HIM...
DAMN HIM TO HELL!

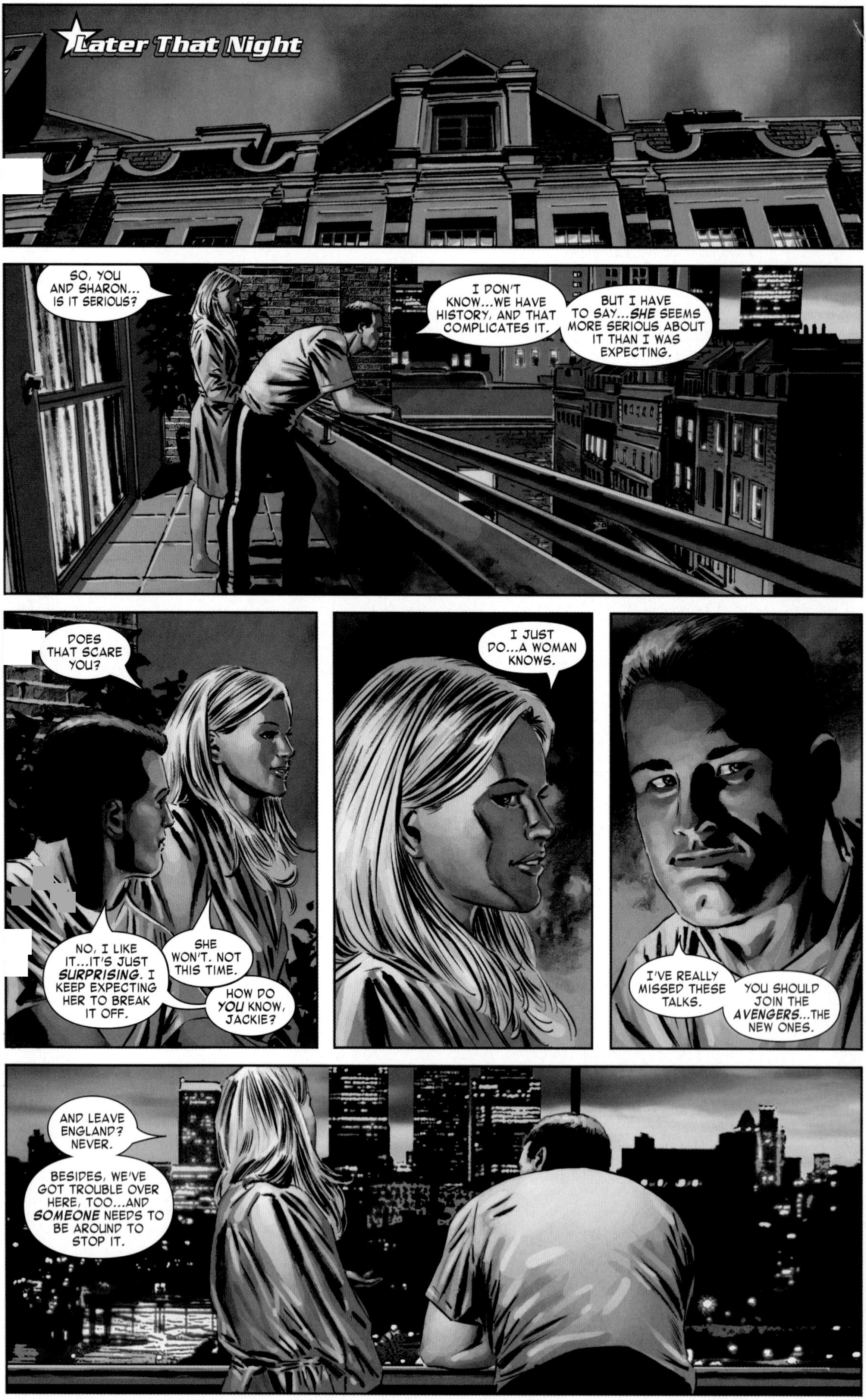
Later That Night
SO, YOU AND SHARON... IS IT SERIOUS?
I DON'T KNOW...WE HAVE HISTORY, AND THAT COMPLICATES IT.
BUT I HAVE TO SAY...SHE SEEMS MORE SERIOUS ABOUT IT THAN I WAS EXPECTING.
DOES THAT SCARE YOU?
NO, I LIKE IT...IT'S JUST SURPRISING. I KEEP EXPECTING HER TO BREAK IT OFF.
SHE WON'T. NOT THIS TIME.
HOW DO YOU KNOW, JACKIE?
I JUST DO...A WOMAN KNOWS.
I'VE REALLY MISSED THESE TALKS.
YOU SHOULD JOIN THE AVENGERS...THE NEW ONES.
AND LEAVE ENGLAND? NEVER.
BESIDES, WE'VE GOT TROUBLE OVER HERE, TOO...AND SOMEONE NEEDS TO BE AROUND TO STOP IT.

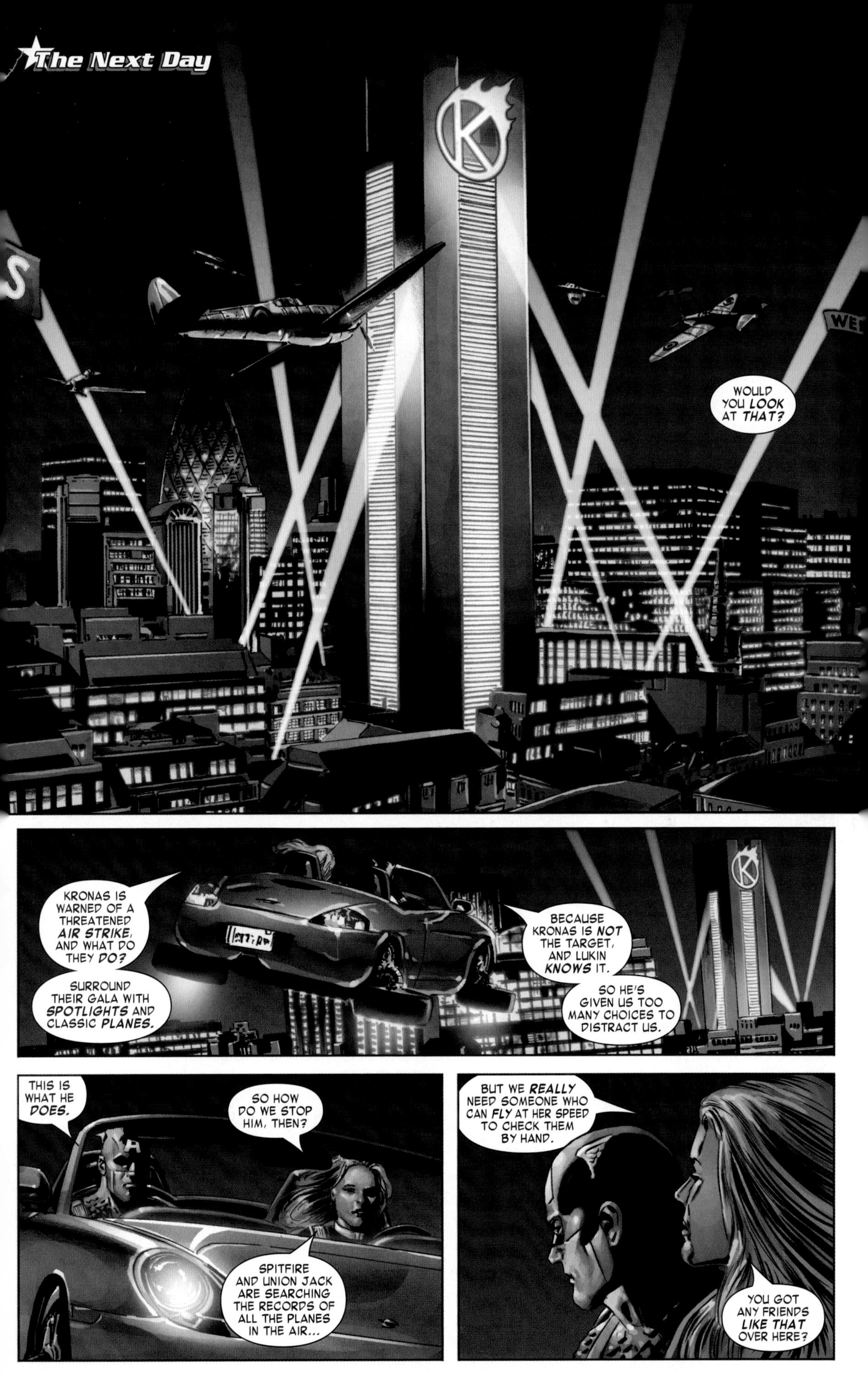
The Next Day
WOULD YOU LOOK AT THAT?
KRONAS IS WARNED OF A THREATENED AIR STRIKE, AND WHAT DO THEY DO?
SURROUND THEIR GALA WITH SPOTLIGHTS AND CLASSIC PLANES.
BECAUSE KRONAS IS NOT THE TARGET, AND LUKIN KNOWS IT.
SO HE'S GIVEN US TOO MANY CHOICES TO DISTRACT US.
THIS IS WHAT HE DOES.
SO HOW DO WE STOP HIM, THEN?
SPITFIRE AND UNION JACK ARE SEARCHING THE RECORDS OF ALL THE PLANES IN THE AIR...
BUT WE REALLY NEED SOMEONE WHO CAN FLY AT HER SPEED TO CHECK THEM BY HAND.
YOU GOT ANY FRIENDS LIKE THAT OVER HERE?

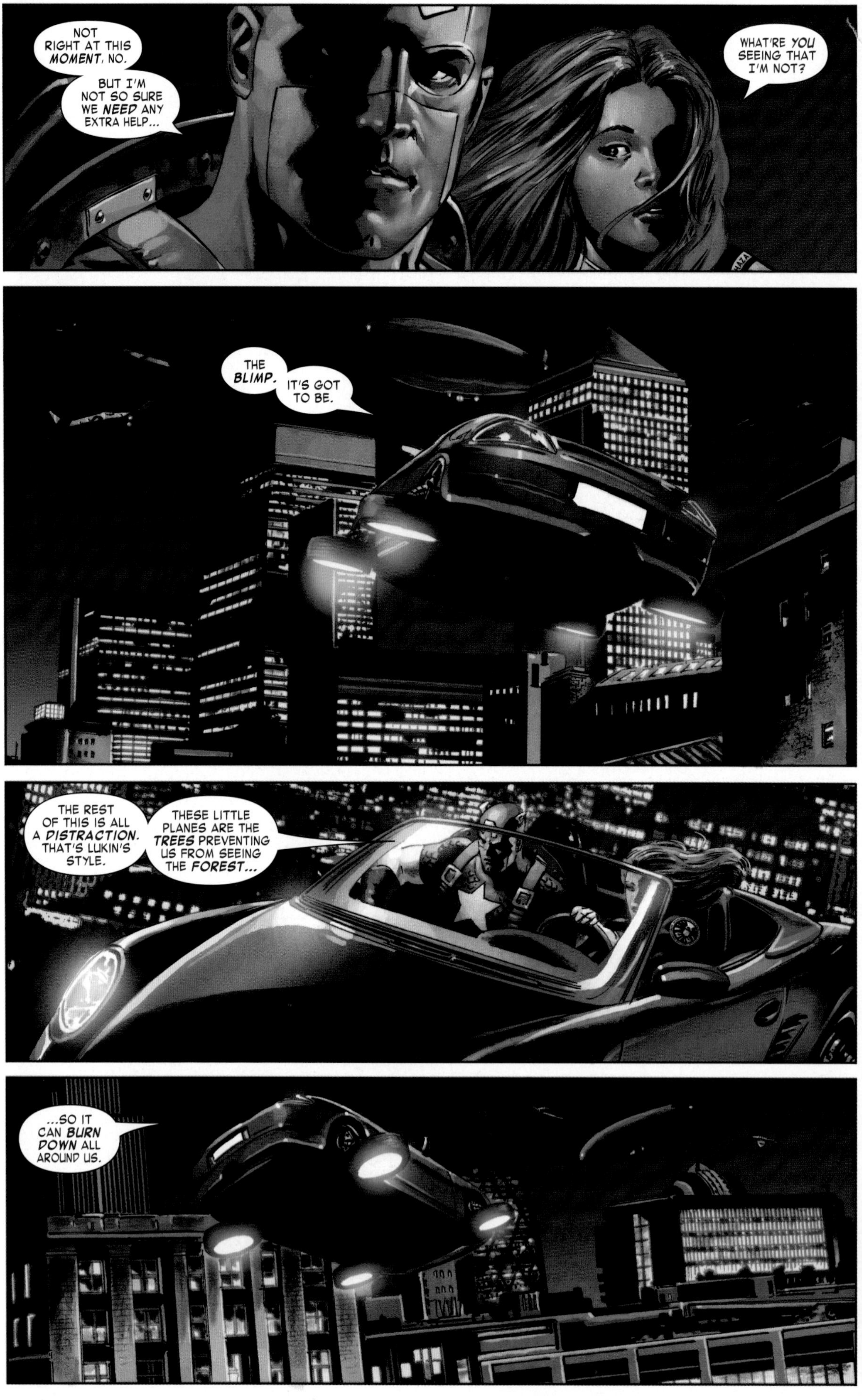
NOT RIGHT AT THIS MOMENT, NO.
BUT I'M NOT SO SURE WE NEED ANY EXTRA HELP...
WHAT'RE YOU SEEING THAT I'M NOT?
THE BLIMP.
IT'S GOT TO BE.
THE REST OF THIS IS ALL A DISTRACTION. THAT'S LUKIN'S STYLE.
THESE LITTLE PLANES ARE THE TREES PREVENTING US FROM SEEING THE FOREST...
...SO IT CAN BURN DOWN ALL AROUND US.

YOU *SEE,* ALEKSANDER?

LEAVE THINGS TO *ME,* AND THEY WILL *ALWAYS* WORK IN OUR FAVOR...

THAT MUST BE WHY CAPTAIN AMERICA IS LONG DEAD, RIGHT?

BECAUSE OF YOUR *EXCELLENT* PLANNING.

PERHAPS YOU SHOULD ACCEPT THAT I AM THE FINER TACTICIAN HERE, SKULL.

I KILLED *YOU,* AFTER ALL.

UNLESS *THIS* WAS MY PLAN ALL ALONG. TO GET INSIDE YOUR HEAD.

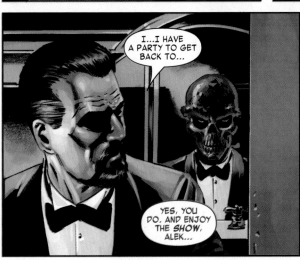

I...I HAVE A PARTY TO GET BACK TO...

YES, YOU DO. AND ENJOY THE *SHOW,* ALEK...

...AS YOU LEARN HOW THINGS ARE DONE *MY WAY.*

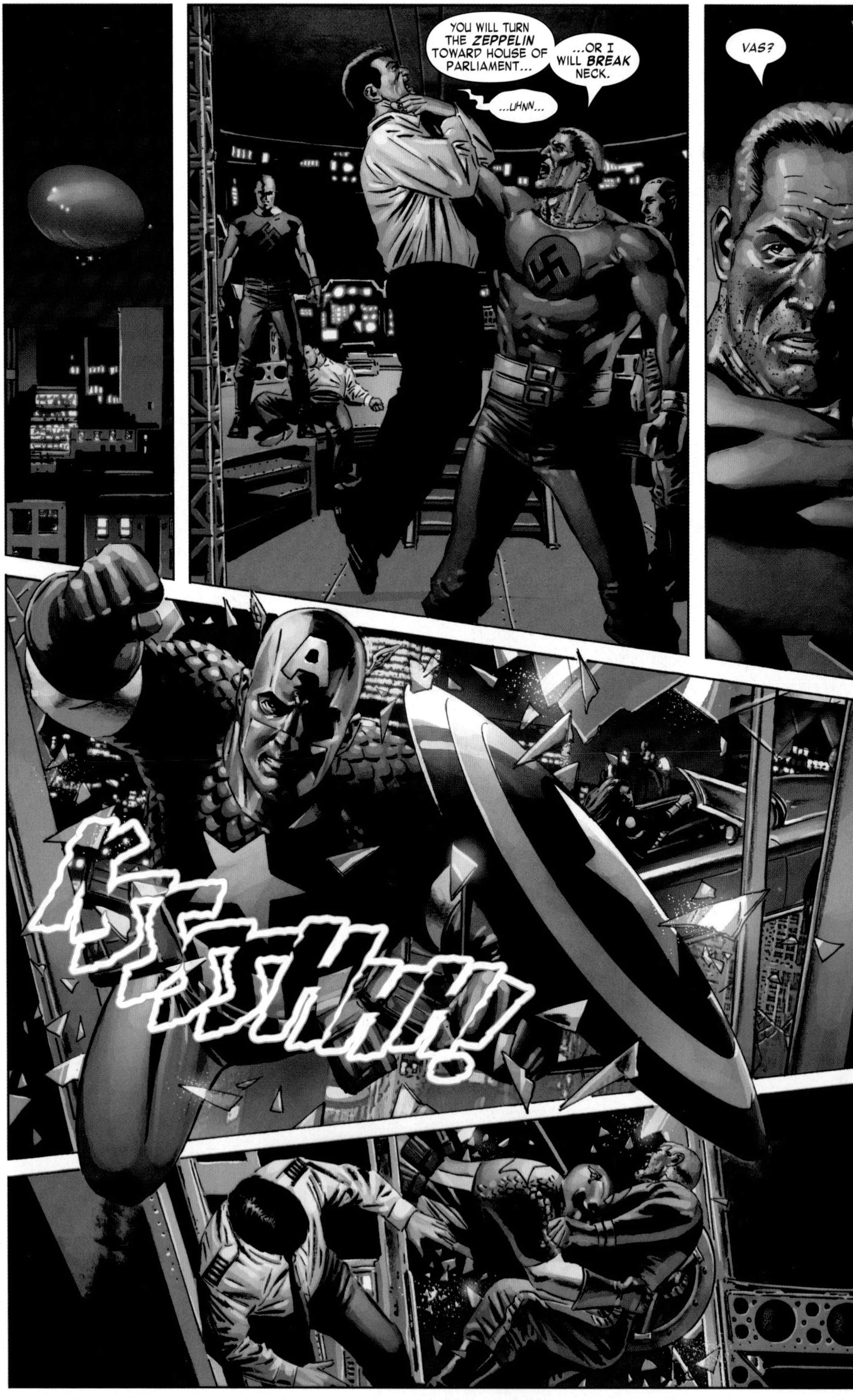
YOU WILL TURN THE ZEPPELIN TOWARD HOUSE OF PARLIAMENT...
...UHNN...
...OR I WILL BREAK NECK.
VAS?

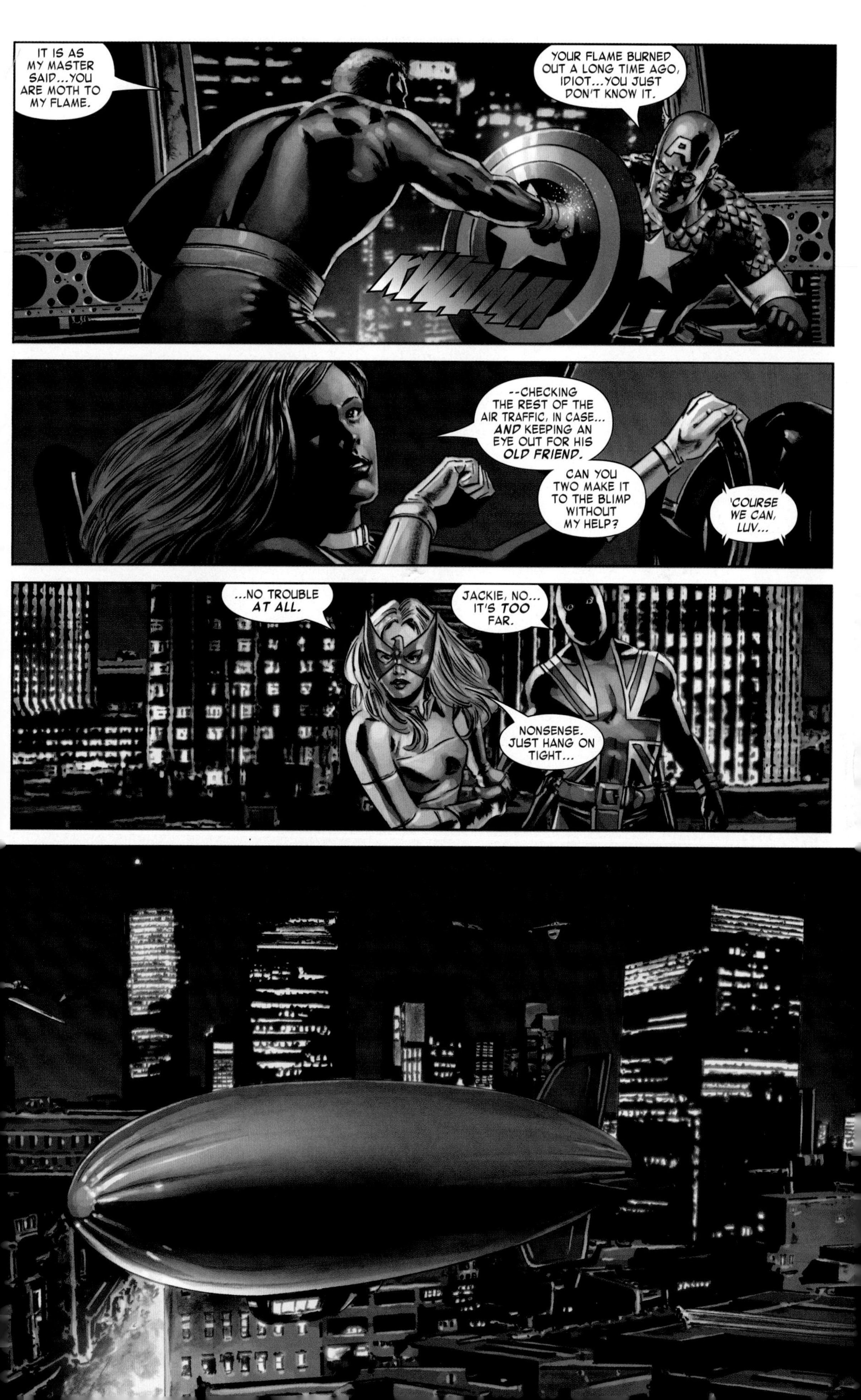
IT IS AS MY MASTER SAID...YOU ARE MOTH TO MY FLAME.
YOUR FLAME BURNED OUT A LONG TIME AGO, IDIOT...YOU JUST DON'T KNOW IT.
KWAMM
--CHECKING THE REST OF THE AIR TRAFFIC, IN CASE... AND KEEPING AN EYE OUT FOR HIS OLD FRIEND.
CAN YOU TWO MAKE IT TO THE BLIMP WITHOUT MY HELP?
'COURSE WE CAN, LUV...
...NO TROUBLE AT ALL.
JACKIE, NO... IT'S TOO FAR.
NONSENSE. JUST HANG ON TIGHT...

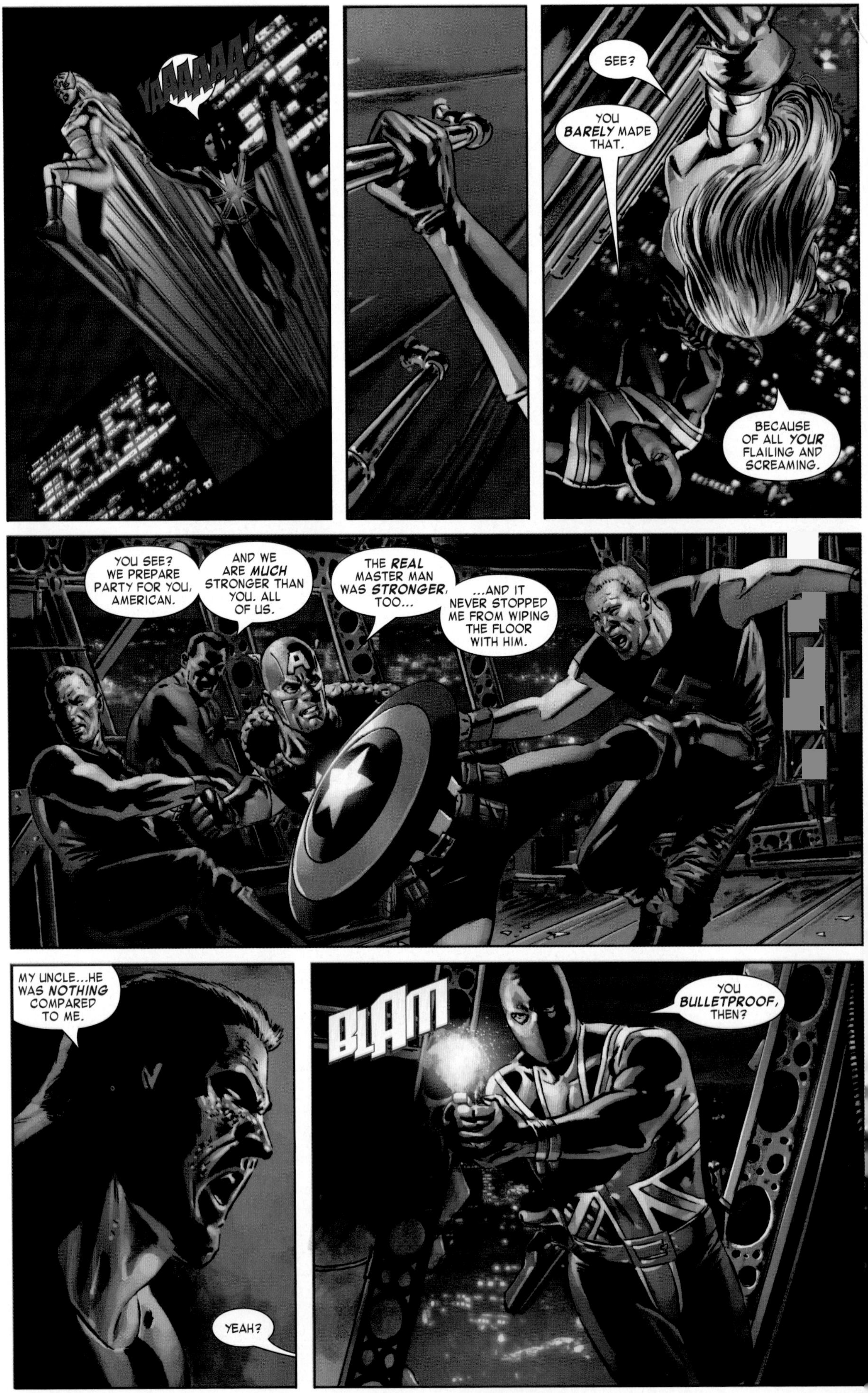

YAAAAAA!
SEE?
YOU BARELY MADE THAT.
BECAUSE OF ALL YOUR FLAILING AND SCREAMING.
YOU SEE? WE PREPARE PARTY FOR YOU, AMERICAN.
AND WE ARE MUCH STRONGER THAN YOU. ALL OF US.
THE REAL MASTER MAN WAS STRONGER, TOO...
...AND IT NEVER STOPPED ME FROM WIPING THE FLOOR WITH HIM.
MY UNCLE...HE WAS NOTHING COMPARED TO ME.
YEAH?
BLAM
YOU BULLETPROOF, THEN?

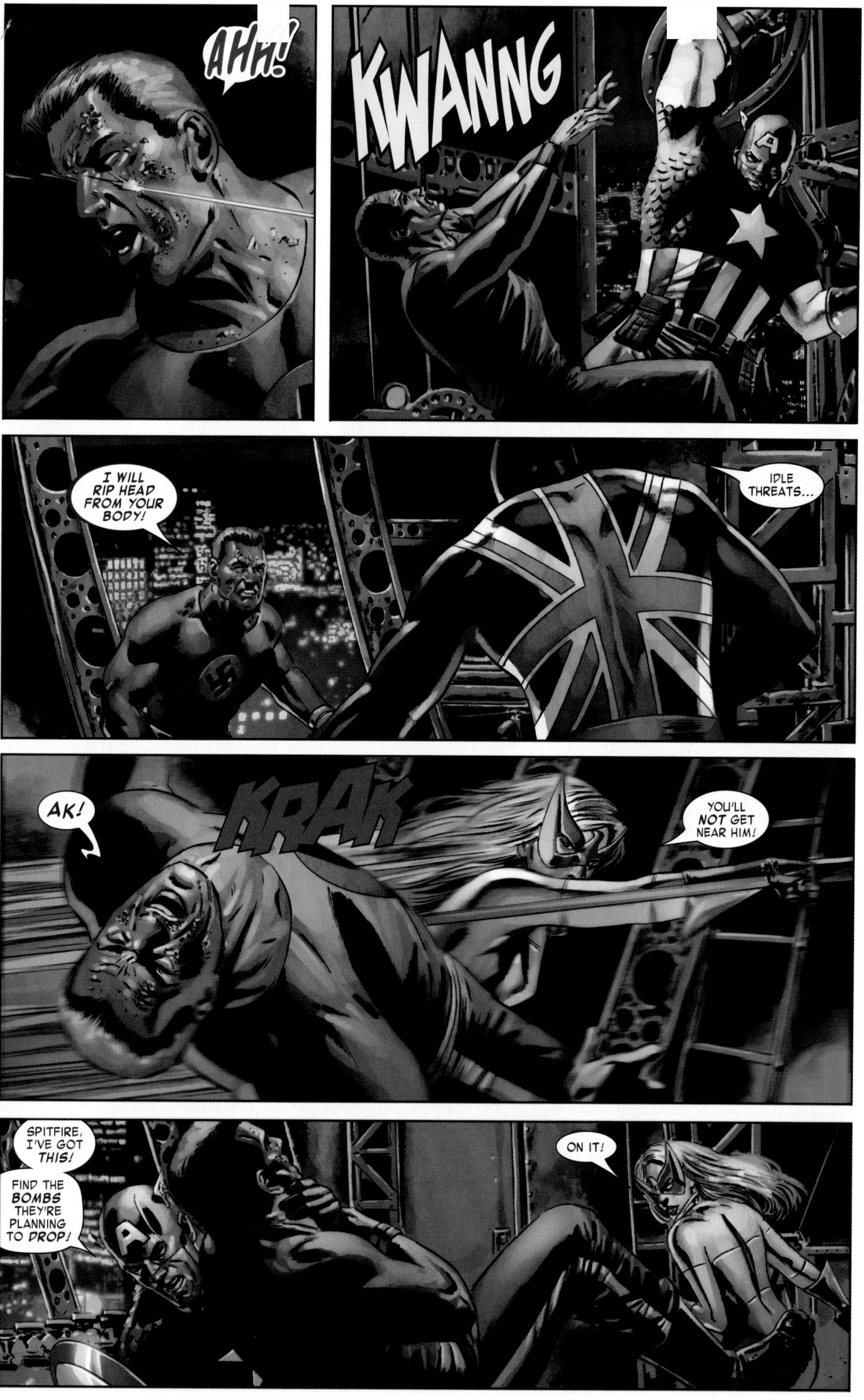
AHH!
KWANNG
I WILL RIP HEAD FROM YOUR BODY!
IDLE THREATS...
AK!
KRAK
YOU'LL NOT GET NEAR HIM!
SPITFIRE, I'VE GOT THIS!
FIND THE BOMBS THEY'RE PLANNING TO DROP!
ON IT!

AND BE *CAREFUL!*

THERE'S *ANOTHER* OF THESE MONSTERS ON BOARD!

NOT FOR LONG...

VAS IS--

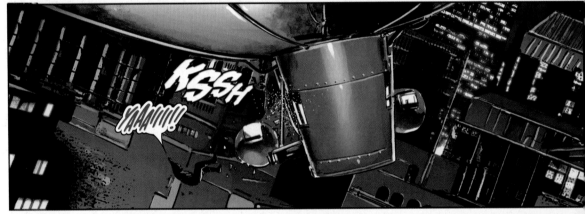

KSSH

YAAAAII!

OH, *DAMN...* CAP, I'VE GOT A PROBLEM...

WHAT?

WELL...I TOOK OUT THAT MASTER RACE THUG. HE'S ON THE ROOFTOPS BELOW, HOPEFULLY *INJURED...*

BUT I MANAGED TO SET THE BLOODY SHIP ON *FIRE* IN THE PROCESS.

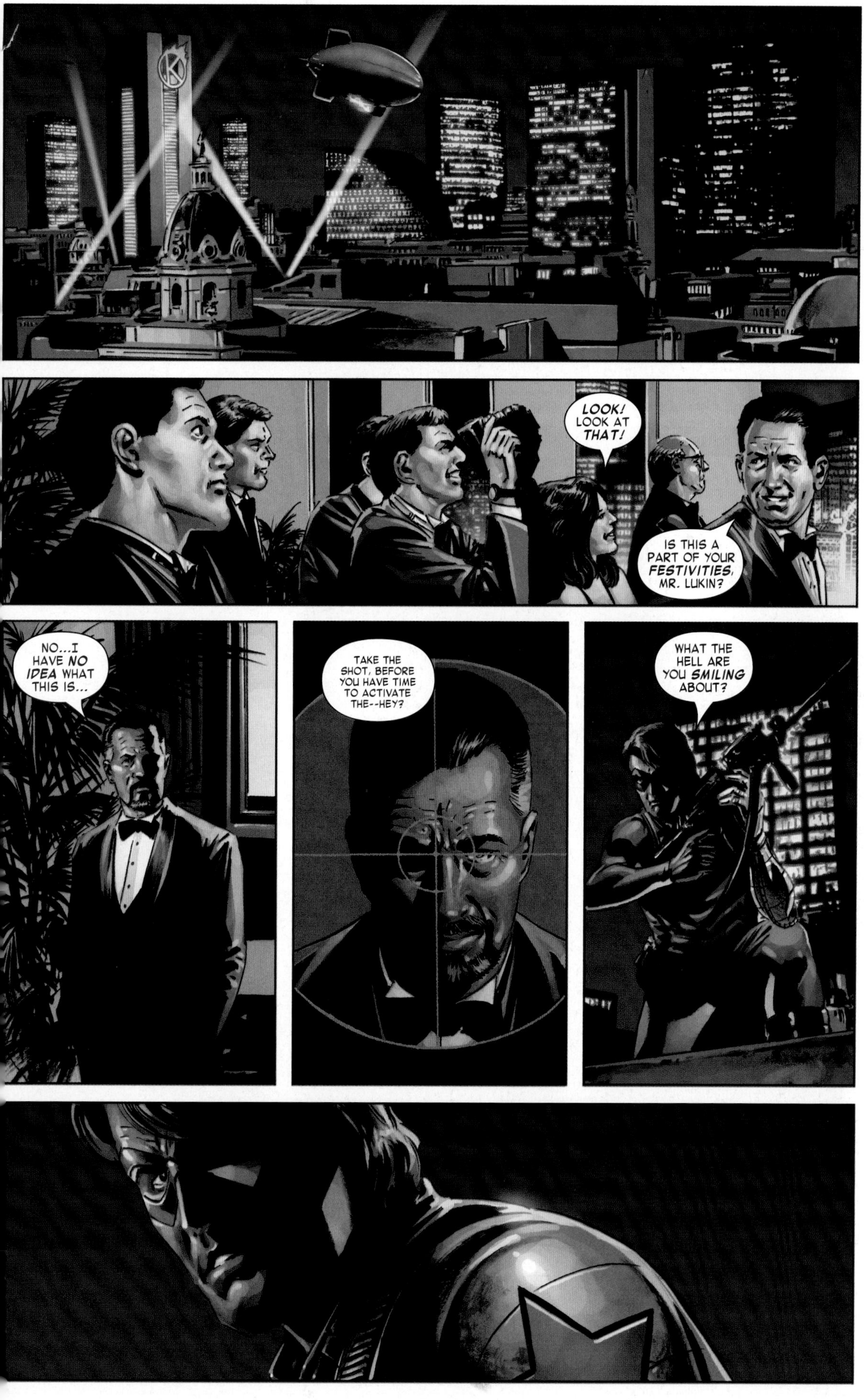
LOOK! LOOK AT THAT!
IS THIS A PART OF YOUR FESTIVITIES, MR. LUKIN?
NO...I HAVE NO IDEA WHAT THIS IS...
TAKE THE SHOT, BEFORE YOU HAVE TIME TO ACTIVATE THE--HEY?
WHAT THE HELL ARE YOU SMILING ABOUT?

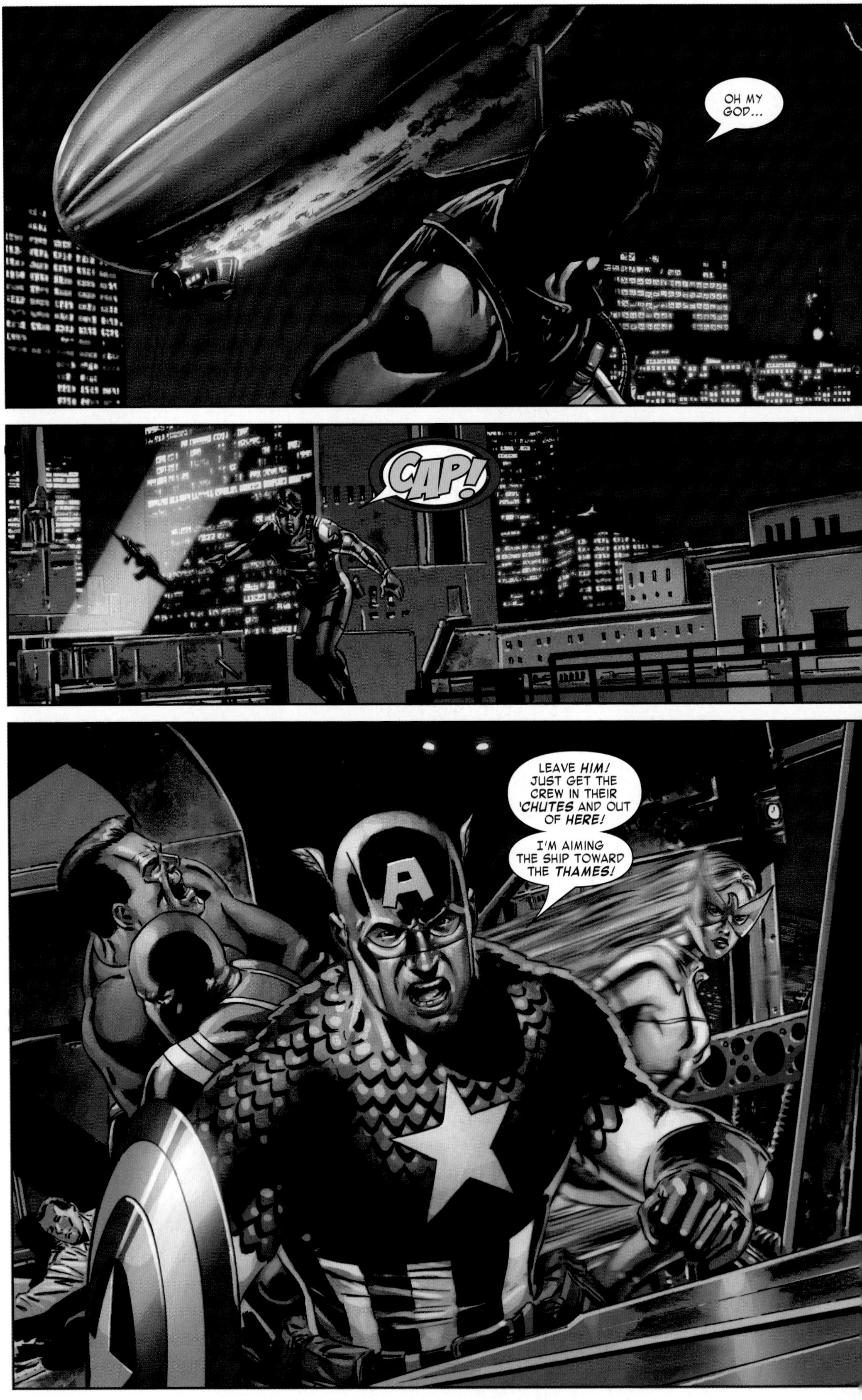
OH MY GOD...
CAP!
LEAVE HIM! JUST GET THE CREW IN THEIR 'CHUTES AND OUT OF HERE!
I'M AIMING THE SHIP TOWARD THE THAMES!

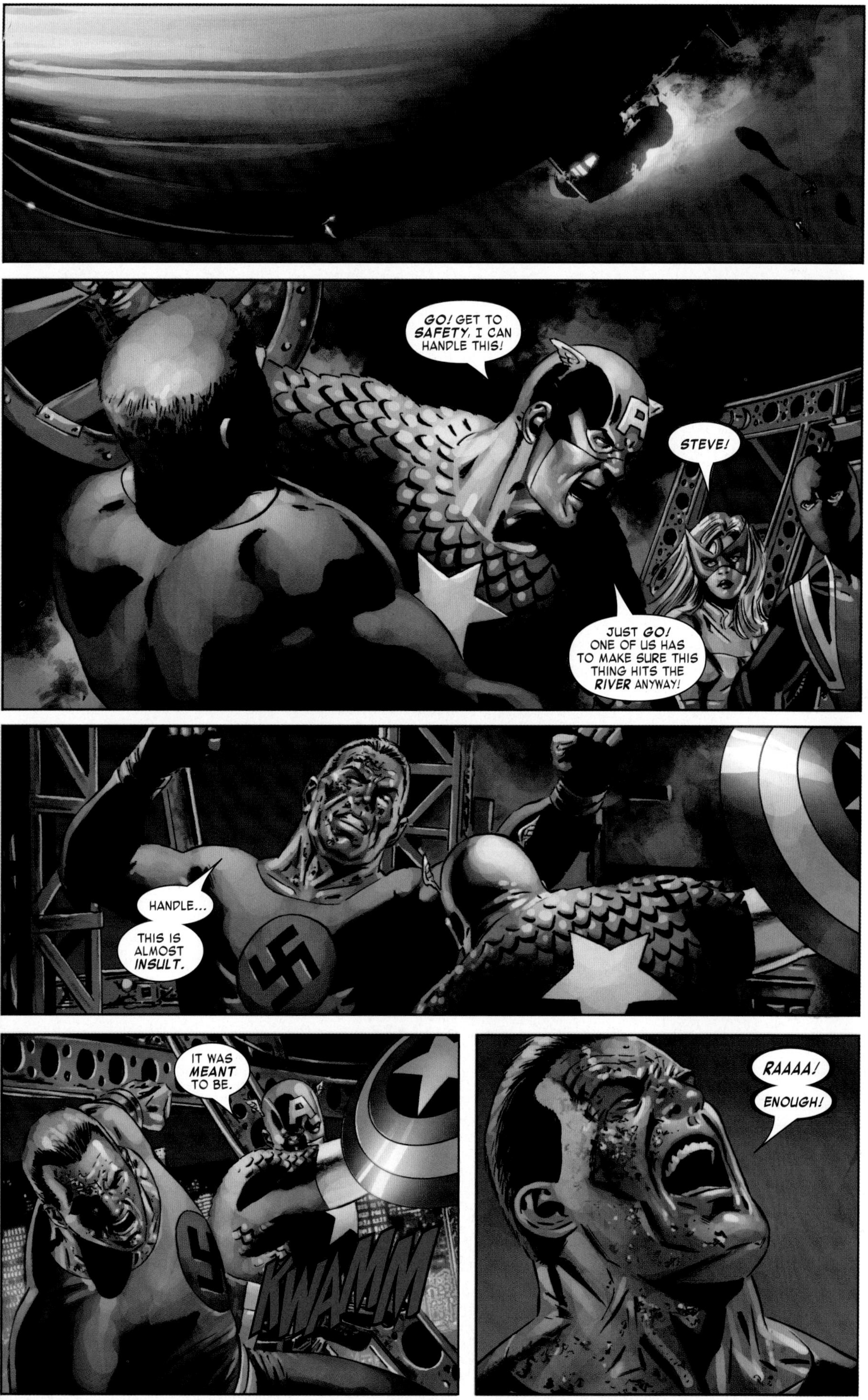
GO! GET TO SAFETY, I CAN HANDLE THIS!
STEVE!
JUST GO! ONE OF US HAS TO MAKE SURE THIS THING HITS THE RIVER ANYWAY!
HANDLE...
THIS IS ALMOST INSULT.
IT WAS MEANT TO BE.
KWAMM
RAAAA!
ENOUGH!

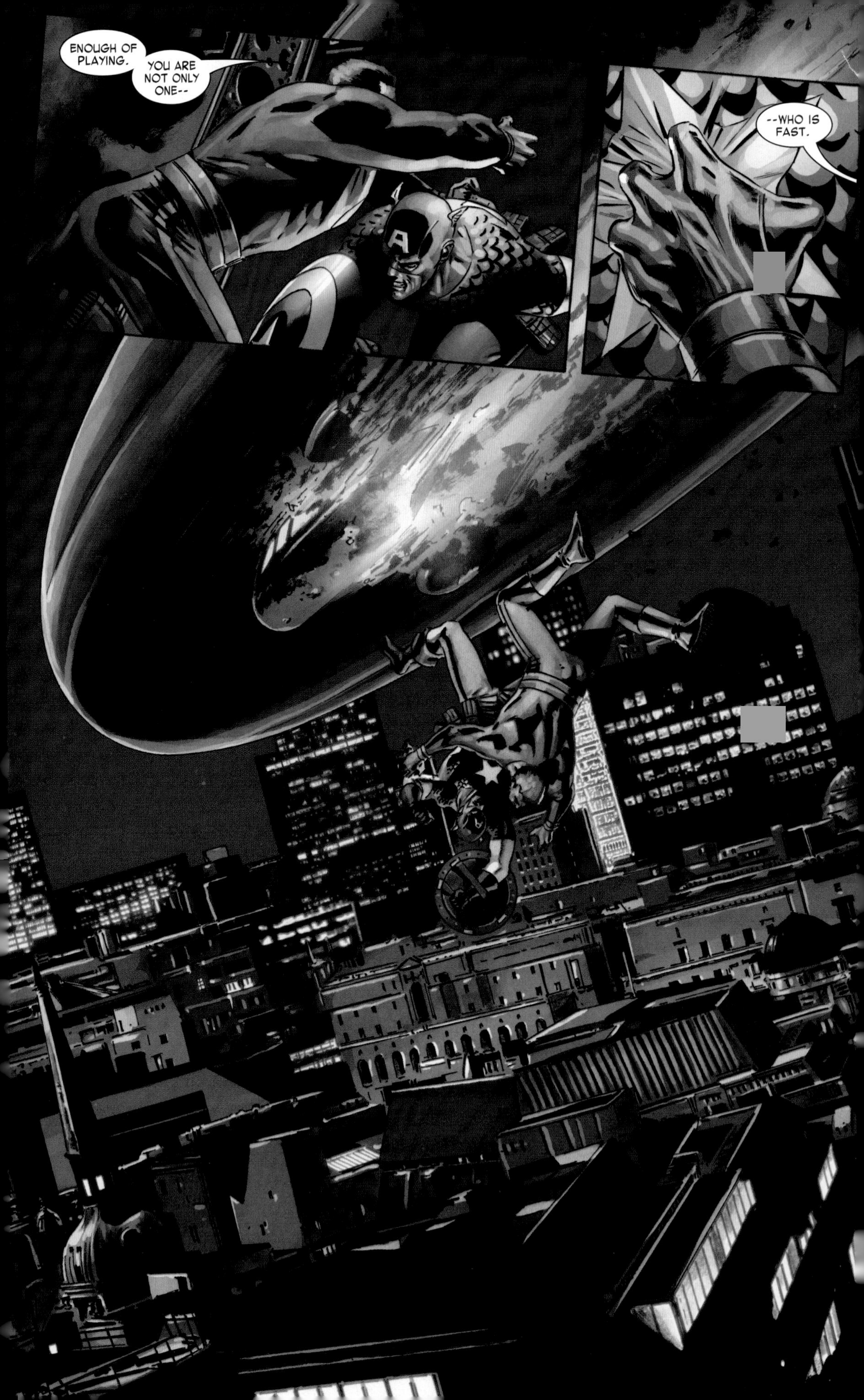
ENOUGH OF PLAYING.
YOU ARE NOT ONLY ONE--
--WHO IS FAST.

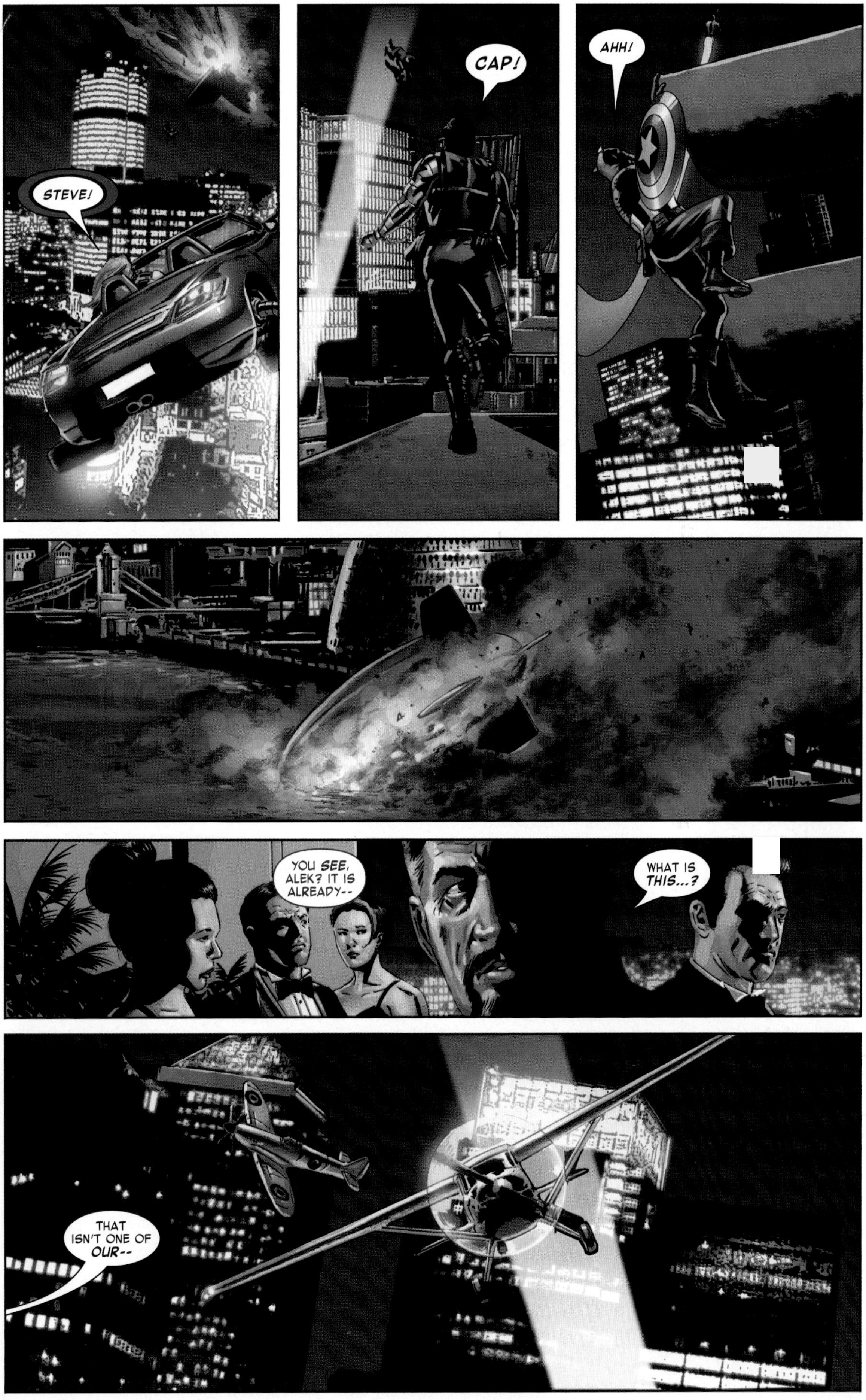
STEVE!
CAP!
AHH!
YOU SEE, ALEK? IT IS ALREADY--
WHAT IS THIS...?
THAT ISN'T ONE OF OUR--

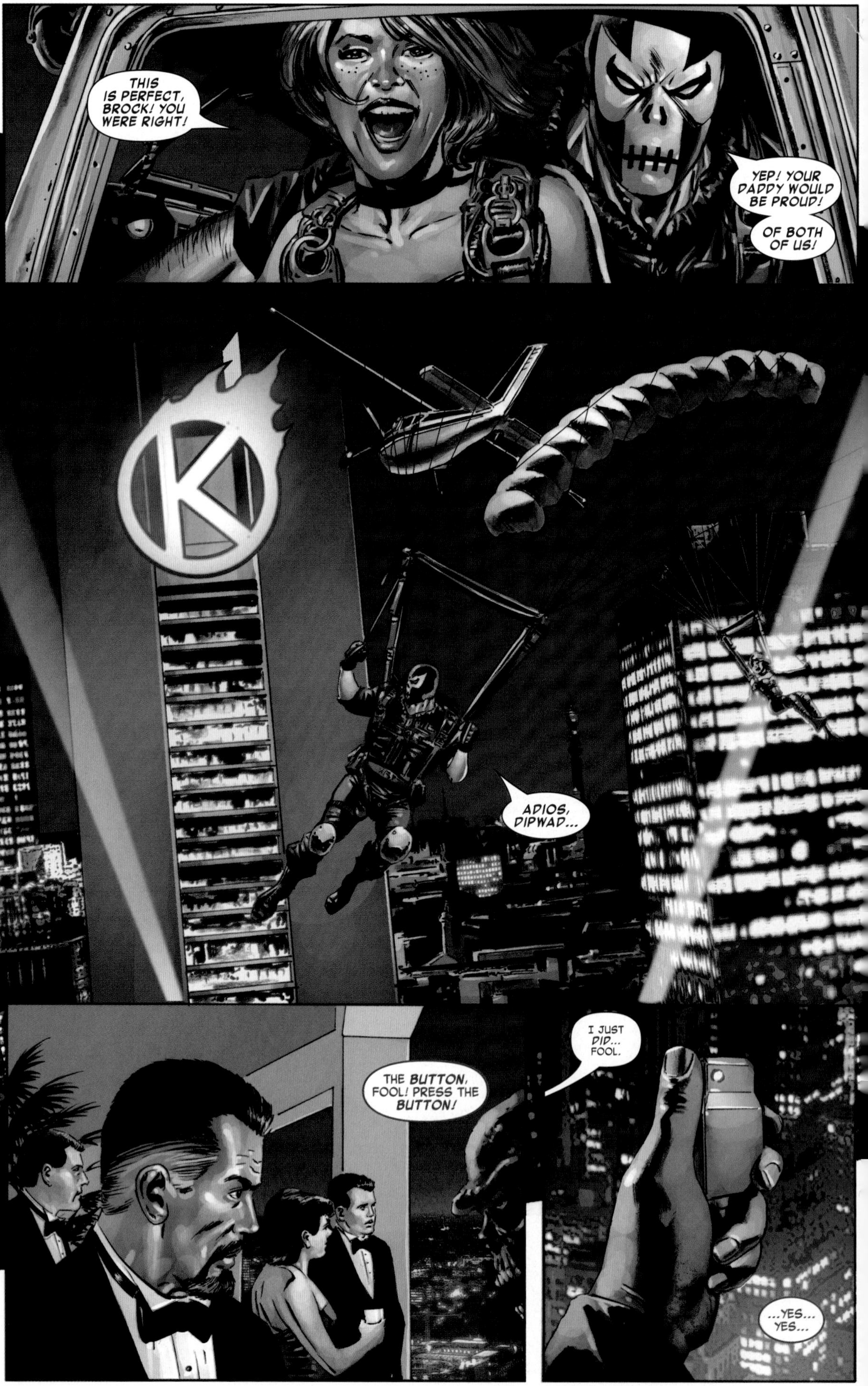

THIS IS PERFECT, BROCK! YOU WERE RIGHT!
YEP! YOUR DADDY WOULD BE PROUD!
OF BOTH OF US!
ADIOS, DIPWAD...
THE BUTTON, FOOL! PRESS THE BUTTON!
I JUST DID... FOOL.
...YES... YES...

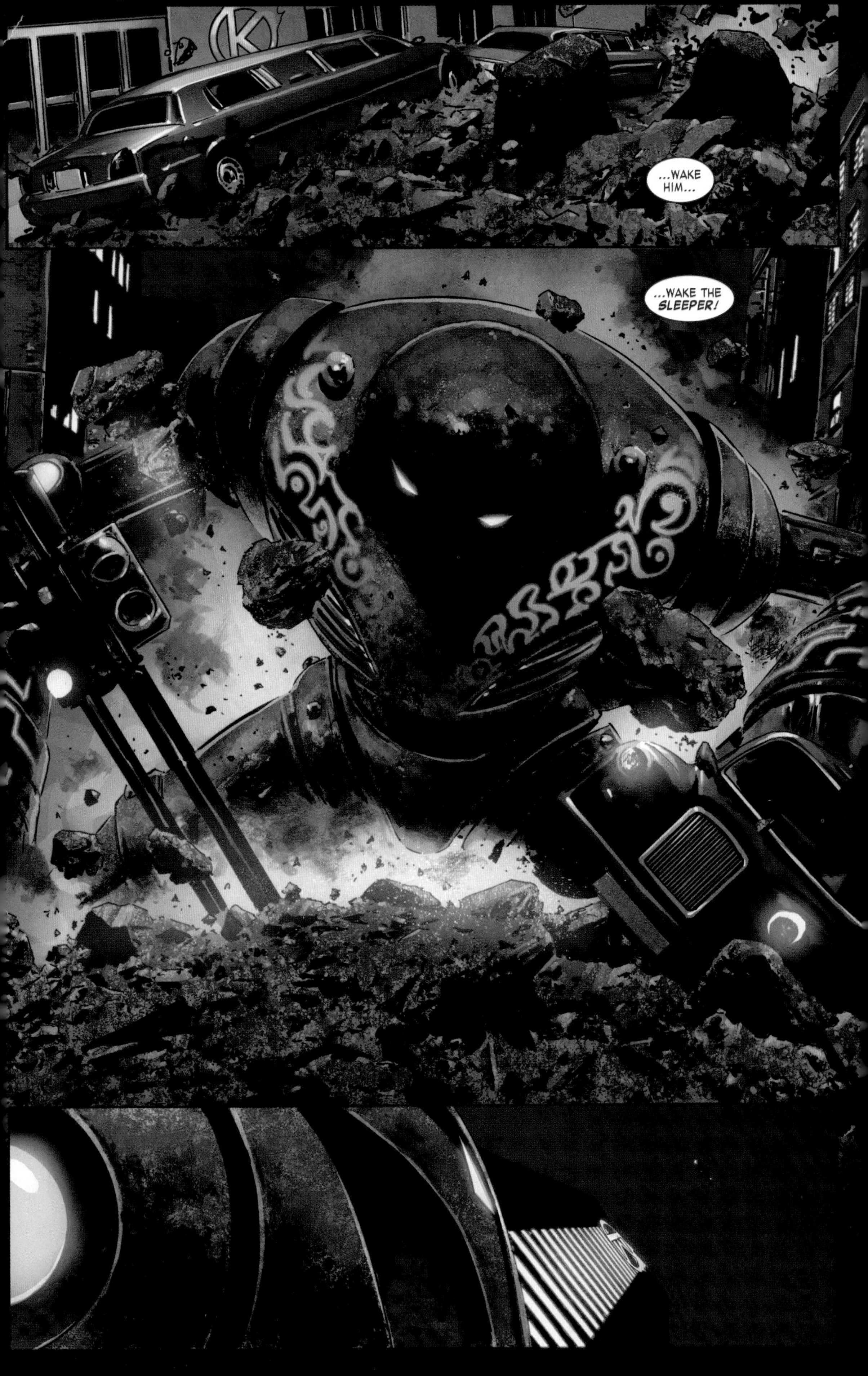
...WAKE HIM...
...WAKE THE SLEEPER!

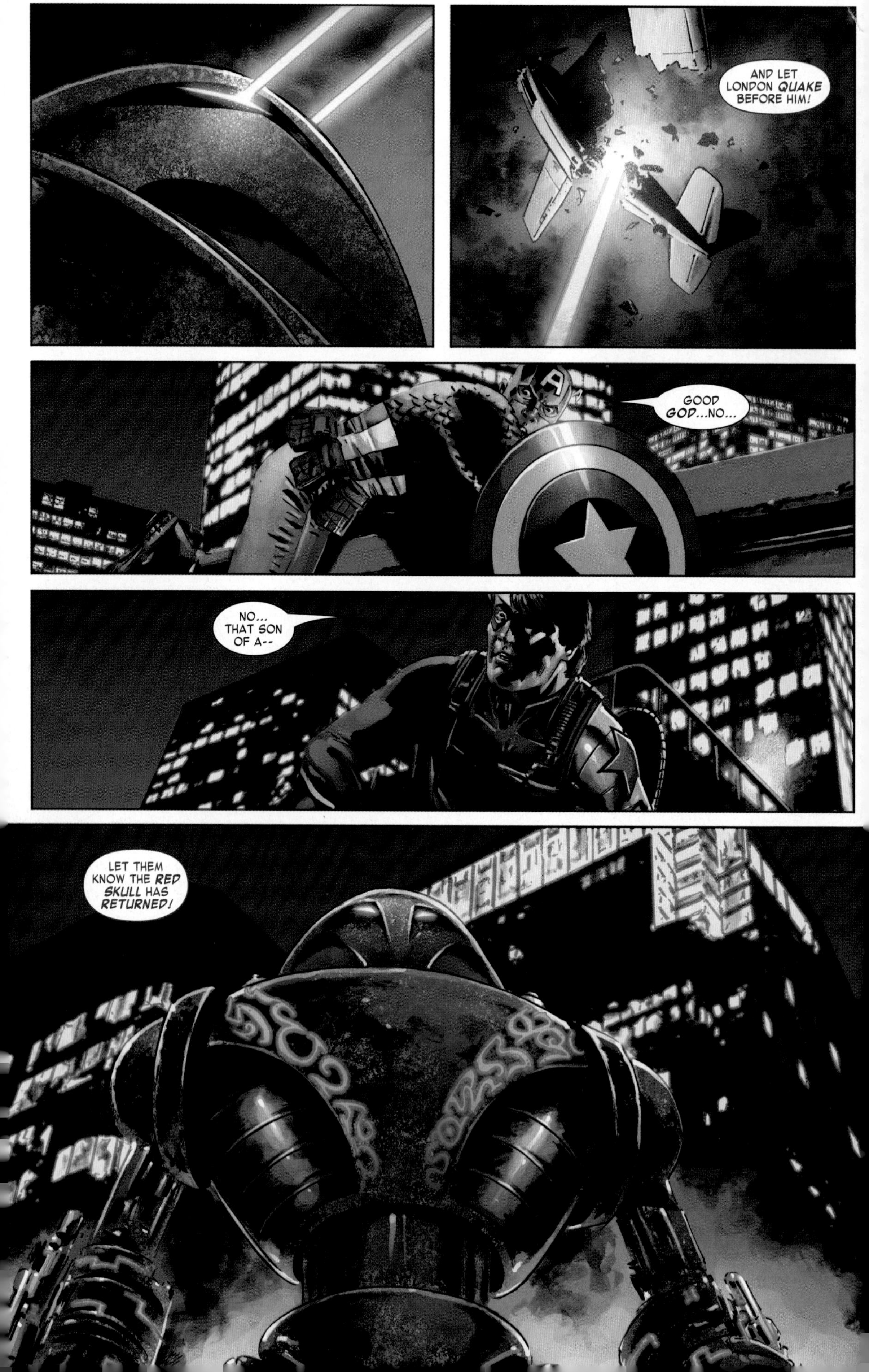
AND LET LONDON QUAKE BEFORE HIM!
GOOD GOD...NO...
NO... THAT SON OF A--
LET THEM KNOW THE RED SKULL HAS RETURNED!

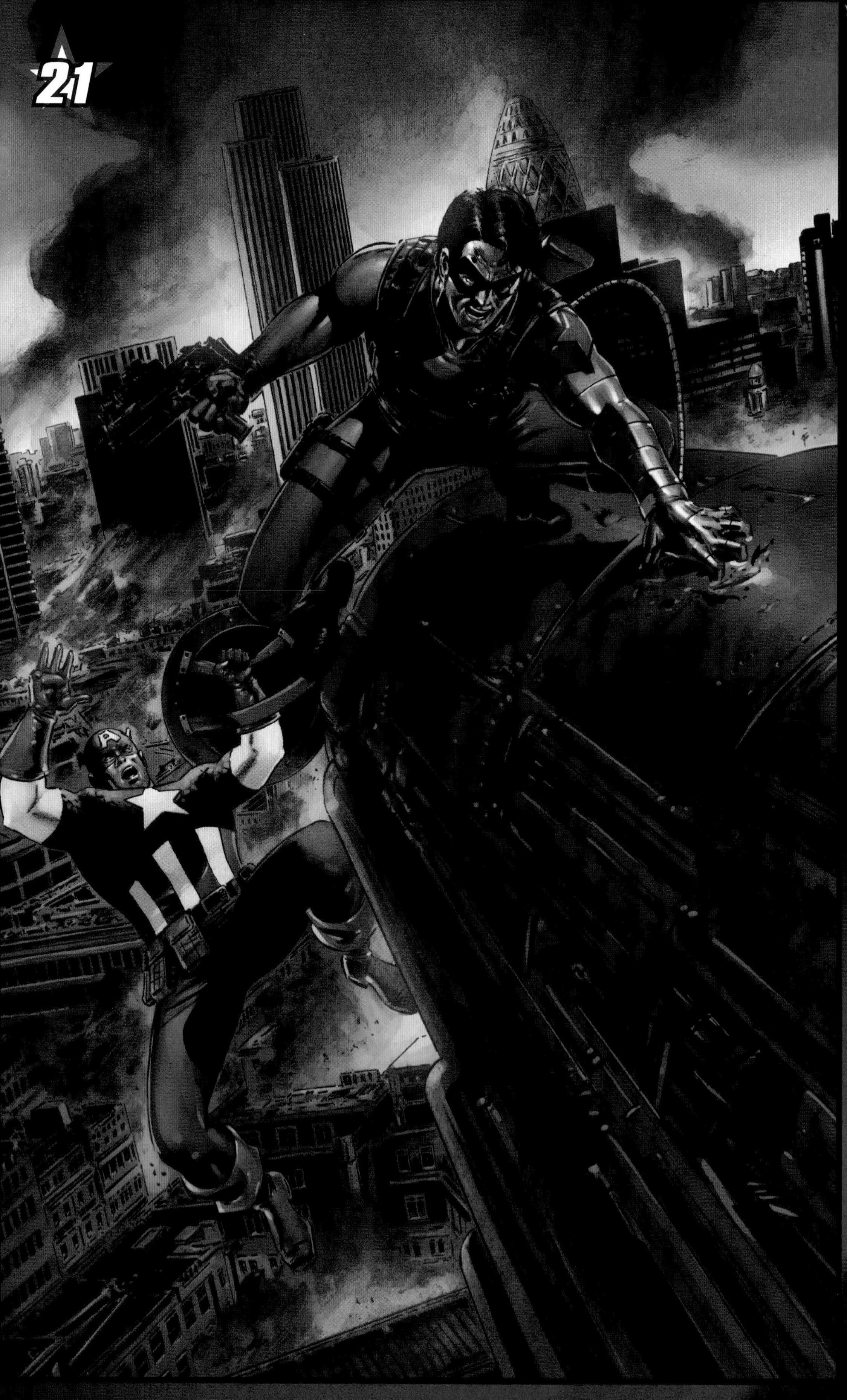
21

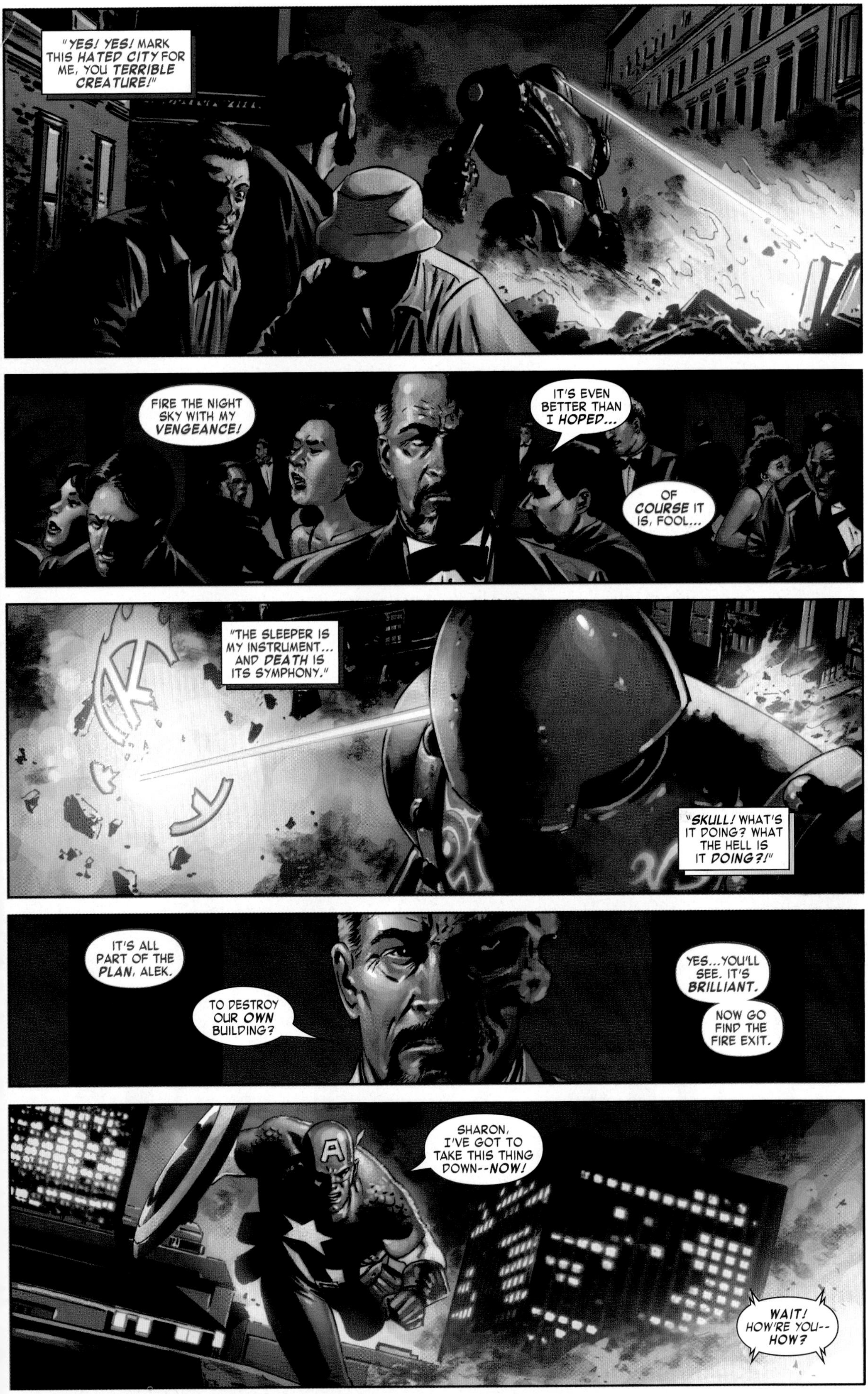
"YES! YES! MARK THIS HATED CITY FOR ME, YOU TERRIBLE CREATURE!"
FIRE THE NIGHT SKY WITH MY VENGEANCE!
IT'S EVEN BETTER THAN I HOPED...
OF COURSE IT IS, FOOL...
"THE SLEEPER IS MY INSTRUMENT... AND DEATH IS ITS SYMPHONY."
"SKULL! WHAT'S IT DOING? WHAT THE HELL IS IT DOING?!"
IT'S ALL PART OF THE PLAN, ALEK.
TO DESTROY OUR OWN BUILDING?
YES...YOU'LL SEE. IT'S BRILLIANT.
NOW GO FIND THE FIRE EXIT.
SHARON, I'VE GOT TO TAKE THIS THING DOWN--NOW!
WAIT! HOW'RE YOU-- HOW?

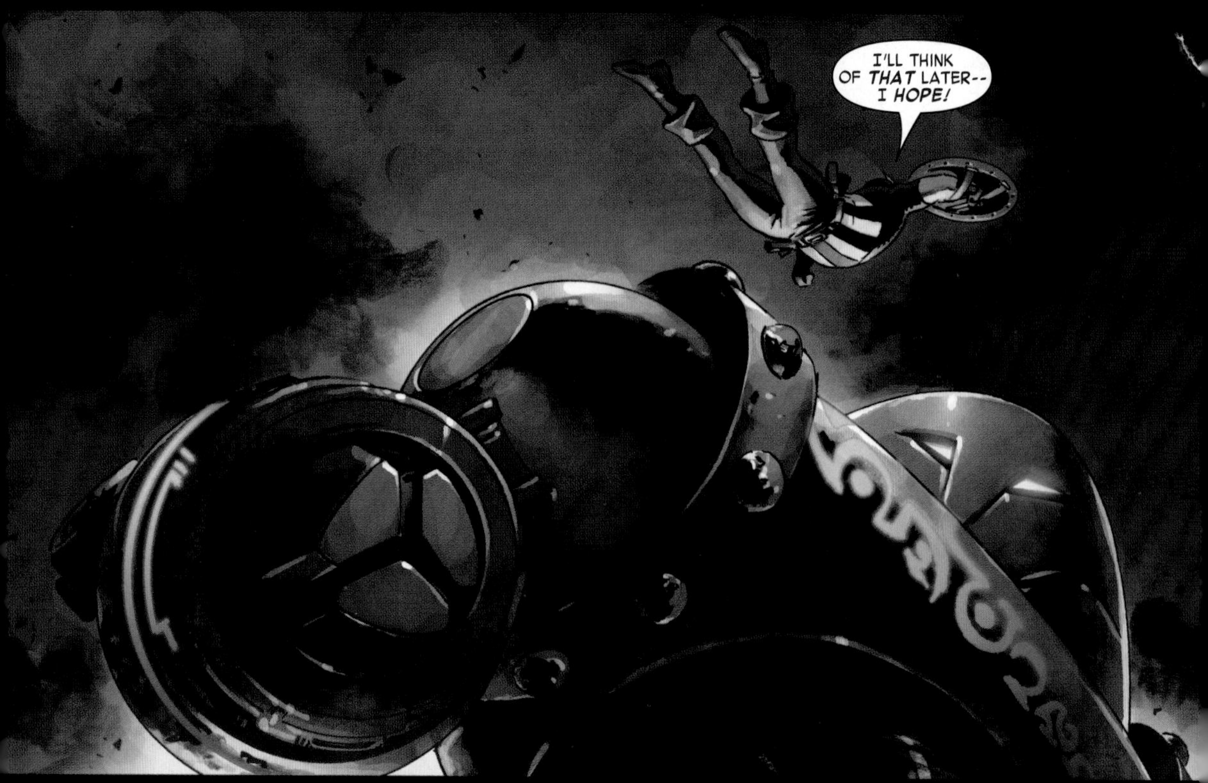
I'LL THINK OF *THAT* LATER-- I HOPE!

TWENTY-FIRST CENTURY BLITZ

CONCLUSION

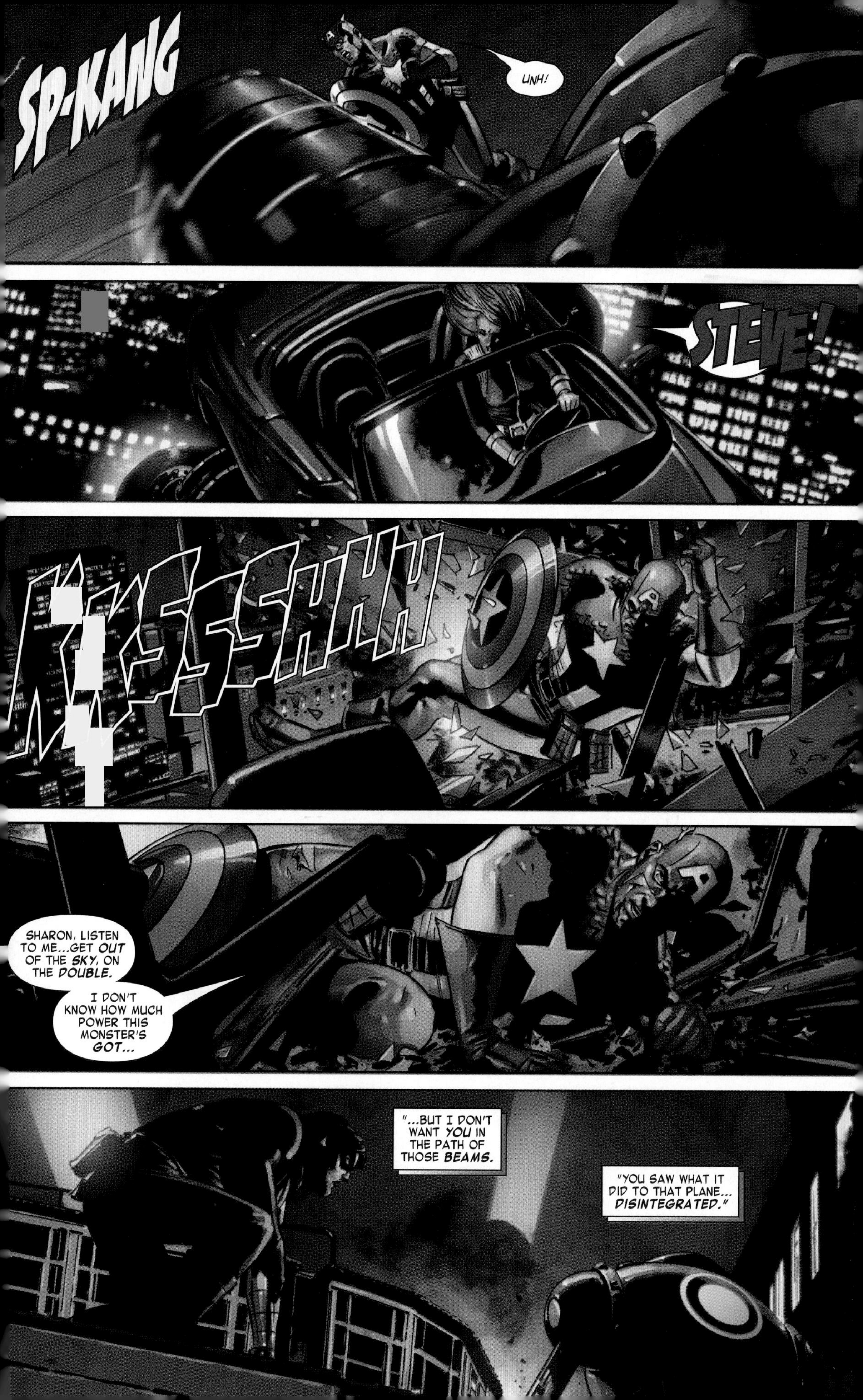
SP-KANG
UNH!
STEVE!
SHARON, LISTEN TO ME...GET OUT OF THE SKY, ON THE DOUBLE.
I DON'T KNOW HOW MUCH POWER THIS MONSTER'S GOT...
"...BUT I DON'T WANT YOU IN THE PATH OF THOSE BEAMS.
"YOU SAW WHAT IT DID TO THAT PLANE... DISINTEGRATED."

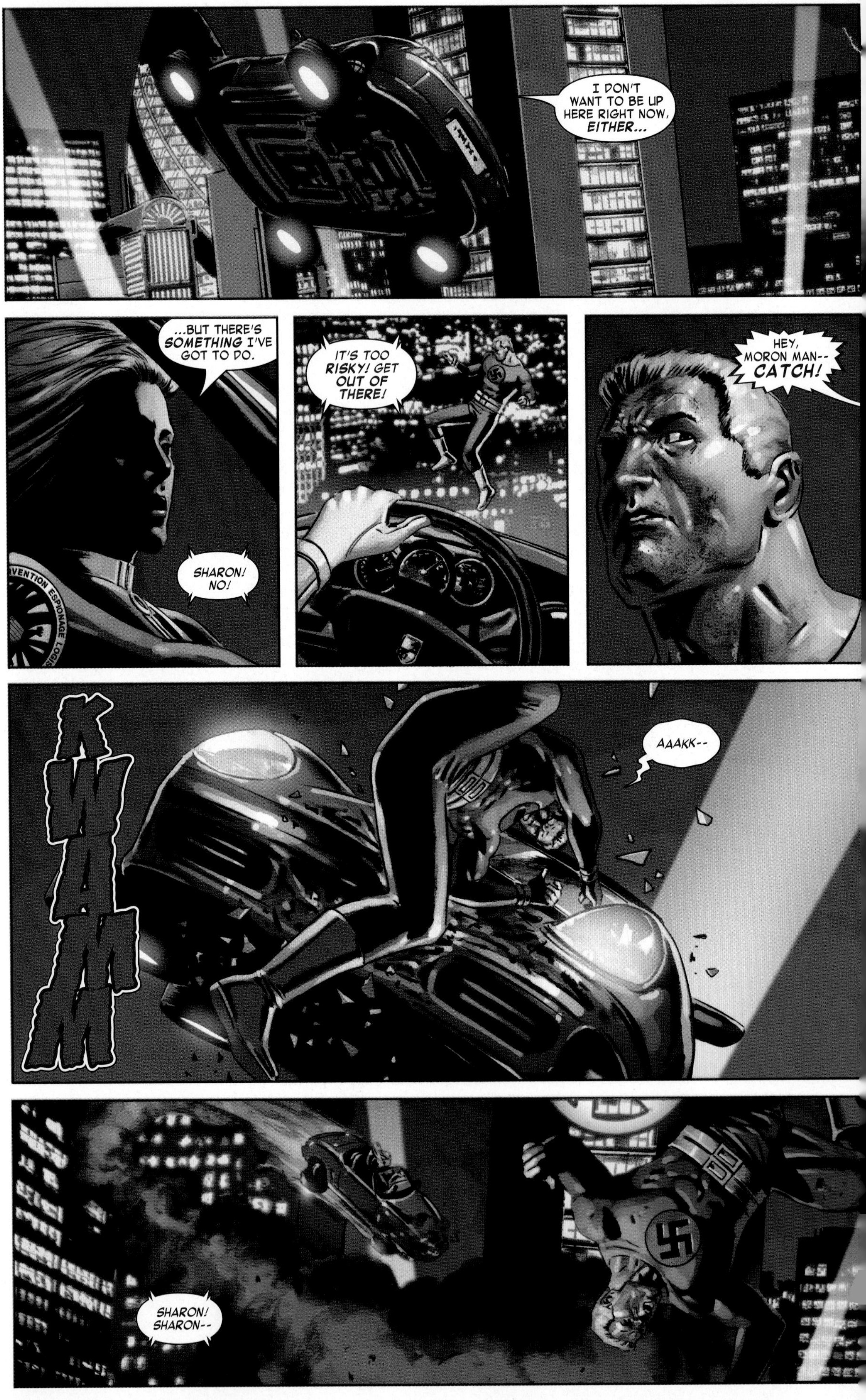
I DON'T WANT TO BE UP HERE RIGHT NOW, EITHER...
...BUT THERE'S SOMETHING I'VE GOT TO DO.
SHARON! NO!
IT'S TOO RISKY! GET OUT OF THERE!
HEY, MORON MAN-- CATCH!
KWAMM
AAAKK--
SHARON! SHARON--

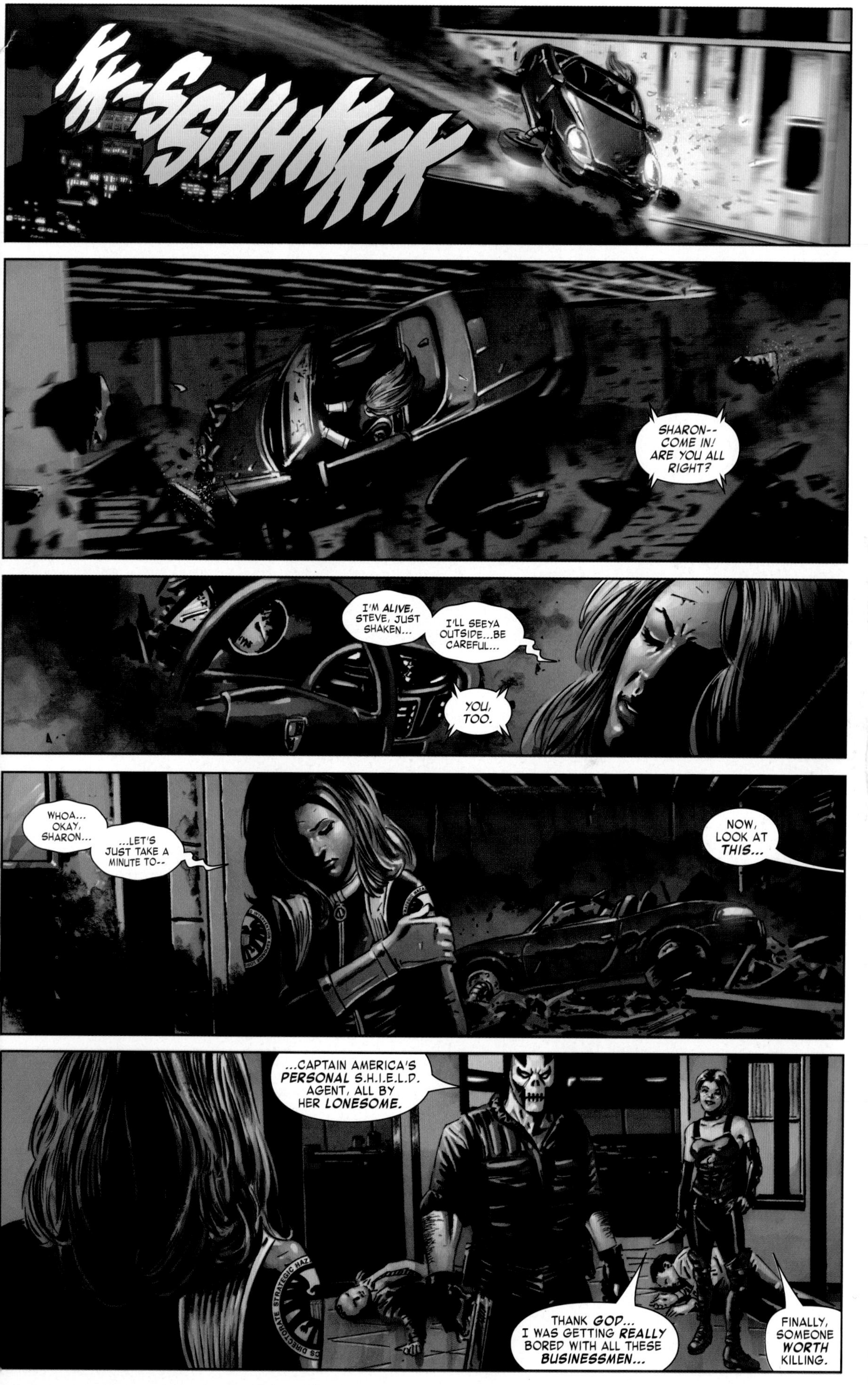
KK-SCHHKKK
SHARON-- COME IN! ARE YOU ALL RIGHT?
I'M ALIVE, STEVE, JUST SHAKEN...
I'LL SEEYA OUTSIDE...BE CAREFUL...
YOU, TOO.
WHOA... OKAY, SHARON...
...LET'S JUST TAKE A MINUTE TO--
NOW, LOOK AT THIS...
...CAPTAIN AMERICA'S PERSONAL S.H.I.E.L.D. AGENT, ALL BY HER LONESOME.
THANK GOD... I WAS GETTING REALLY BORED WITH ALL THESE BUSINESSMEN...
FINALLY, SOMEONE WORTH KILLING.

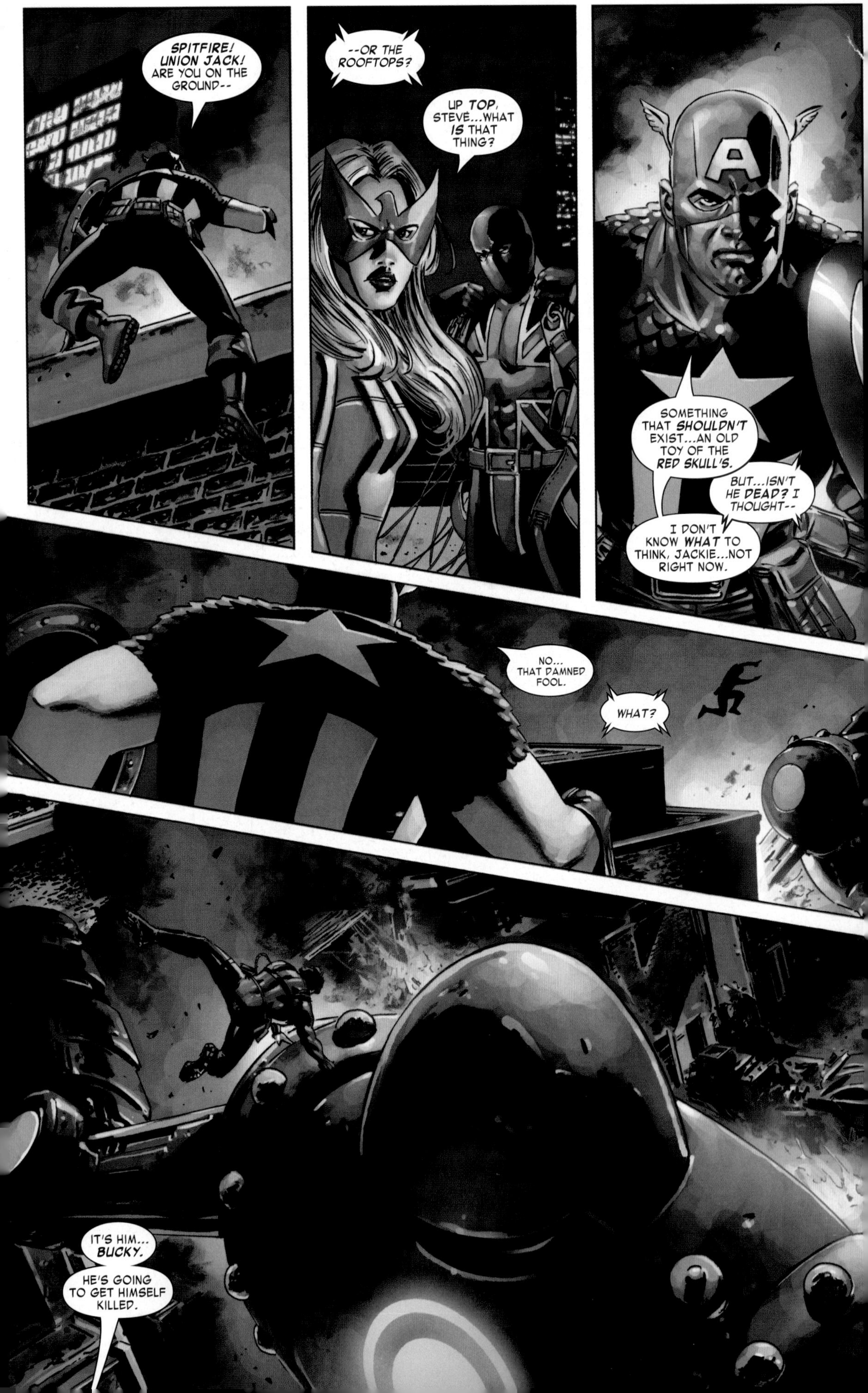
SPITFIRE! UNION JACK! ARE YOU ON THE GROUND--
--OR THE ROOFTOPS?
UP TOP, STEVE...WHAT IS THAT THING?
SOMETHING THAT SHOULDN'T EXIST...AN OLD TOY OF THE RED SKULL'S.
BUT...ISN'T HE DEAD? I THOUGHT--
I DON'T KNOW WHAT TO THINK, JACKIE...NOT RIGHT NOW.
NO... THAT DAMNED FOOL.
WHAT?
IT'S HIM... BUCKY.
HE'S GOING TO GET HIMSELF KILLED.

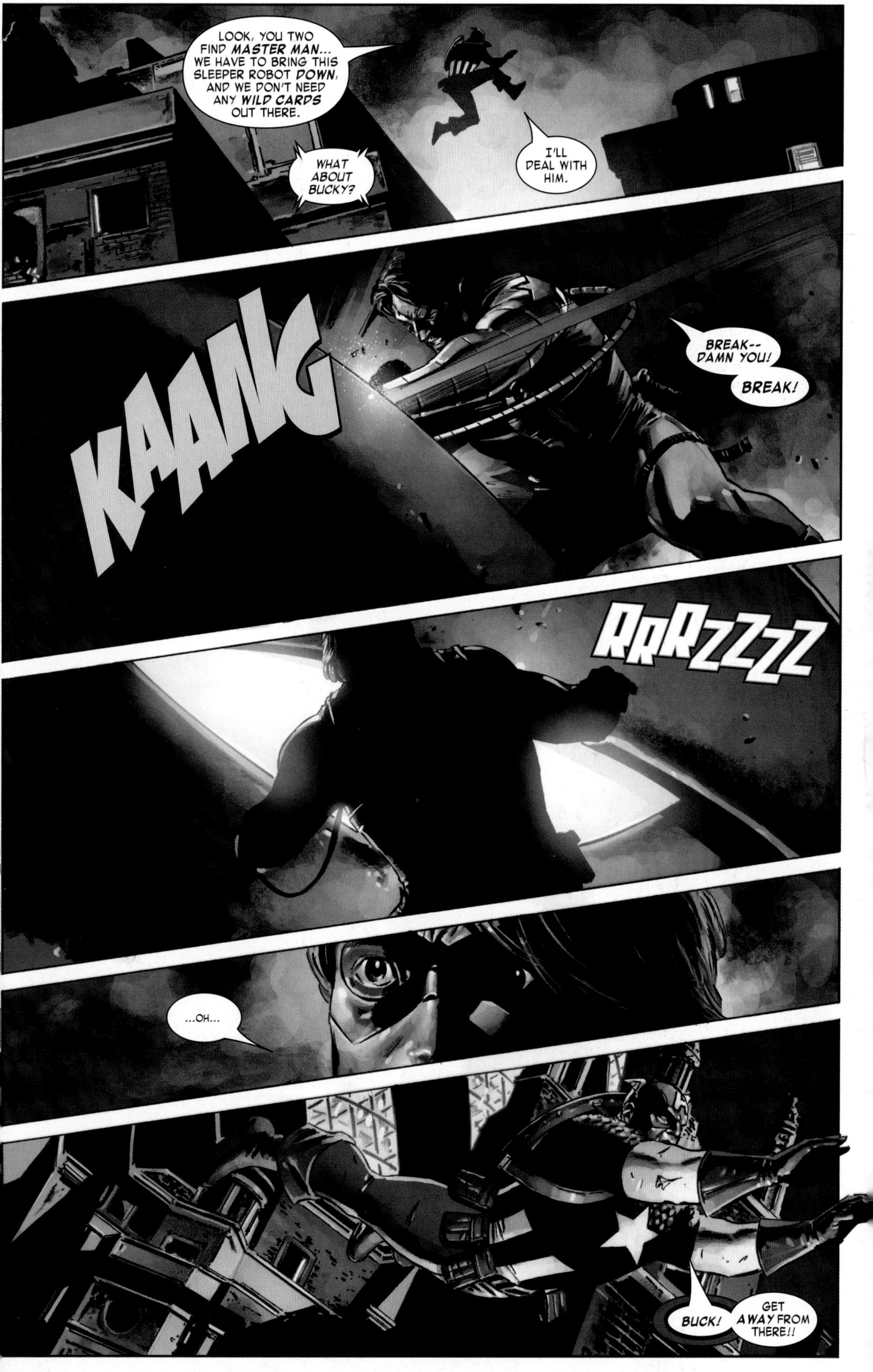

LOOK, YOU TWO FIND MASTER MAN... WE HAVE TO BRING THIS SLEEPER ROBOT DOWN, AND WE DON'T NEED ANY WILD CARDS OUT THERE.
WHAT ABOUT BUCKY?
I'LL DEAL WITH HIM.
KAANG
BREAK-- DAMN YOU!
BREAK!
RRRZZZZ
...OH...
BUCK!
GET AWAY FROM THERE!!

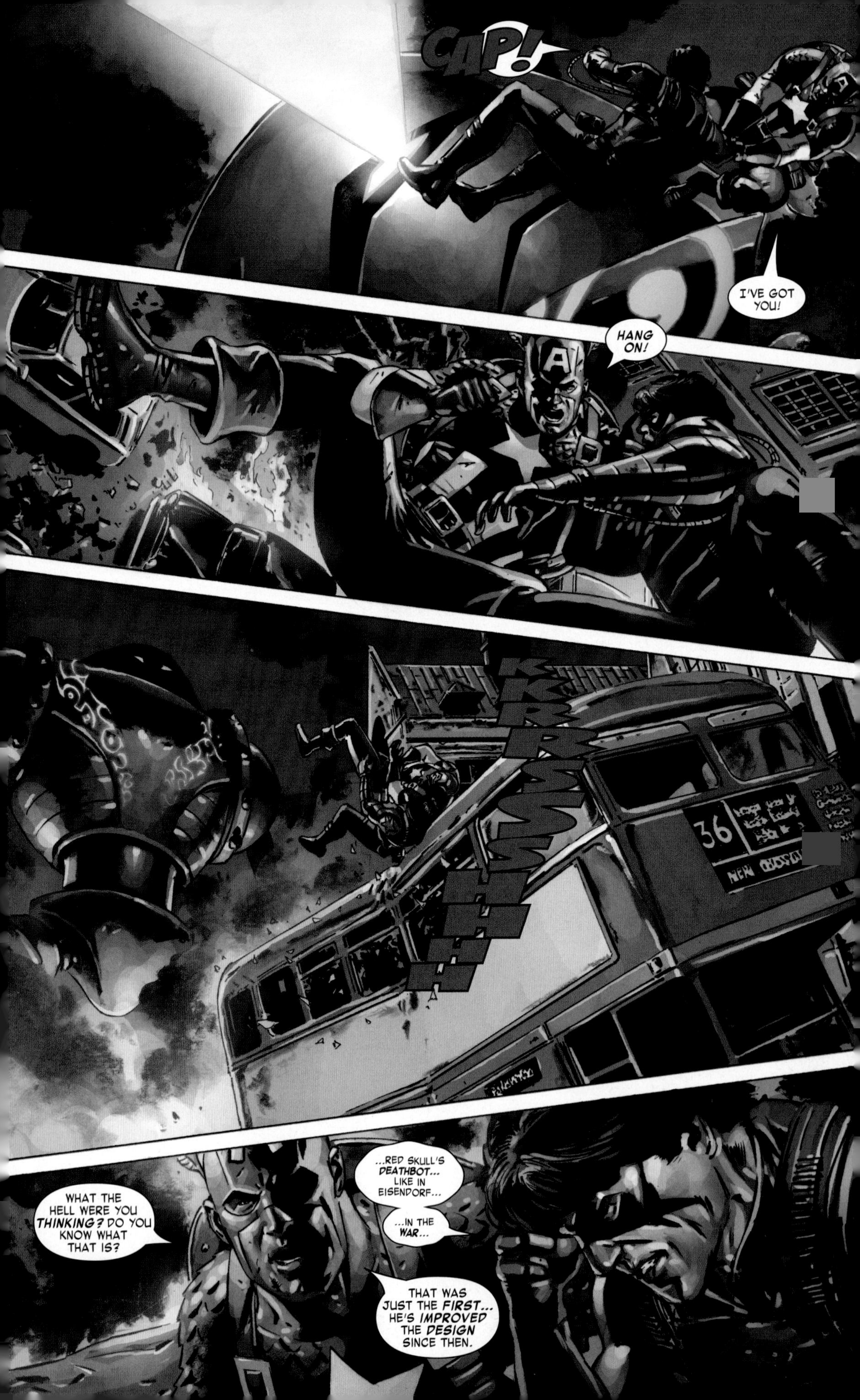
CAP!
I'VE GOT YOU!
HANG ON!
KRRRAAASSSHHHH
36
WHAT THE HELL WERE YOU THINKING? DO YOU KNOW WHAT THAT IS?
...RED SKULL'S DEATHBOT... LIKE IN EISENDORF...
...IN THE WAR...
THAT WAS JUST THE FIRST... HE'S IMPROVED THE DESIGN SINCE THEN.

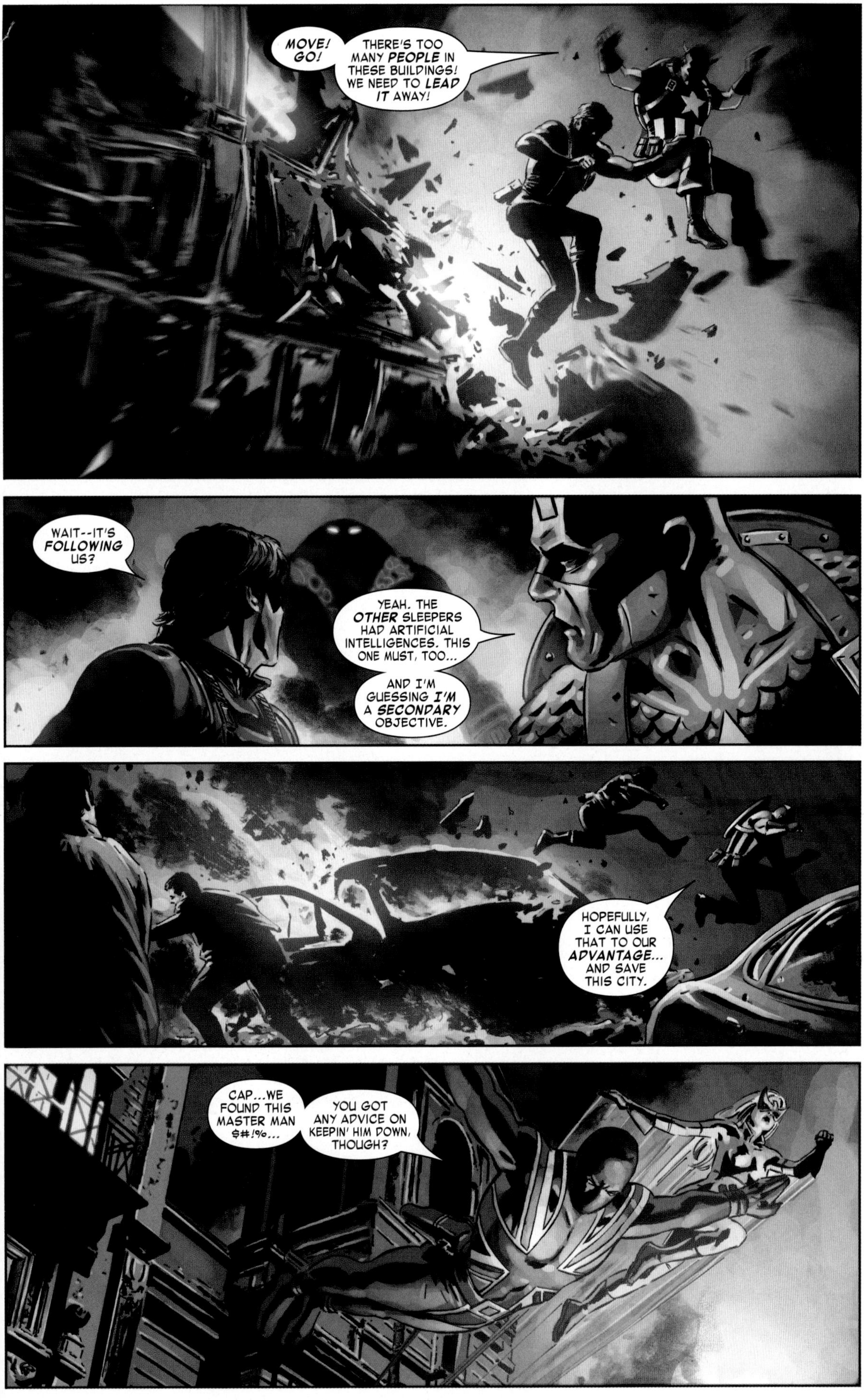
MOVE! GO!
THERE'S TOO MANY PEOPLE IN THESE BUILDINGS! WE NEED TO LEAD IT AWAY!
WAIT--IT'S FOLLOWING US?
YEAH. THE OTHER SLEEPERS HAD ARTIFICIAL INTELLIGENCES. THIS ONE MUST, TOO...
AND I'M GUESSING I'M A SECONDARY OBJECTIVE.
HOPEFULLY, I CAN USE THAT TO OUR ADVANTAGE... AND SAVE THIS CITY.
CAP...WE FOUND THIS MASTER MAN $#!%...
YOU GOT ANY ADVICE ON KEEPIN' HIM DOWN, THOUGH?

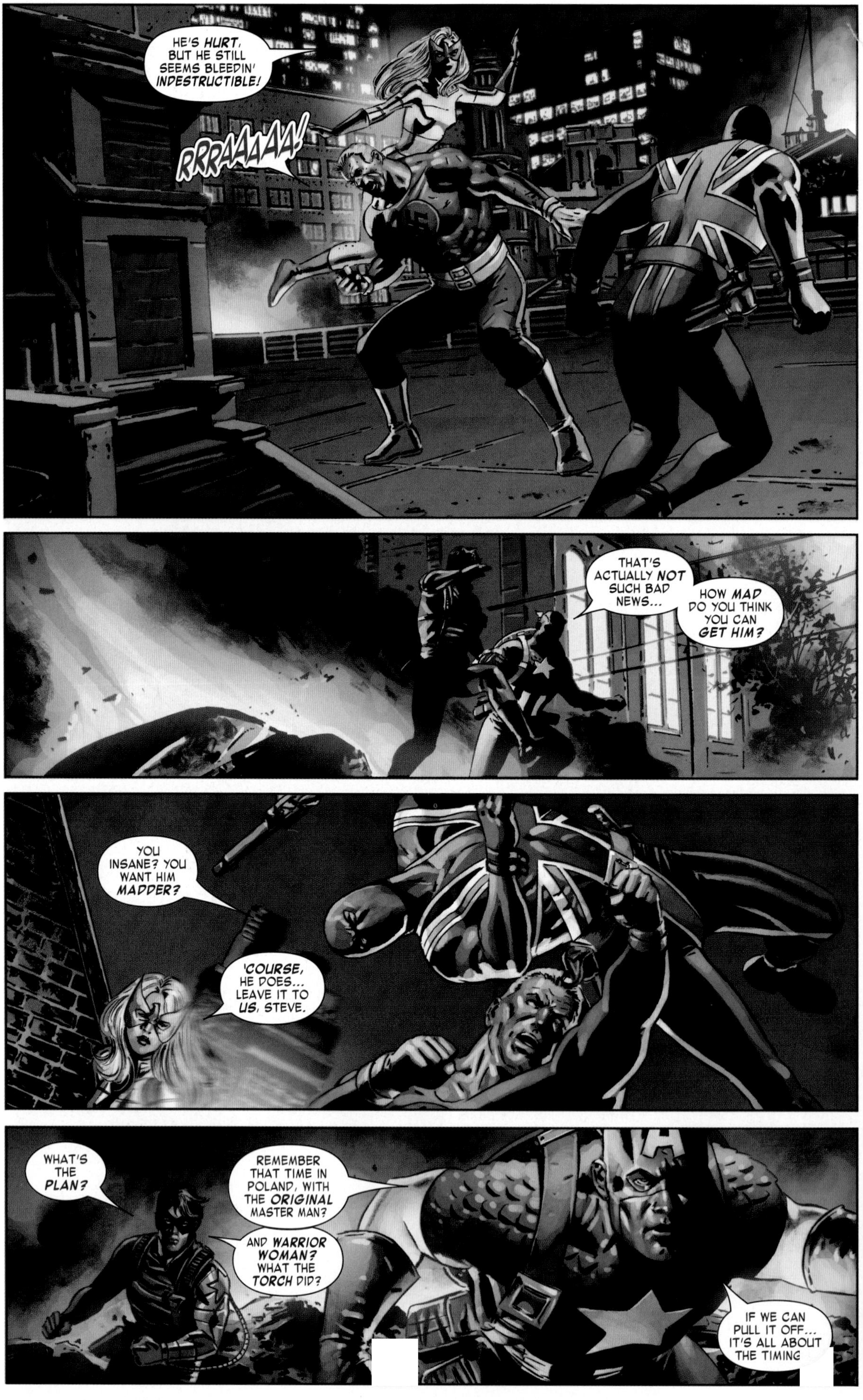
HE'S HURT, BUT HE STILL SEEMS BLEEDIN' INDESTRUCTIBLE!
RRRAAAAAA!
THAT'S ACTUALLY NOT SUCH BAD NEWS...
HOW MAD DO YOU THINK YOU CAN GET HIM?
YOU INSANE? YOU WANT HIM MADDER?
'COURSE, HE DOES... LEAVE IT TO US, STEVE.
WHAT'S THE PLAN?
REMEMBER THAT TIME IN POLAND, WITH THE ORIGINAL MASTER MAN?
AND WARRIOR WOMAN? WHAT THE TORCH DID?
IF WE CAN PULL IT OFF... IT'S ALL ABOUT THE TIMING

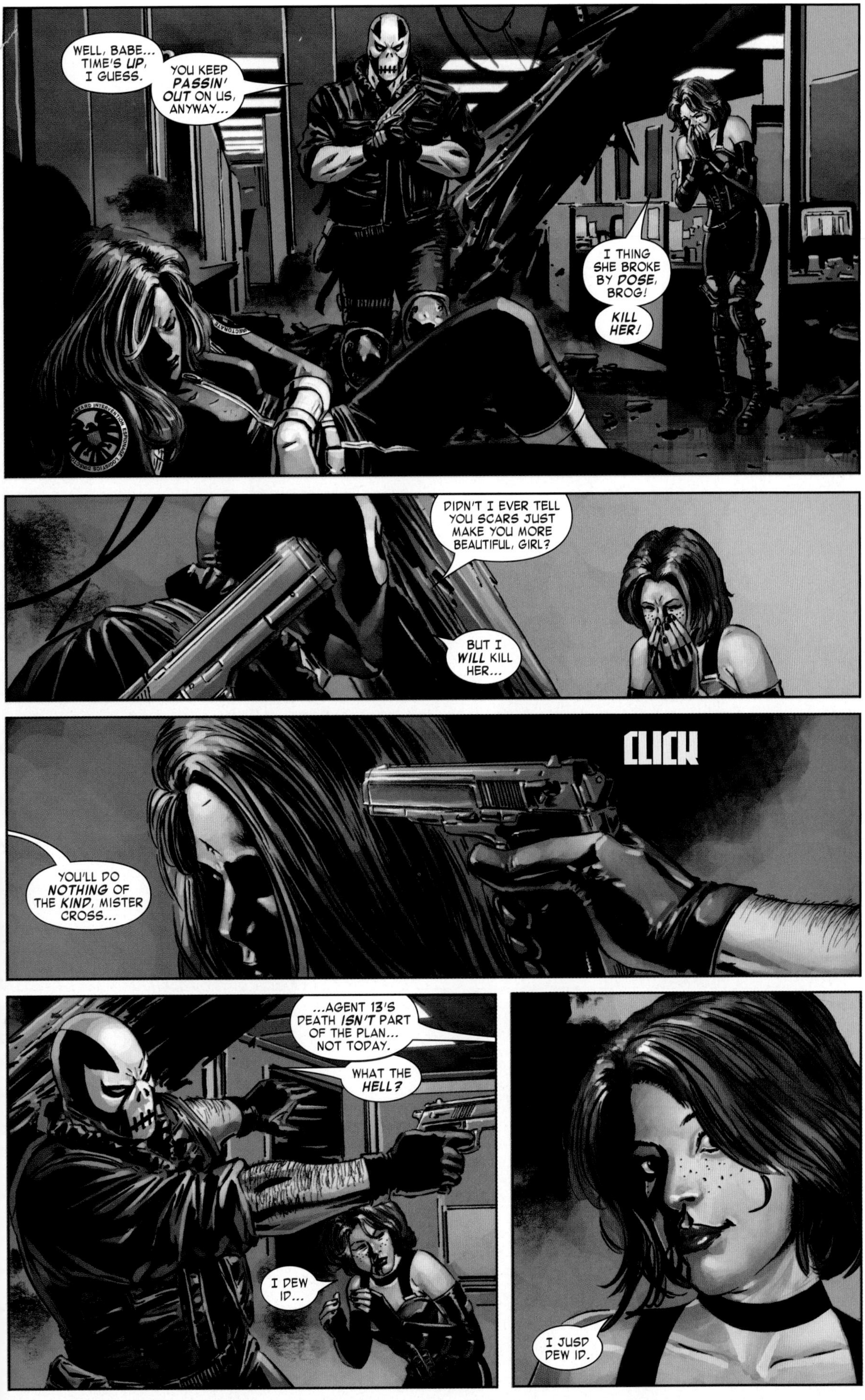
WELL, BABE... TIME'S UP, I GUESS.
YOU KEEP PASSIN' OUT ON US, ANYWAY...
I THING SHE BROKE BY DOSE, BROG!
KILL HER!
DIDN'T I EVER TELL YOU SCARS JUST MAKE YOU MORE BEAUTIFUL, GIRL?
BUT I WILL KILL HER...
CLICK
YOU'LL DO NOTHING OF THE KIND, MISTER CROSS...
...AGENT 13'S DEATH ISN'T PART OF THE PLAN... NOT TODAY.
WHAT THE HELL?
I DEW ID...
I JUSD DEW ID.

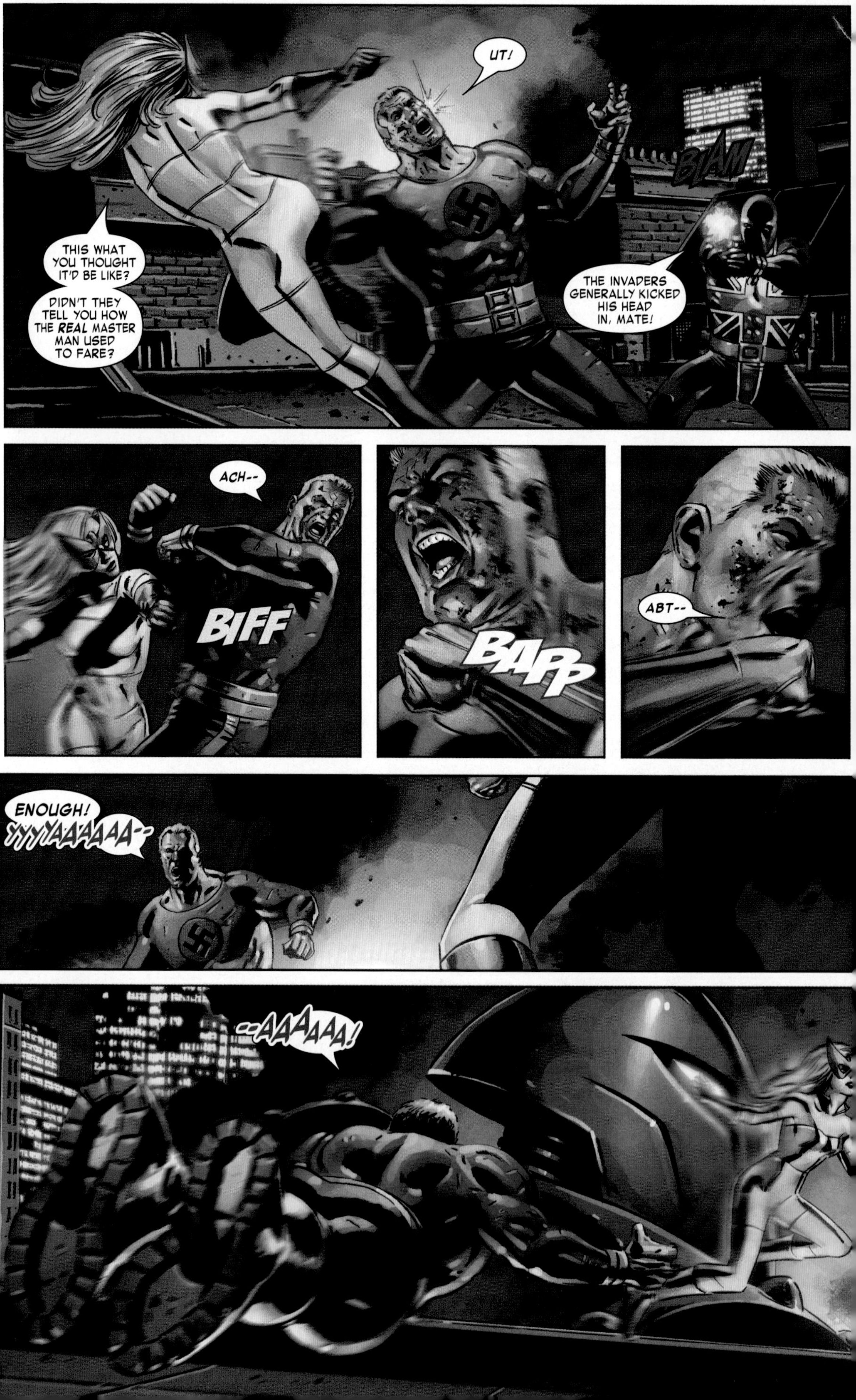
UT!
BLAM
THIS WHAT YOU THOUGHT IT'D BE LIKE?
DIDN'T THEY TELL YOU HOW THE REAL MASTER MAN USED TO FARE?
THE INVADERS GENERALLY KICKED HIS HEAD IN, MATE!
ACH--
BIFF
BAPP
ABT--
ENOUGH!
YYYYAAAAAA--
--AAAAAA!

KK-BLANG!

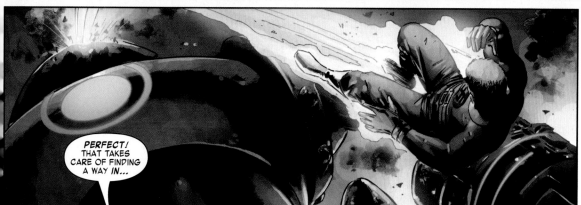

PERFECT! THAT TAKES CARE OF FINDING A WAY IN...

HERE, BUCK--TAKE THIS.

WHAT IS IT?

CONCUSSION CHARGE...I'LL KEEP IT BUSY, YOU HIT THE TARGET.

WAIT...CAP, I DON'T--WE NEED TO--

THERE'S NO TIME... WE'LL TALK LATER.

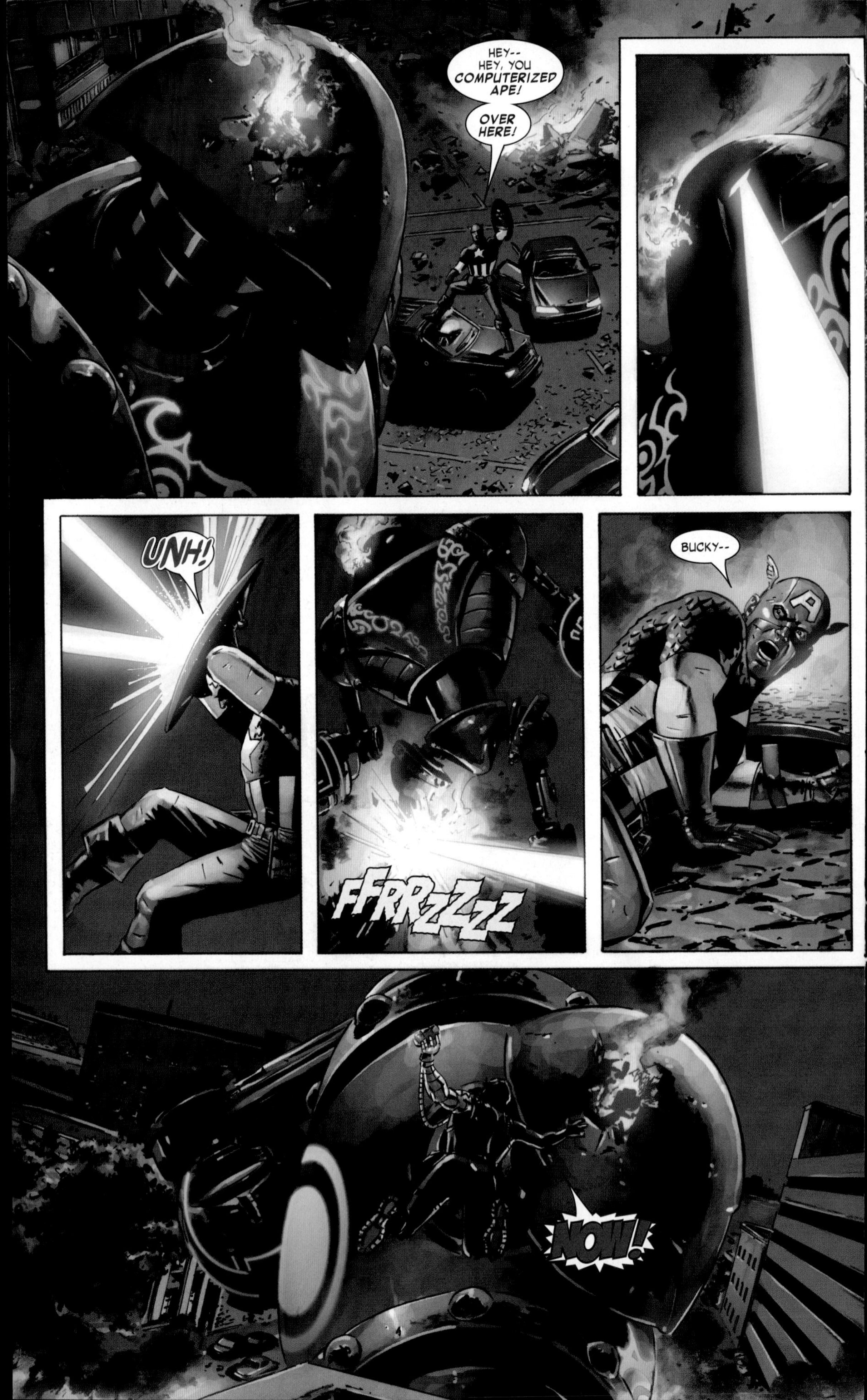
HEY--
HEY, YOU COMPUTERIZED APE!
OVER HERE!
UNH!
FFRRZZZZ
BUCKY--
NOW!

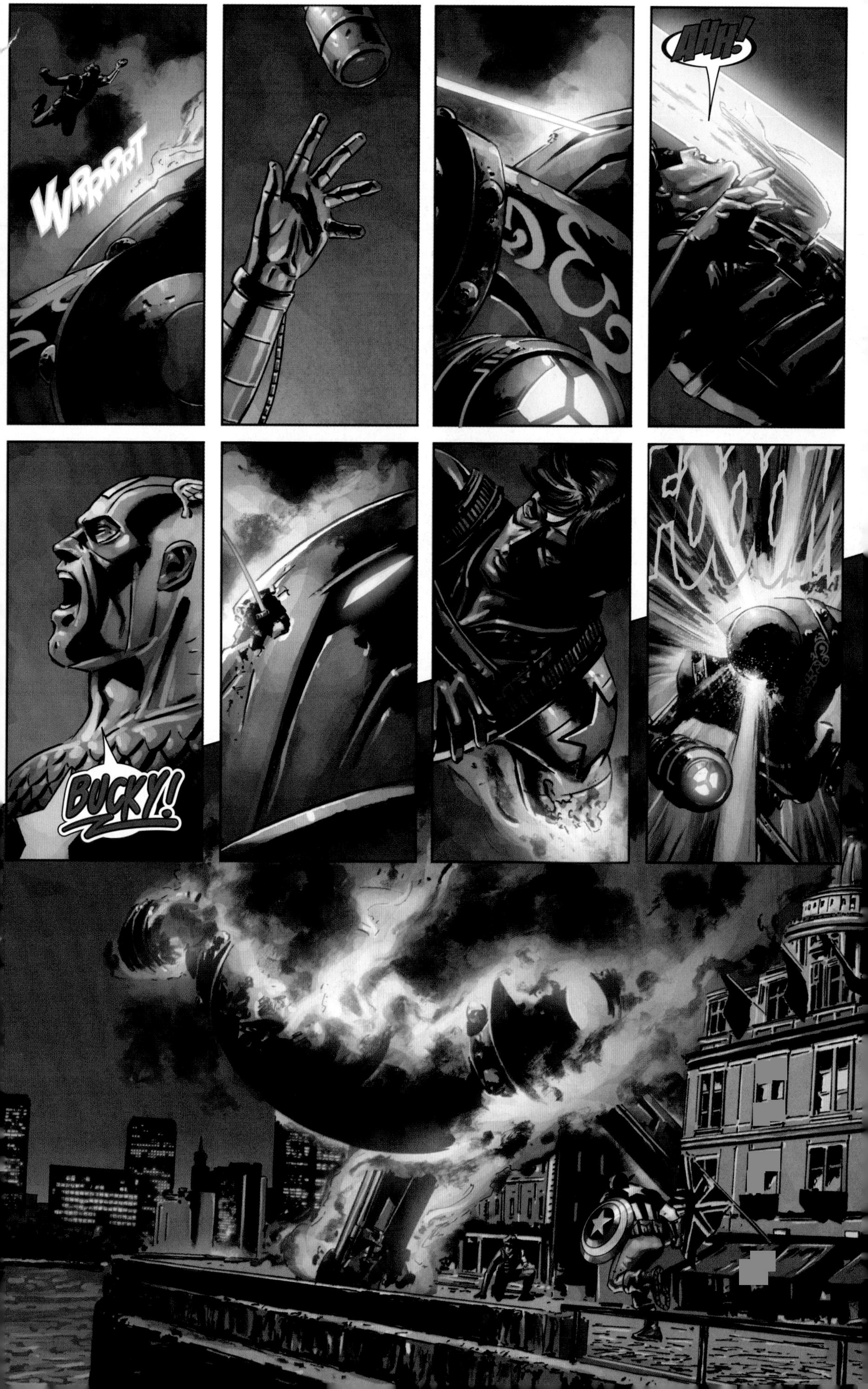
VVRRRRRT
AHH!
BUCKY!

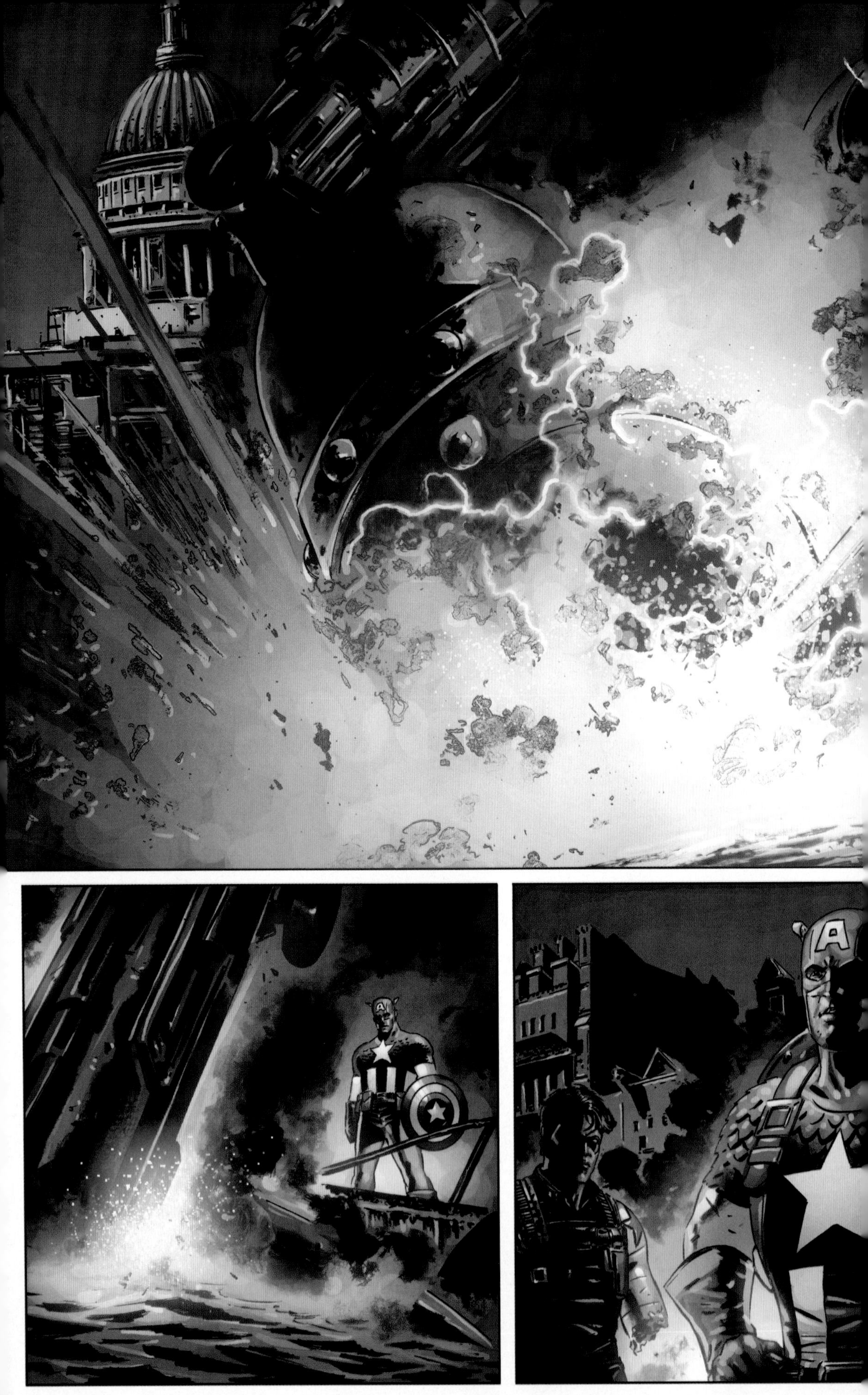

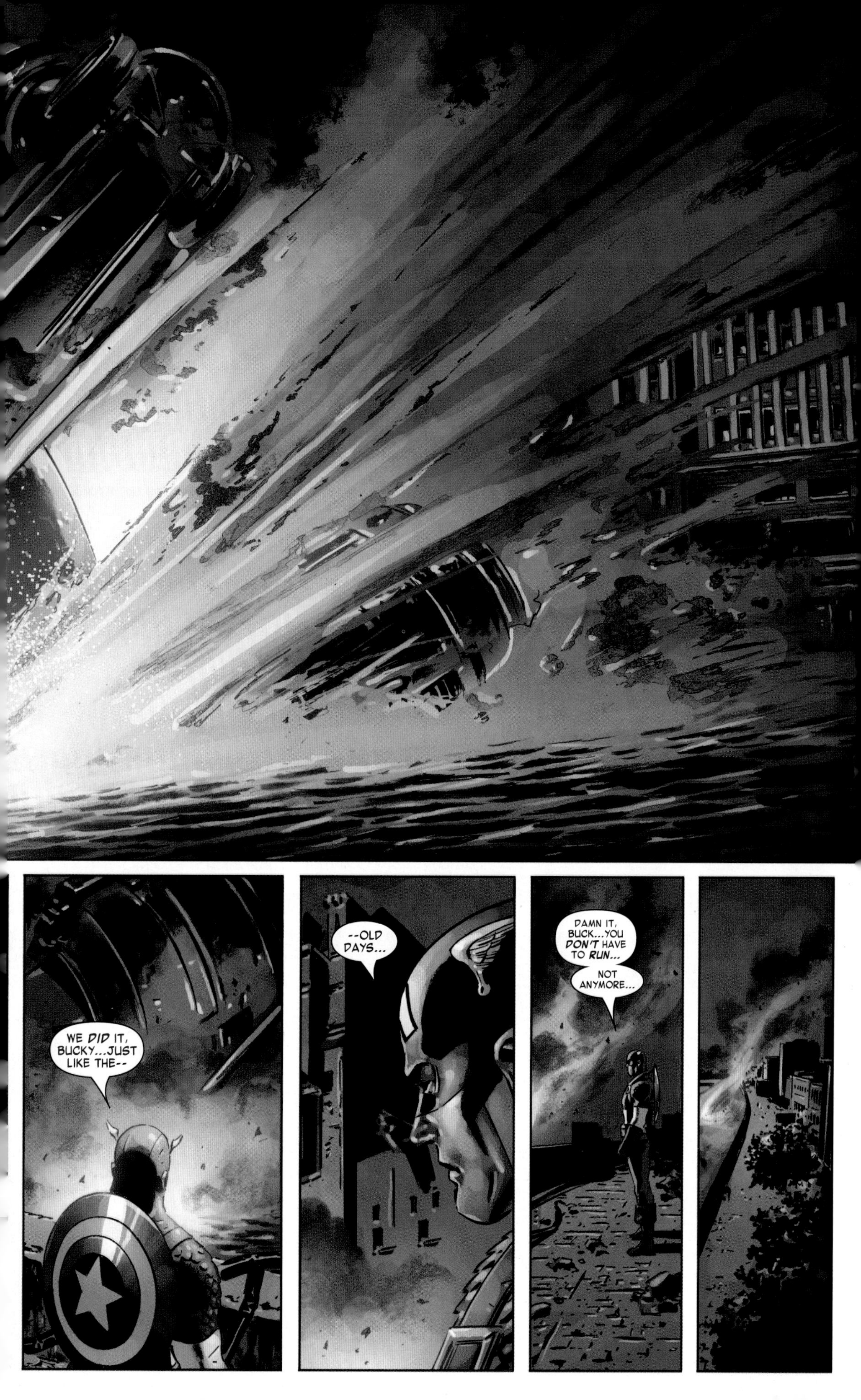
WE DID IT, BUCKY...JUST LIKE THE--
--OLD DAYS...
DAMN IT, BUCK...YOU DON'T HAVE TO RUN...
NOT ANYMORE...

YOU DID NOT *SERIOUSLY* THINK THAT THE RED SKULL COULD BE *KILLED*?

CONSIDER THIS NIGHT A *SAMPLING* OF MY IDEA OF FUN... AND KNOW THAT IT IS ONLY THE *BEGINNING!*

THE MESSAGE, RECEIVED EARLY THIS MORNING FROM INTERNATIONAL TERRORIST, THE *RED SKULL*, CLAIMED CREDIT FOR THE DESTRUCTION LAST NIGHT.

THE RED SKULL *WAS* REPORTED DEAD NEARLY *A YEAR AGO* BY THE INTELLIGENCE COMMUNITY, BUT *CLEARLY*, THOSE REPORTS WERE IN *ERROR*.

ALONG WITH THE *ROBOT* USED TO ATTACK THE CITY, AUTHORITIES *ALSO* CAPTURED SEVERAL GERMAN YOUTHS WHO REFERRED TO THEMSELVES AS THE *MASTER RACE*...

CE" CAPTURE

ECIAL.....SPECIAL REPO

...THESE SUPER-MEN AND THE SO-CALLED *SLEEPER* ROBOT WERE SUBDUED BY *CAPTAIN AMERICA*, WORKING WITH *UNION JACK* AND *SPITFIRE*, ALL OF WHOM DECLINED COMMENT...

AMERICA

ECIAL REPORT.....SPECIAL REPO

HOWEVER, *RECLUSIVE KRONAS* C.E.O. *ALEKSANDER LUKIN* SURPRISED THE WORLD BY ISSUING *THIS* PUBLIC STATEMENT...

THIS ATTACK ON MY COMPANY, ON *KRONAS*, IS AN ATTACK ON US *ALL*...

THESE MEN IN MASKS, WHETHER WORKING *ALONGSIDE* THE LAW OR *AGAINST* IT, CAN BE ALLOWED TO BRING US TERROR NO MORE!

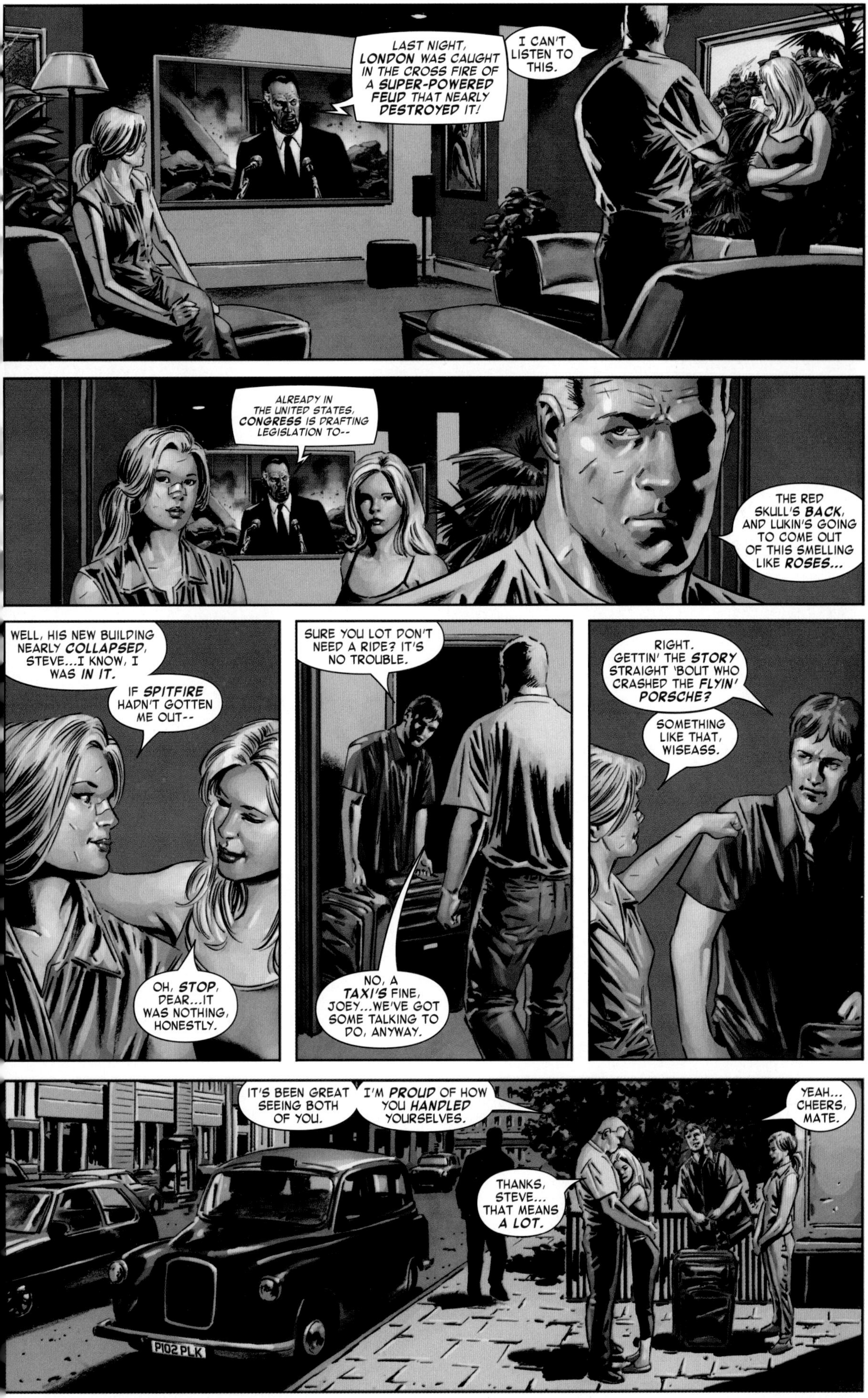
LAST NIGHT, LONDON WAS CAUGHT IN THE CROSS FIRE OF A SUPER-POWERED FEUD THAT NEARLY DESTROYED IT!
I CAN'T LISTEN TO THIS.
ALREADY IN THE UNITED STATES, CONGRESS IS DRAFTING LEGISLATION TO--
THE RED SKULL'S BACK, AND LUKIN'S GOING TO COME OUT OF THIS SMELLING LIKE ROSES...
WELL, HIS NEW BUILDING NEARLY COLLAPSED, STEVE...I KNOW, I WAS IN IT.
IF SPITFIRE HADN'T GOTTEN ME OUT--
OH, STOP, DEAR...IT WAS NOTHING, HONESTLY.
SURE YOU LOT DON'T NEED A RIDE? IT'S NO TROUBLE.
NO, A TAXI'S FINE, JOEY...WE'VE GOT SOME TALKING TO DO, ANYWAY.
RIGHT. GETTIN' THE STORY STRAIGHT 'BOUT WHO CRASHED THE FLYIN' PORSCHE?
SOMETHING LIKE THAT, WISEASS.
IT'S BEEN GREAT SEEING BOTH OF YOU.
I'M PROUD OF HOW YOU HANDLED YOURSELVES.
THANKS, STEVE... THAT MEANS A LOT.
YEAH... CHEERS, MATE.
P102 PLK

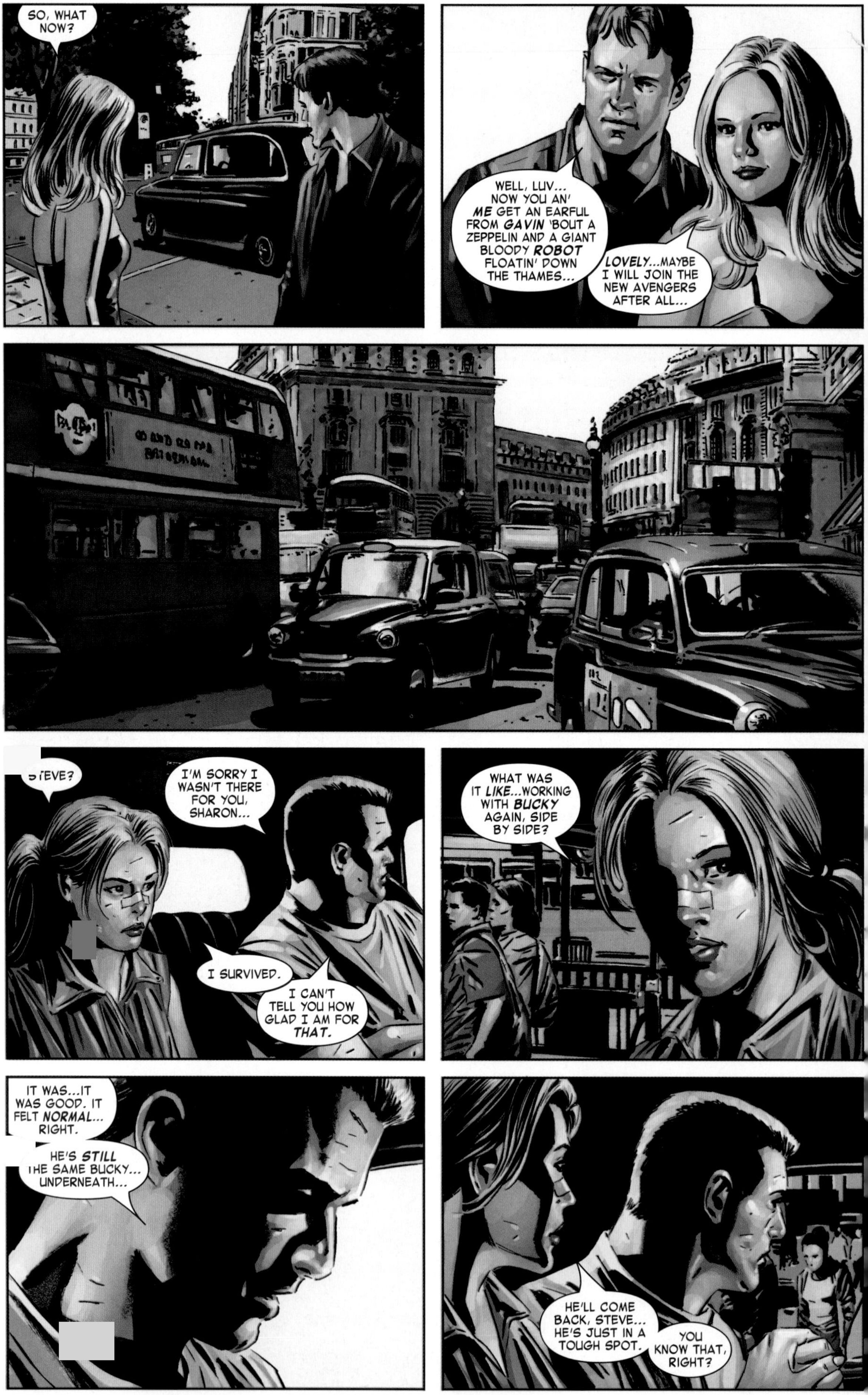
SO, WHAT NOW?
WELL, LUV... NOW YOU AN' ME GET AN EARFUL FROM GAVIN 'BOUT A ZEPPELIN AND A GIANT BLOODY ROBOT FLOATIN' DOWN THE THAMES...
LOVELY...MAYBE I WILL JOIN THE NEW AVENGERS AFTER ALL...
STEVE?
I'M SORRY I WASN'T THERE FOR YOU, SHARON...
I SURVIVED.
I CAN'T TELL YOU HOW GLAD I AM FOR THAT.
WHAT WAS IT LIKE...WORKING WITH BUCKY AGAIN, SIDE BY SIDE?
IT WAS...IT WAS GOOD. IT FELT NORMAL... RIGHT.
HE'S STILL THE SAME BUCKY... UNDERNEATH...
HE'LL COME BACK, STEVE... HE'S JUST IN A TOUGH SPOT.
YOU KNOW THAT, RIGHT?

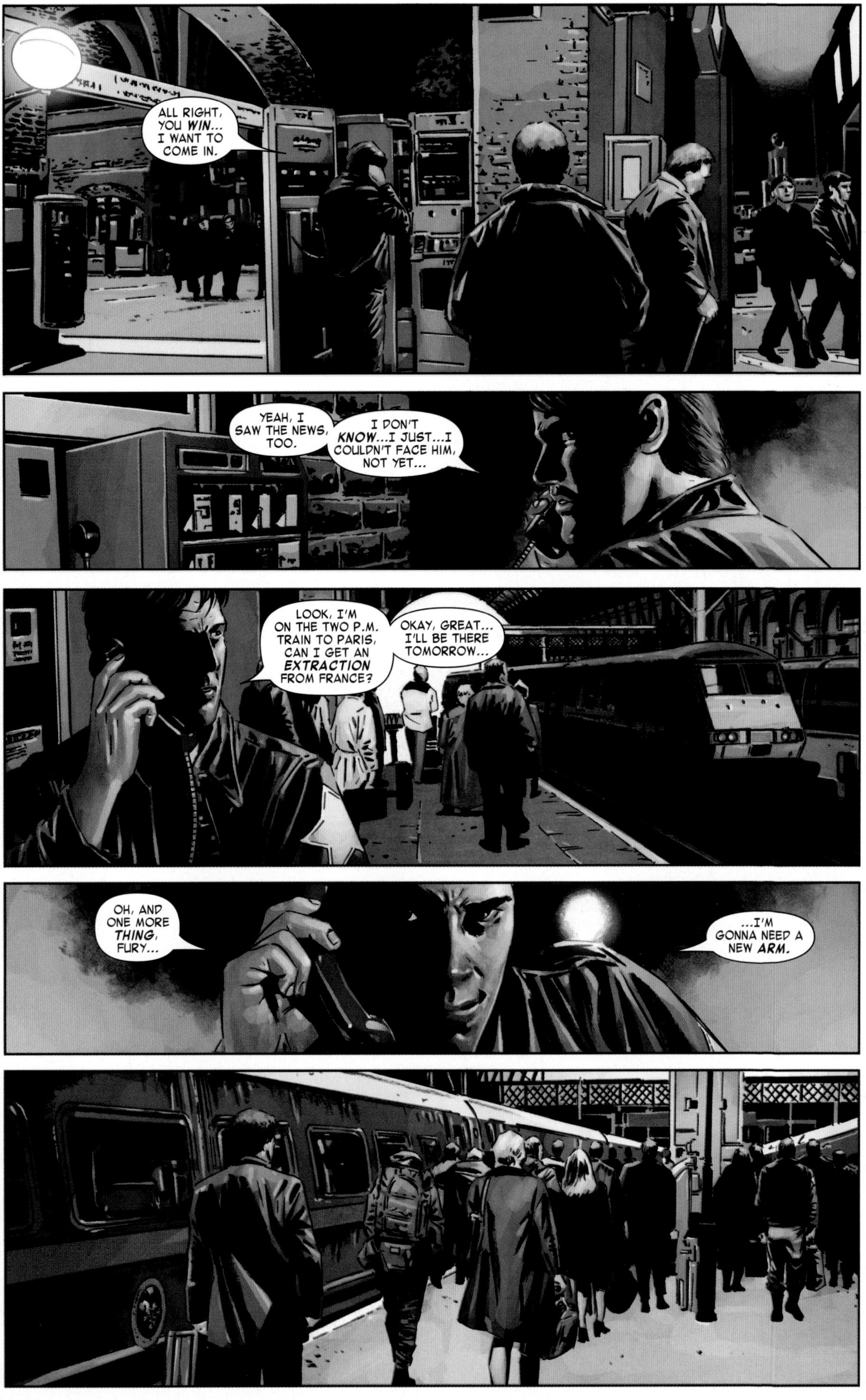
ALL RIGHT, YOU *WIN*... I WANT TO COME IN.
YEAH, I SAW THE NEWS, TOO.
I DON'T *KNOW*...I JUST...I COULDN'T FACE HIM, NOT YET...
LOOK, I'M ON THE TWO P.M. TRAIN TO PARIS, CAN I GET AN *EXTRACTION* FROM FRANCE?
OKAY, GREAT... I'LL BE THERE TOMORROW...
OH, AND ONE MORE *THING*, FURY...
...I'M GONNA NEED A NEW *ARM.*

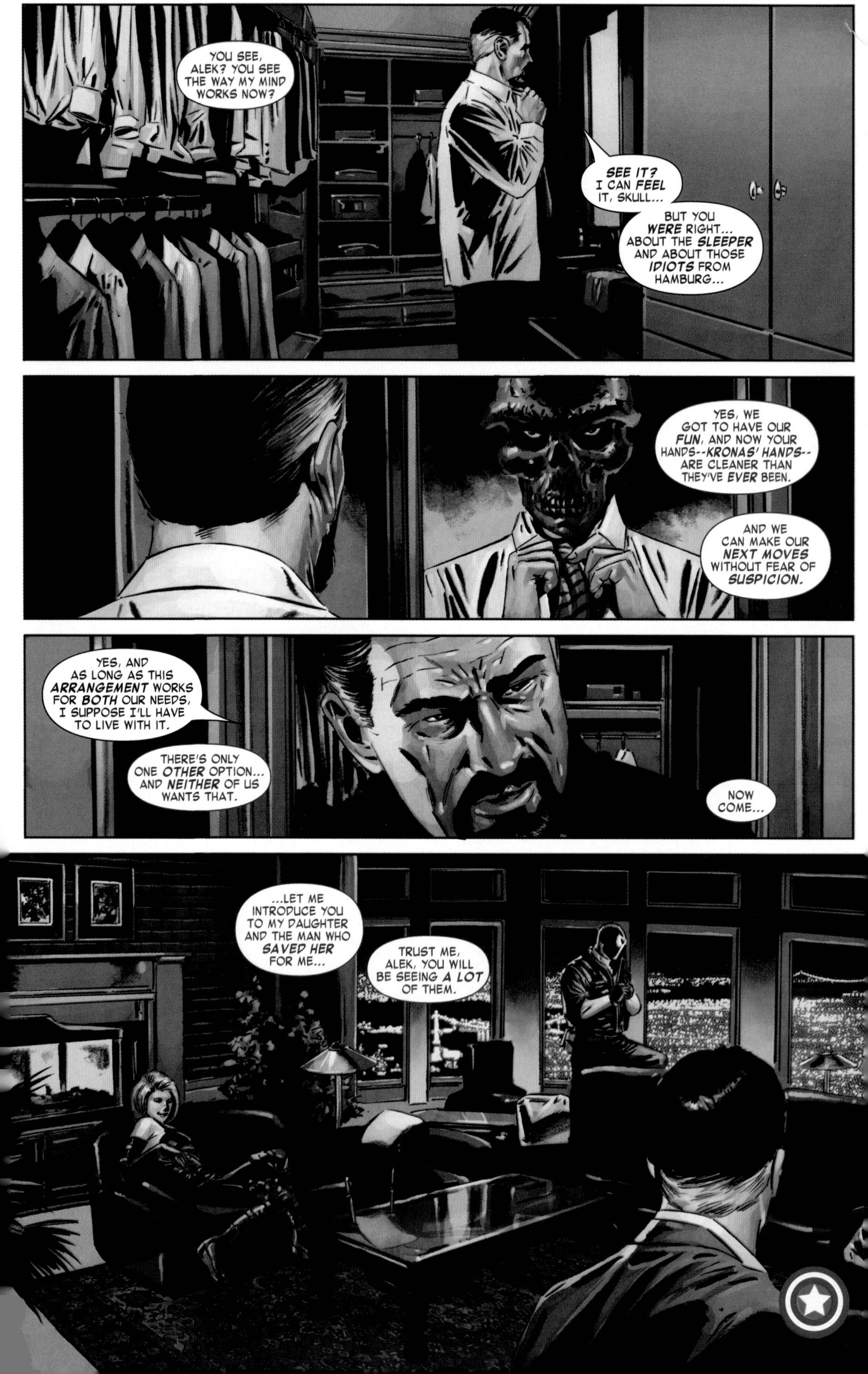
YOU SEE, ALEK? YOU SEE THE WAY MY MIND WORKS NOW?
SEE IT? I CAN FEEL IT, SKULL...
BUT YOU WERE RIGHT... ABOUT THE SLEEPER AND ABOUT THOSE IDIOTS FROM HAMBURG...
YES, WE GOT TO HAVE OUR FUN, AND NOW YOUR HANDS--KRONAS' HANDS--ARE CLEANER THAN THEY'VE EVER BEEN.
AND WE CAN MAKE OUR NEXT MOVES WITHOUT FEAR OF SUSPICION.
YES, AND AS LONG AS THIS ARRANGEMENT WORKS FOR BOTH OUR NEEDS, I SUPPOSE I'LL HAVE TO LIVE WITH IT.
THERE'S ONLY ONE OTHER OPTION... AND NEITHER OF US WANTS THAT.
NOW COME...
...LET ME INTRODUCE YOU TO MY DAUGHTER AND THE MAN WHO SAVED HER FOR ME...
TRUST ME, ALEK, YOU WILL BE SEEING A LOT OF THEM.

MARVEL SPOTLIGHT

ED BRUBAKER • OFFICIAL HANDBOOK

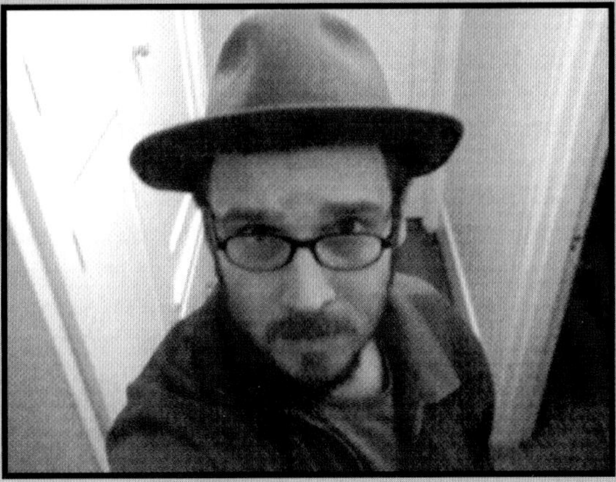

REAL NAME: Ed Brubaker
DATE OF BIRTH: 1966
PLACE OF BIRTH: Naval Hospital, Bethesda, MD
OCCUPATION: Comic book writer
PLACE OF RESIDENCE: Seattle, WA
WEBSITE: www.edbrubaker.com
FIRST COMICS APPEARANCE: *Dark Horse Presents #65, 1992*
FIRST MARVEL COMICS APPEARANCE: *Captain America #1, 2005*

HISTORY: Ed Brubaker was born into the life of a Navy brat, in the tow of an enlisted dad who carried his family around various ports of call after his service in the Vietnam War. Very early in his life, Ed found himself living at the now-infamous Guantanamo Bay Naval Base, a US Navy installation located in a small parcel of US-controlled land on the southeastern tip of Cuba. For age four to seven, Ed was a citizen of "Gitmo," and to him, it was a great place to be a little kid while his dad served in Naval intelligence. Ed and his siblings enjoyed spending balmy summer days playing out on the base and getting to watch *Planet of the Apes* and kung fu movies at the outdoor movie theater, and on one pivotal day in Ed's life, his dad came home with hundreds of comics that were given to him by co-workers whose kids no longer wanted them! If that wasn't enough to turn him into a comics zombie, the fact that the base PX sold only Marvel Comics turned him into a Marvel zombie!

His early love for comics manifested in a desire to become not a writer, but a pencil artist. In Ed's young mind, his first projects would include *Captain America, Spider-Man,* and *X-Men*, so that should give you some idea of where his leanings were. But then he turned fourteen and his discovery of punk rock and alternative and European comics changed all the default settings of his pop-culture mind. From then on, he stopped looking at what the mainstream offered altogether, preferring books like *American Splendor* to *Captain America.*

Though a terribly bright kid, Ed hated school. He liked learning but hated regurgitating information in the form of tests, and he never went to college. The bug to write, however, was definitely a part of him, and he found himself writing pulp fiction material at the request of artist friends like Eric Shanower, who took a script Ed wrote for him and turned it into a story that was printed in *Dark Horse Presents #65-68* as "An Accidental Death." Ed's first story was a critical hit, to the degree that it was nominated for an Eisner Award!

Ed's career path continued to yield lucky breaks when his "Accidental Death" partner Shanower was approached by Vertigo, and he pulled Ed along with him. His indie snobbishness having placed him completely out of touch with mainstream comics for over a decade, Ed developed a pitch for Vertigo under the misimpression that they were a "young adult" imprint. Surprisingly, his pitch for the satiric *Prez* was accepted, this one by the very mainstream DC Comics! Later, Ed's talent was recognized by two DC editors, Shelly Roeberg and the late Lou Stathis, who were both early advocates of Ed's writing. Shelly insisted that Ed fashion another proposal for Vertigo, which resulted in *Scene of the Crime*, a noirish detective mini-series that was published in 1998.

Scene of the Crime was Ed's big breakthrough in mainstream comics, getting him more recognition than ever before and hooking him up with artist Michael Lark, a creative partner-in-crime that he has worked with on various projects ever since. From that point on, Ed's workload has never lightened up. In fact, he soon found fans in DC's Bat office and was asked to pitch a Batman project that turned into *Batman: Gotham Noir*, a one-shot in collaboration with Sean Phillips, another artist with whom he would build a strong creative association. Finding himself at home creating mainstream comics with a sense of populist fun, it wasn't long before he was writing more Bat books, like *Batman, Catwoman* and *Gotham Central.* During this time, he also wrote *Point Blank, Sleeper* and a run on *Authority* for DC imprint Wildstorm, and all the while, the awards and critical acclaim kept coming his way.

His move to Marvel came with the hopes that he could take on a bigger and more influential writing role than he was able to achieve at DC. That wish came true instantly, as his first book with Marvel, a revamp of *Captain America*, was not only the critical hit he was accustomed to, but a commercial hit as well! Ed was allowed to play around with critical elements of Cap's past, a brave feat which proved to pump up the enthusiasm of a franchise that had grown somewhat stale in the eyes of longtime readers. He was also able to craft a pivotally important tale in *X-Men: Deadly Genesis*, which brought to light several long lost characters from the X-Men's past. His next major project is to continue the story he set up in *Deadly Genesis* in the pages of the X-Men's flagship title, *Uncanny X-Men.* He's come a long way from Guatnanamo, but Ed Brubaker has arrived as one of Marvel's most creative – and most important – writers of the decade.

THE ED BRUBAKER MARVEL COMICS LIBRARY:

Books of Doom #1-6 (2006)
Captain America #1-up (2005-06)
Captain America 65th Anniversary Special (2006)
Marvel Spotlight: Ed Brubaker/Billy Tan (2006)
Uncanny X-Men #475-up (2006)
Wha...Huh??? (2005)
X-Men: Deadly Genesis #1-6 (2006)
Daredevil #82-up (2006)

COLLECT 'EM IN TRADE:

Fantastic Four: Books of Doom Premiere HC
Captain America: Winter Soldier Vol. 1 Premiere HC/TPB
Captain America: Winter Soldier Vol. 2 Premiere HC/TPB
Captain America: Red Menace Vol. 1 TPB
X-Men: Deadly Genesis Premiere HC

THE SPOTLIGHT INTERVIEW

Marvel Spotlight had the opportunity to speak with Ed Brubaker on multiple occasions recently to cover his overall writing career and his tenure at Marvel, which is a good thing because there is lots to talk about! His indie career writing gritty crime comics took him to DC, where he advanced his game with highly acclaimed work on *Scene of the Crime* and *Sleeper*, and settled into a long run on *Catwoman* with Darwyn Cooke. Looking at the last couple years at Marvel alone, Ed had transformed *Captain America* into one of Marvel's biggest fan-favorites, picked up *Daredevil* from Brian Michael Bendis and made it even *more* popular than it already was, and delivered two mini-series that have become essential reading in their respective canons: *X-Men: Deadly Genesis*, the story that sets up his ongoing series on *Uncanny X-Men* and *Books of Doom*, the mini-series that explored the history of Marvel's greatest villain. Throw in his upcoming crime book on Marvel imprint Icon, and like we said, there is lots to talk about! So let's get crackin', Ed!

SPOTLIGHT: Let me ask you about a sort of stereotype that has surrounded your career before coming to Marvel, that Ed Brubaker is the "crime guy." You are so at home in the genre, and at the same time so incredibly successful at it, that it has logically followed in some people's minds that that is all that you can or want to do. But I'm sure that there have been points where you may have felt that you didn't want to be "the crime guy."

ED: I feel like I'm a pulp writer, in a way. All of that has been out of being able to understand the structure of mysteries and crime stories, which has been so helpful in writing super-hero stories, because the basic plot of a mystery is still the same as any kind of pulp adventure, and super-heroes grew out of the pulps. But also, I never want to be pigeonholed. If there is any comic book guy that is someone that I would look at as a career model at all, it would be Alan Moore, in the way that he is someone who does every genre. *Dead Enders* was a sci-fi romance comic, you know? *(Laughter.)* For a long time I was trying to convince someone at DC to let me do a romance comic. Because *Lowlife*, my comic that I wrote and drew myself, was sort of a semi-autobiographical comic, but a lot of it had to do with romantic ups and downs.

I like all kinds of stuff. It just turned out that I thought I was going to be "Mr. Serious Alternative Cartoonist Who Only Writes Very Serious Fiction or Autobiography", and then I wound up discovering mystery fiction, after having previously dismissed it. I always thought it was kind of stupid for some reason, even though I loved mystery movies. But I sort of became obsessed with them in my late 20s and early 30s.

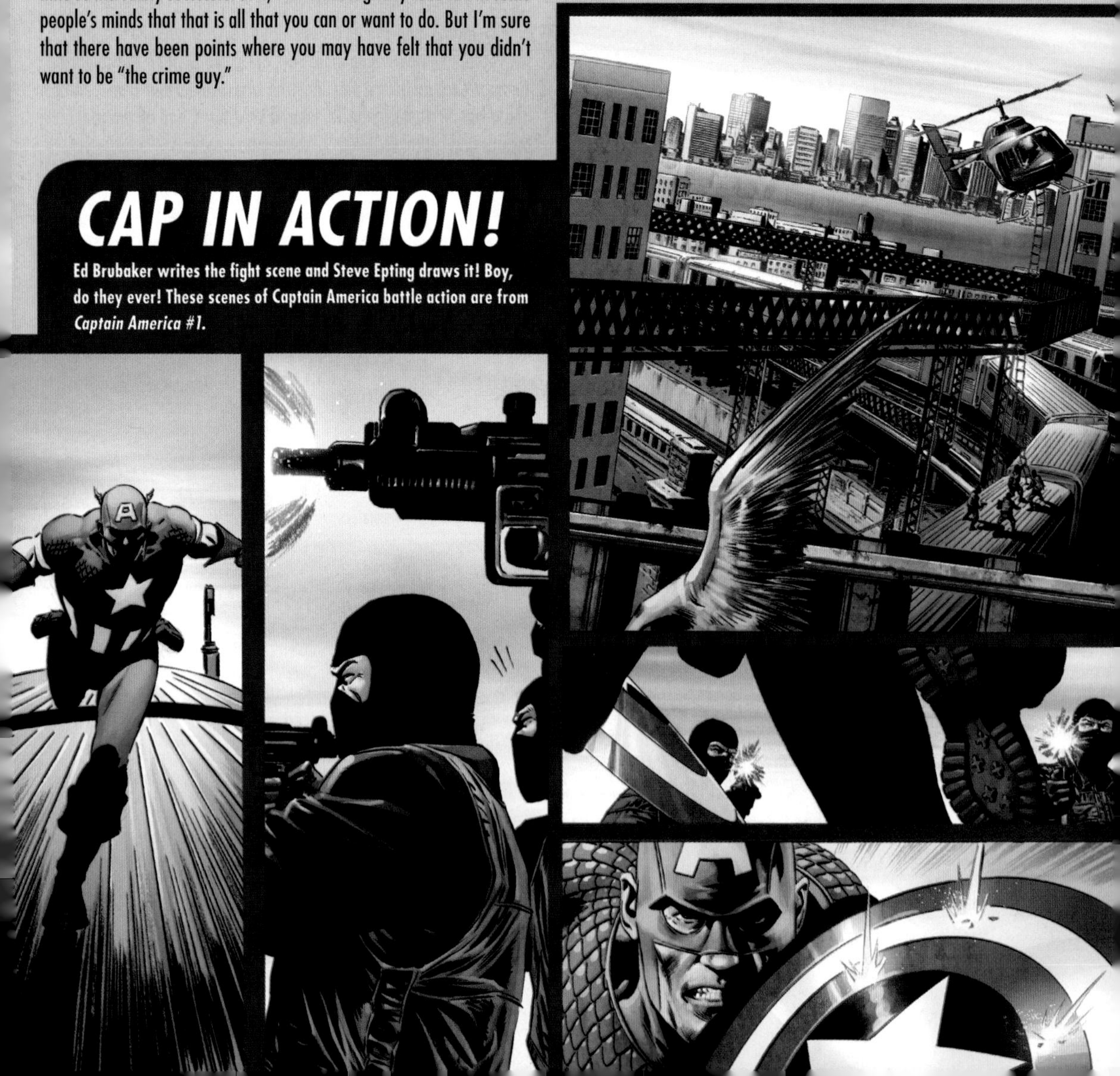

CAP IN ACTION!

Ed Brubaker writes the fight scene and Steve Epting draws it! Boy, do they ever! These scenes of Captain America battle action are from *Captain America #1*.

WITH ED BRUBAKER

I discovered Ross Macdonald and basically read every book that guy ever wrote and realized that he had grown out of the pulps. I read a bunch of Raymond Chandler, and became obsessed and read all his novels, and Dashiell Hammett, and soaked in all this stuff over a number of years, to the point where I realized that I was full of it for dismissing that genre as serious literature.

A lot of people forget that Shakespeare was a popular writer. He wasn't trying to write serious literature; he was just writing like everybody else, he was writing to earn a living and to survive and entertain people. It's only now through the passage of time that he's regarded as a serious artist, just like Chandler and Ross Macdonald are now considered some of the great writers of the 20th century. They were pretty well dismissed by the intelligentsia at the time. Chandler had this great quote that if Shakespeare had been alive in the 20s, he'd have been working for the pulps, because that was the magazine that reached the widest amount of readers. That's what all writers want to do: to reach a ton of people. I sort of became obsessed with that and then I started writing mysteries. I went from being someone who pretty much only read really serious fiction, non-fiction and really arty comics to being someone who embraced the pulp aspects of the medium and actually enjoyed that stuff on just a pure, "reading for enjoyment" level.

It was a pure accident through Steve Weissman, a cartoonist who is a good friend of mine who does a book called *Yikes*, that I had Ross Macdonald forced on me. Through that I think I rediscovered a love of reading for pure enjoyment. It opened my mind and now I realize that in my late teens and early 20s, I think I was full of it in the same way that almost all teenagers and young people tend to be full of it. I thought I knew everything about life and art and what was important, when in reality, reading for enjoyment, and writing things for people that they can get lost in- on a pure enjoyment level- is not a trivial thing in the least. I think that's what I hate about how dismissive, for instance, the *Comics Journal* and a lot of the alternative comics people are about mainstream comics. They're unwilling to see the craft or just read something for enjoyment. Everything has to be something that should be hung up on a museum wall.

SPOTLIGHT: The kind of writing that wants to supposedly "change your life!"

ED: Exactly! But you never know who's going to change your life. Reading Ross MacDonald changed my life, even more than Shakespeare! And I love reading Shakespeare! *(Laughter.)* But I really don't mind if people want to see me as "the crime guy." I hope they do, because I have a crime comic coming out! *(Laughter.)*

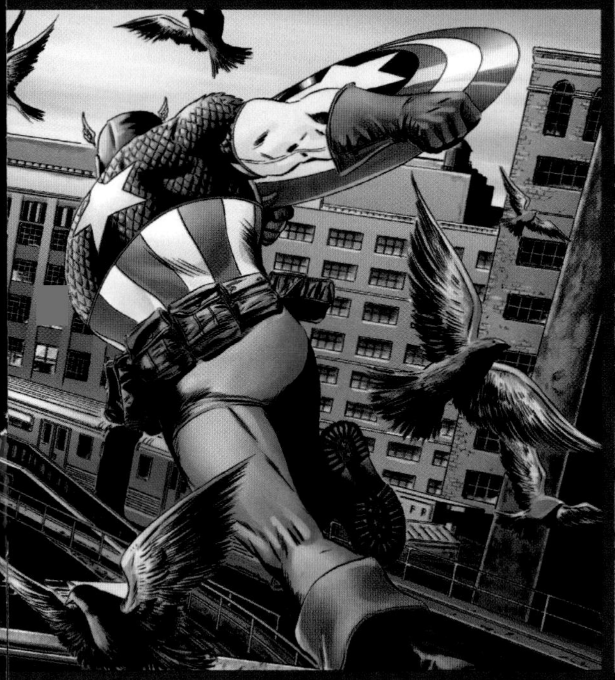

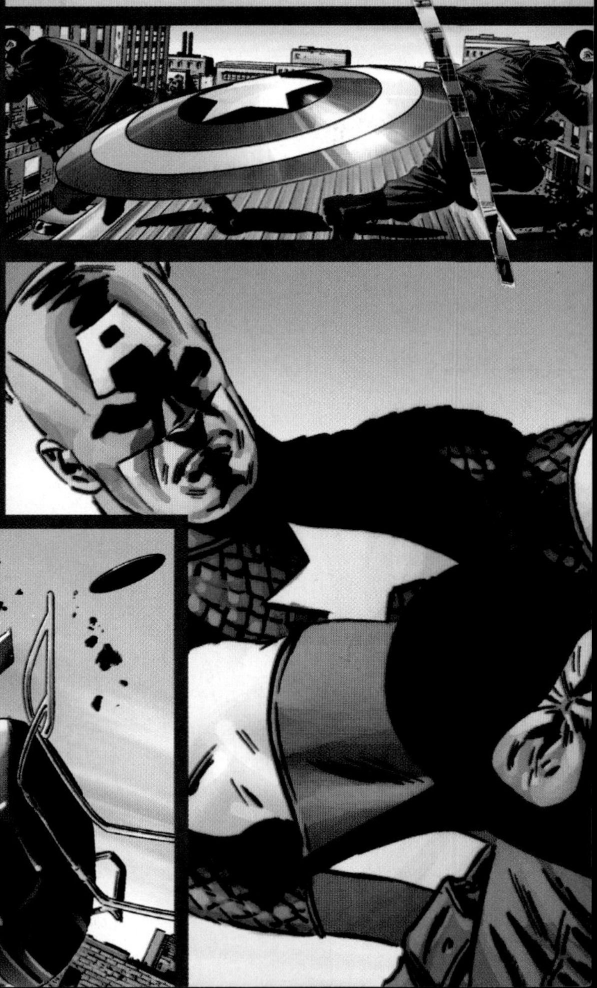

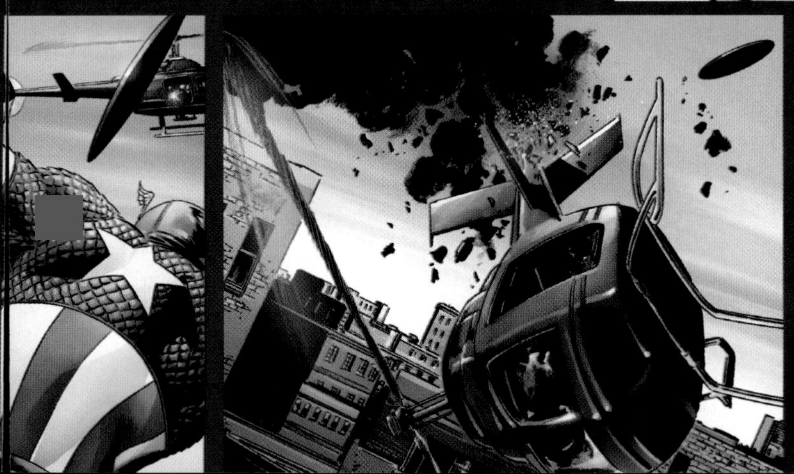

SPOTLIGHT: Another thing about your career of late is that you have been given the opportunity by Marvel to come in on your books and really shake things up. Daredevil, Captain America, and now the X-Men, you've really created some defining moments in their respective legacies.

ED: I guess to some degree, but other than bringing Bucky back in *Captain America*, I don't think that anything that I've done is the kind of thing that anybody else shouldn't be able to do on their books; it's just that most people are afraid to do it. I think the thing that I learned in the Bat Office at DC over the three or four years that I was there was that if you don't do stuff like that on your books, nobody is going to remember you. I mean, there are people who like my *Batman* run, but more people remember my *Catwoman* run, which is where I really took risks and really shook things up and did things that people felt like you shouldn't be able to get away with in a *Catwoman* comic. Like when I had someone yanking an eye out and feeding it to somebody. *(Laughter.)*

SPOTLIGHT: Mmmmm.....yummy....

ED: The implications of that act and what it does to readers, the people remember those *Catwoman* stories more than they remember almost anything I did on Batman. The reason I was able to take risks on *Catwoman* is that nobody cared about her at the time. Her book was on the verge of cancellation before I got offered the gig, and I was pretty much told I could do anything I wanted, so I thought, "Cool! I'll make it a pulp comic!" I had seen what Brian was doing with *Daredevil* and I thought I could do a similar thing with *Catwoman*. I could have the East End be her neighborhood and just tell the kind of stories I wanted to tell, even though it's a super-hero comic.

So that was a bit of a breakthrough, and when I came to Marvel, I had been in comics steadily since 1998 so I had a good six years of steady writing under my belt, so I knew the basic chops of the job. And I also knew the characters really well, like Cap and Daredevil, and I had these gut instincts on what I should do to shake them up. Conveniently, Joe, Axel Alonso and Tom had already gone through this huge argument about the idea of bringing Bucky back. I didn't know it at the time, and so when I talked to Joe about taking the job, I said, "Well if I do it, I want to bring Bucky back." *(Laughter.)* My theory is that every person who has ever written Cap, if you're writing it right, you want to bring Bucky back. If you're writing it wrong, it means you're being too reverential to everything that came before. You don't want to piss on everything that came before, but at the same time you don't want to hold up everything that came before as The Gospel that cannot ever be altered, because then you just get stagnant.

SPOTLIGHT: As part of the responsibility for handling these types of revolutionary change, do you fear for potential fan backlash?

ED: There were times where Brevoort and I were talking before *Captain America #6* came out where I was saying, "Maybe we should have Bucky be a robot!" *(Laughter.)* I was sort of getting cold feet, but at the same time, Tom and I were both alternately nervous and excited about it, because we thought we had a really good story. That was my feeling. I thought, "If you're going to do something like that, you can't just do it as shock value, you have to do it because it adds something to Captain America." As a writer, you can't bring Bucky back just because that is something you wanted to do since you were four years old. You have to actually make it part of the story. Like, why is that an interesting story? How does it affect Captain America? What does that do that hasn't been done to Captain America in a long time, or ever?

The story of Captain America to me has always been one of a guy and his teenage partner who lived four years side by side in World War II seeing the harshest stuff in the world and still being heroes at the end of the day, no matter what it took. The tragedy for Captain America was the Stan Lee retcon where Bucky got blown up. I remember, as a kid, just being so upset about that, how there was no actual comic where Bucky blew up.

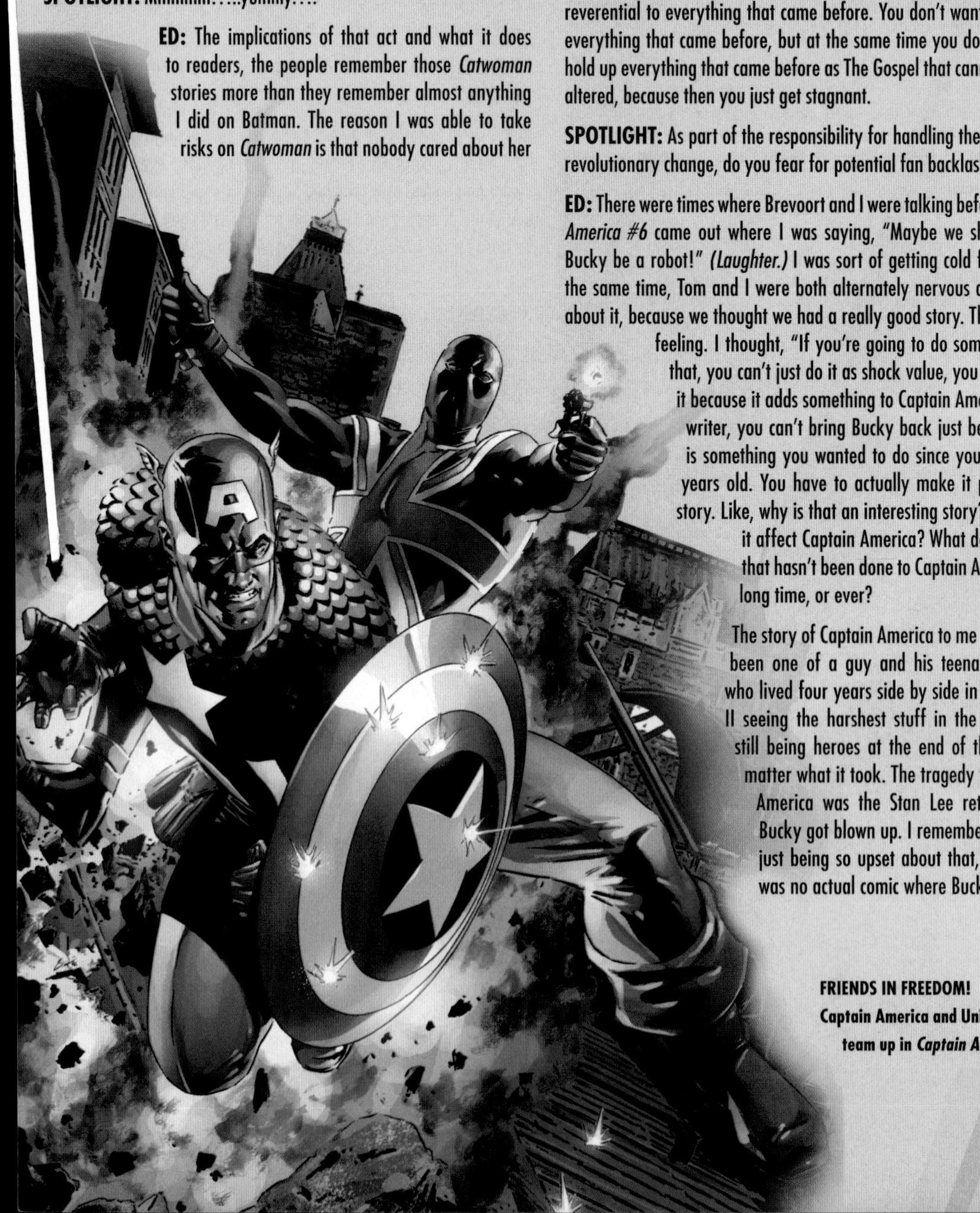

FRIENDS IN FREEDOM!
Captain America and Union Jack team up in *Captain America #19*.

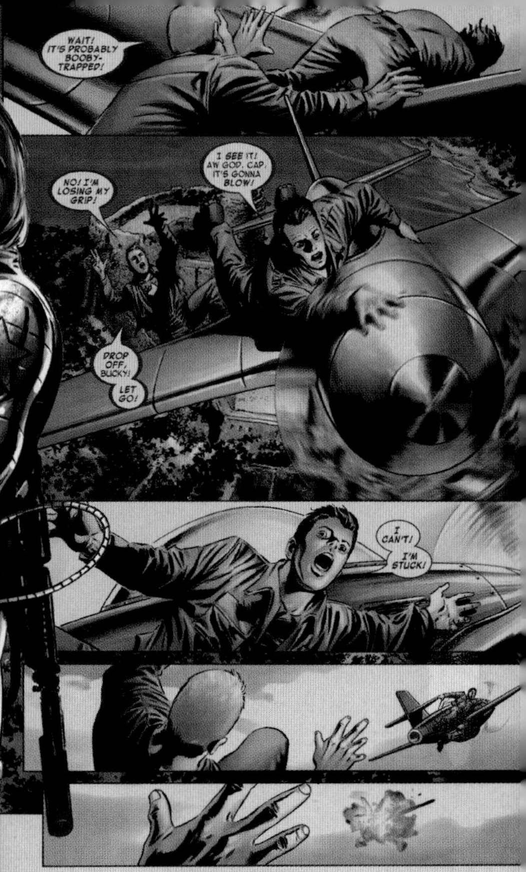
WAIT! IT'S PROBABLY BOOBY-TRAPPED!
NO! I'M LOSING MY GRIP!
I SEE IT! AW GOD, CAP, IT'S GONNA BLOW!
DROP OFF, BUCKY!
LET GO!
I CAN'T! I'M STUCK!

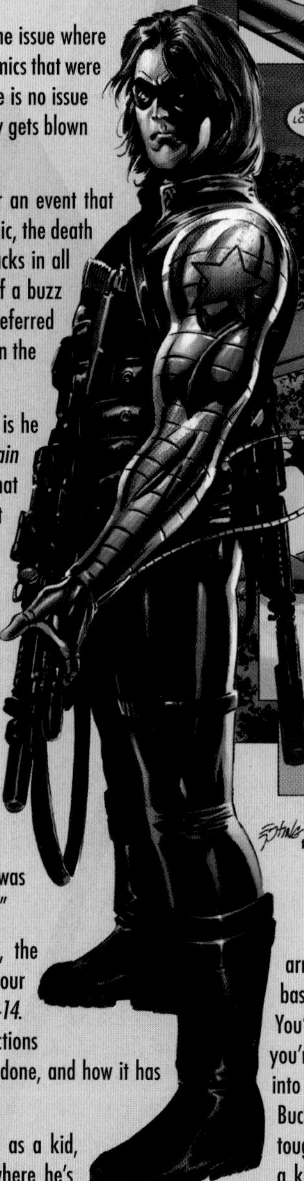

DON'T CALL IT A COMEBACK! He's been here for years! Bucky surfaces in the Marvel Universe in Ed's Winter Soldier epic!

I had the issue where Gwen Stacy died, I had the issue where Uncle Ben gets killed, and they were actually comics that were part of the run, but when I found out that there is no issue of *Captain America* that I could buy where Bucky gets blown up, I was really upset.

SPOTLIGHT: That's an interesting insight. For an event that never was actually portrayed in any Marvel comic, the death of Bucky is one of the most referenced flashbacks in all of Marvel comics: Bucky hanging off the end of a buzz bomb, or drone plane, or however it has been referred to over the years, has been an indelible image in the minds of Marvel readers.

ED: I always thought, if there's no comic, how is he dead? Having now read every issue of *Captain America* multiple times over the last few years, that story has been told something like eight different ways! *(Laughter.)* There are so many different versions of that story, but he's always on a plane, it always blows up. So I thought, "Why does he have to blow up?" I mean, Cap was found, and he has the super-soldier serum, and I thought, "Well, what if there's a story where Bucky didn't die?" I remember talking to Mark Waid about this, and he was like, "Oh, I don't know if I would have ever brought Bucky back." And I'm like, "But you *did* bring Bucky back for something like two issues in your run!" Because *everybody* wants to bring Bucky back! I was just like, "Let's bring him back and let him stay!"

SPOTLIGHT: And so you brought him back, the process of which provided the storyline for your Winter Soldier epic in *Captain America #1-14.* What are some of your observations and reflections about that whole enterprise now that it's been done, and how it has influenced the Captain America mythos?

ED: Bucky was one of my favorite characters as a kid, reading *Tales of Suspense,* those old stories where he's running around with a machine gun taking on the Nazis. I always thought Bucky was so cool. I also liked the fact that Captain America, of all Marvel heros, was the only one who had actual time pass in his life. There's a certain amount of time, a five-year period, where time did definitely pass for Captain America. In all the current Marvel and DC comics, time doesn't actually pass, at least not in the right way. We always look back that the time of the origin is ten to twelve years in the past. Well, for Cap, ten to twelve years is the time that he woke up in *Avengers #4,* but before that, he had five years of being Captain America that can never be changed. There's this five year period where they grew, they aged....Bucky, the Human Torch, Namor, they fought for five years in a war!

So Bucky is not a teenager when he died, unless he was nine years old when he became Bucky. My feeling was that Bucky was fifteen or sixteen, and when he got blown up, he was twenty or twenty-one. By the end of the war, he's a man, not a teenage sidekick. I always thought he'd be an interesting character because he was different from Cap. Brevoort and I talked about that a lot, because we thought that Bucky was really the kind of kid who would have picked on Cap when he was a skinny guy. He was the brawler of his group. He was an army brat, and army brats get into a lot of fights. Growing up on military bases, I've seen plenty of them and been in plenty of them. You're a military brat, you're moving every two years, and you're having to go to a new school and you're having to get into fights. It's just a whole different life. And on top of that, Bucky is an army brat orphan! *(Laughter.)* He's gonna be a tough little mother. I looked at that and thought, if we had a kick ass enough story, we could do anything. If you've figured your story out enough that it excites you, your editor, and the artist you're working with, then you're set.

You know that most of the people who complain are going to probably still keep reading it, but we were worried that we were going to alienate a bunch of people with *Cap.* So we really wanted to make sure that this was a very organic story and that it made sense, and that it had a purpose, and the gratifying thing about this is that the majority of the people who were really against the idea of bringing back Bucky have been won over because what we're doing with that story is not what people expected. It's funny, there were people who were actually more angry about the WWII flashbacks, where we had a page that showed why Bucky was actually worthwhile to the Invaders.

SPOTLIGHT: Actually, that was my favorite sequence in the book! The depiction of Bucky as a down and dirty special ops kind of battlefield soldier was very arresting, made you stop in your tracks as a reader.

ED: Michael Lark is giving me that page. I don't have it yet, but he's giving it to me. I'll have it framed on my wall for the rest of my life. I saw that whole scene in my mind after my first conversation with Tom Brevoort, when we were talking about Bucky. I was like, "Why is

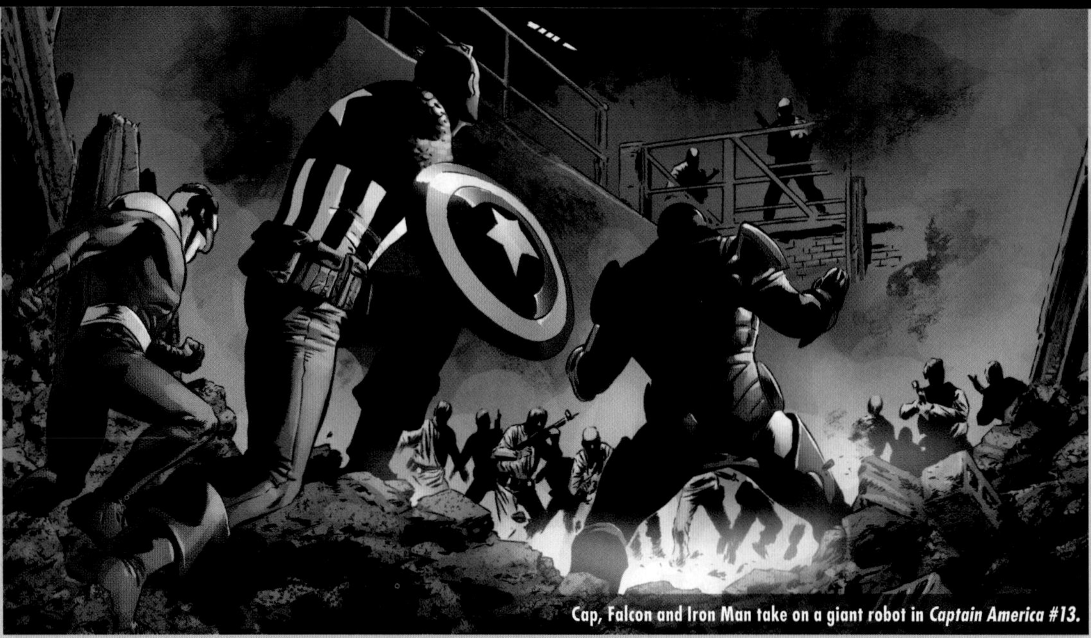

Cap, Falcon and Iron Man take on a giant robot in *Captain America #13.*

a teenage kid running around with a super soldier, the prince of Atlantis, and two guys that can light themselves on fire? All Bucky can do is hold a gun!" *(Laughter.)*

SPOTLIGHT: Well, we know now that wasn't all he could do!

ED: Tom was like, "What if Bucky was not just some kid trained by Captain America?" Cap is given this job by the military, and Bucky is on the military base, so obviously he's gotten military training, too. There's gotta be a better reason for Bucky being the sidekick; that whole idea of him being a symbol of being against the Hitler Youth was kinda lame, and Tom said, "Bucky is this scrapper, he's a fighter, and that's what makes him worthwhile, and he can do things that Captain America can't be seen to be doing." A lot of folks got mad about that. They didn't think that Bucky would do anything that Cap wouldn't do. My feeling is that I don't think Cap *wouldn't* do them, but while there are news reporters in the trenches with him, shooting newsreel footage, you don't want to have Captain America, who is the symbol of all of America, being shown gutting people with a knife. "It's not like Cap didn't do the same things every other soldier had to do."

That's what really bugged me about Cap in the late 80s and early 90s, when they completely sissified Captain America. Here's a guy who fought in WWII for five years and you're telling me he never killed anybody? It was war. What use is a super soldier who won't kill anybody? So I completely ignored that. I was like, "No, Captain America and Bucky killed people. The Invaders killed people. It was a war, and in war, soldiers kill people."

SPOTLIGHT: Have you thought of doing any more classic Cap stories set in that time period?

ED: I'm doing one right now, and Gene Colan is going to be drawing it. I wrote the opening scene for him, but we had to put it off for a little while, but he should be working on that. I finish up the script in about a month. It's going to be a forty-page story.

SPOTLIGHT: And Gene is going to do all of that?

ED: Yes! He's got an inker and a colorist and he's really excited about it. It should be out next summer. It was going to be just a single issue, but Gene wanted to do more, and so I suggested we just do an annual. I bugged Tom Brevoort about it and so we're going to do it as an annual. But you know, it has to stand on its own. It's set in WWII. I asked Gene, "What do you want to draw?" And he said, "Let's do darkness and rain." And I was like, "Captain America, World War II, darkness and

Continued on Second Page Following

BUCKY, BEHIND ENEMY LINES: Trained to exact lethal tactics against the Nazis, Bucky was very good at what he did! (Flashback scene from *Captain America #5.*)

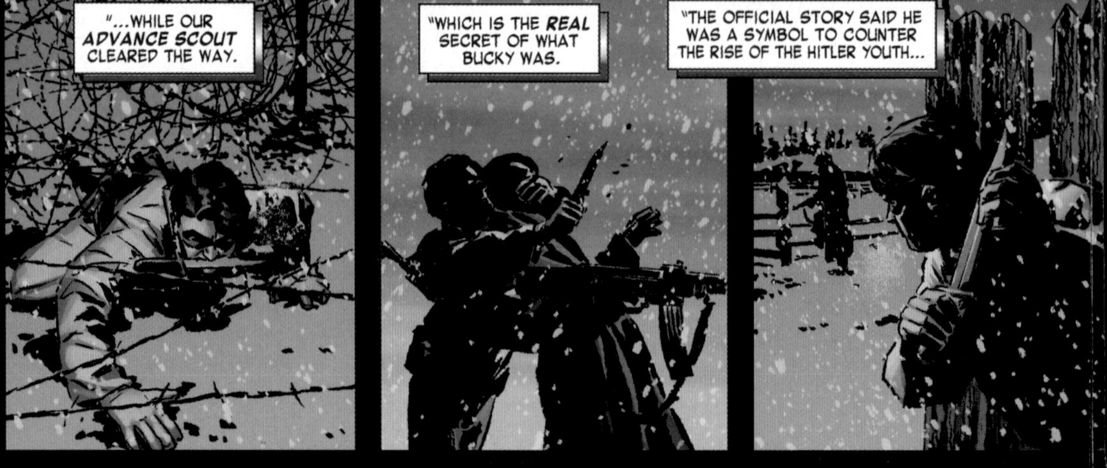
"...WHILE OUR ADVANCE SCOUT CLEARED THE WAY.
"WHICH IS THE REAL SECRET OF WHAT BUCKY WAS.
"THE OFFICIAL STORY SAID HE WAS A SYMBOL TO COUNTER THE RISE OF THE HITLER YOUTH...

THE RETURN OF DOOM

Recently, Dr. Doom made his grand return in the pages of J. Michael Straczynski's *Fantastic Four.* Shortly before that, Ed Brubaker took on the task of updating the "good" doctor's origin for a new generation. That came in the form of *Books of Doom,* a six-issue miniseries that was beautifully illustrated by artist Pablo Raimondi. Ed's story delves not only into the history, but also the mind of Dr. Doom. The story is told through a series of interviews with Doom, and others who knew him throughout his rise to power. But all may not be as it seems. Explains Brubaker, "With a character like Dr. Doom, he's so bombastic, that when he's telling you his life story, it's like you can tweak the details around a little bit to make it so that he is coming across as the hero, because everyone likes to come across as the hero in their story."

Certain things remain constant, though. There are pivotal moments in anyone's life, but Brubaker centers Doom's story around moments that would make the word "pivotal" seem to be mere condescension. As many readers know, Doom's mother, a gypsy sorceress, was long ago condemned to Hell for dealing with dark forces. Brubaker discovered this aspect as a young reader. As he relates it, "It was a story that Gerry Conway and Gene Colan did, where Dr. Doom was going to basically try to free his mother's soul from Hell. I remember reading that and thinking my whole life that that was this key element to understanding Dr. Doom, that his mother was trapped in Hell, and that he was trying to free her soul, which adds this tragic element to Dr. Doom."

The final turning point for Doom comes due to his other parent. Persecuted and on the run through the snow-driven Bavarian mountains, his father freezes to death, holding his son in his arms trying to keep him warm. This was dealt with only in passing in Doom's original origin story, but Brubaker sees it as worth more exploration. "He can't move, because his father's arms are frozen around him, and he's sitting there waiting for hours for someone to come rescue him. That's what drove him insane, what made him think of his mother's soul, and I used that as this pivotal moment where he goes from being a strange but normal and harmless kid, to the guy who becomes the megalomaniac that invents things that freeze people, and burns them, and sends them off to other dimensions."

FANTASTIC FOUR: BOOKS OF DOOM
BRUBAKER • RAIMONDI

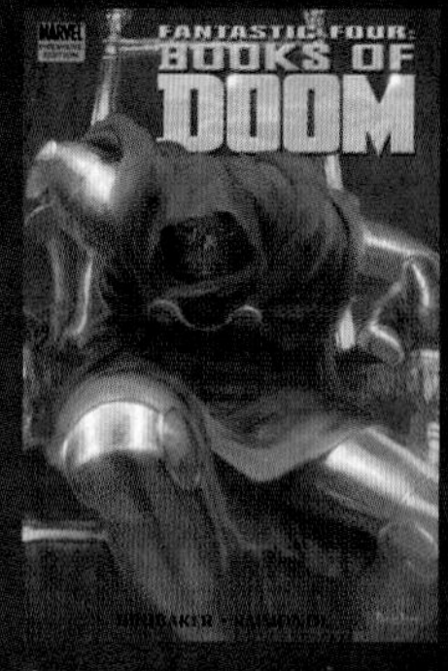

There are of course, the controversies. One of the longest-running debates in the fan community is "What lies behind Doctor Doom's mask?" Different creators have had different answers over the years. Even Stan Lee and Jack Kirby reportedly disagreed, with Stan feeling Doom should be hideously scarred, while Jack opined that the ultimate irony would have Doom scared of facing the world with nothing more than a simple, tiny scar; an inconsequential blemish blown to huge proportions by Doom's megalomaniacal vanity. Longtime *FF* writer John Byrne combined these approaches, suggesting that Doom started off with a simple scar, but in his desire to cover it up, put his mask on fresh from the forge, thus irreparably burning his face. Brubaker has his own take, but he self-effacingly acknowledges it will remain a matter of debate. "If you read the Kirby origin story, Stan Lee has it written in there about, 'Don't worry about the mask cooling, he doesn't care.' So you can see where Byrne got that from, but I thought it was a bit much. I don't know. People probably think that about everything that I change! *(Laughter.)*"

Books of Doom is a moving and intriguing character piece starring the premiere villain in the Marvel Universe. It's out now in Premiere Hardcover, at finer stores everywhere. Don't miss it!

— by Matt Adler

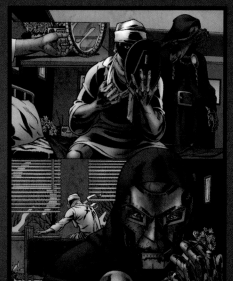

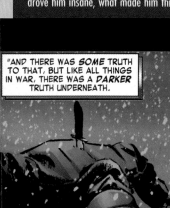

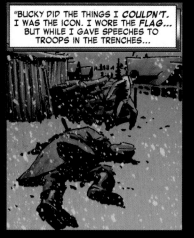

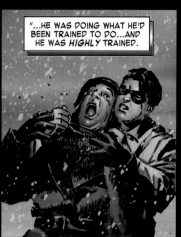

"AND THERE WAS SOME TRUTH TO THAT, BUT LIKE ALL THINGS IN WAR, THERE WAS A DARKER TRUTH UNDERNEATH.
"BUCKY DID THE THINGS I COULDN'T. I WAS THE ICON. I WORE THE FLAG... BUT WHILE I GAVE SPEECHES TO TROOPS IN THE TRENCHES...
"...HE WAS DOING WHAT HE'D BEEN TRAINED TO DO...AND HE WAS HIGHLY TRAINED.

rain. Okay, I've got it." *(Laughter.)* So it's an anniversary kind of annual, a special thing, but for me, Gene Colan is one of my favorite artists of all time, and to get a chance to work with him, it's amazing. Now, if they could get me John Romita…

SPOTLIGHT: Speaking of great artists, you've got to believe that part of the way that *Captain America* has been resonating with fans is because of the work that Steve Epting and Michael Lark have done in drawing your scripts.

ED: Michael did all the flashbacks and I love the way he did them, but I would have loved to have seen Steve do them. He's done some of the flashback scenes in later issues, and it seems like nobody even notices that they're not drawn by Michael. *(Laughter.)* I don't think their styles could be any more different, other than that they're both fairly realistic. I had a list of about two or three people that I wanted to draw Cap, and his name was near the top of it because of the stuff that I saw from *El Cazador*, and some of the covers he had done with Cap on them. He came up in my first conversation with Brevoort, and they were looking for a monthly for him, and I was like, "Get him!" The only problem with Steve is that he's a little bit slow. He can't keep a monthly schedule, because he pencils and inks himself. I mean, you've seen what his stuff looks like — it's mind blowing.

To me, I feel like I'm working in the classic era again. I think that's a large reason why some of those old time Cap fans are still around, even if the idea of bringing Bucky back horrified them. The reality of ˙ is that it looks like a classic comic in a lot of ways. Steve's biggest in﹍nces as an artist are obviously John Romita, John Buscema, the classi﹍﹍r-hero guys.

There's that st﹍﹍﹍ #1 where Cap is throwing his shield as he's leaping off a building onto ﹍﹍﹍﹍train, and the way that Cap is drawn in there, it was like a combination of ﹍﹍﹍d Buscema, it was so amazing. But the sequence of the action….as much as I﹍﹍﹍ Epting's stuff, when I got those pages, I was like, "Oh my God! I am never giving up this artist!" When Cap is fighting those terrorists on the rooftop of that train, and it's like a six-page sequence, it sells you on how cool Captain America is. He throws his shield, and it cuts through

the tail-fin of a helicopter, and when his shield comes back he catches it and he's running straight at these guys. The choreography of that scene might be the best action we've actually done in the book until maybe issue #13, when we had Cap, Iron Man and Falcon fighting together. That was totally bad. I should have probably not forced Steve to do an issue with twelve pages of action right before I gave him the big finale of Cap and Bucky fighting. But he doesn't mind drawing all action.

SPOTLIGHT: One of the things that is notable about Cap are those elegant and vibrant fight scenes. How do you approach writing fight scenes? Do you have particular ideas of choreography in mind when you are writing?

ED: A little bit of it is giving the artist a lot of leeway to make it work the way they want to., especially with Michael and Steve. With Steve, I've noticed that when I tell him, "Okay, here's what basically has to happen, and here's basically the amount of space you have to do it," he winds up using a lot more panels than I would expect him to use. Initially, I thought we don't need that many panels, so with Steve I tend to give him leeway to do what he wants, but I tend to write a fairly choreographed action scene for him, but often it's just "Someone punches someone and they go flying." *(Laughter.)* I know he'll make that look cool. Also, with Steve, I've found I can describe something that sounds impossible, and he'll just draw it and it looks amazing, so I take that liberty sometimes. *(Laughter.)*

With Michael, I tell him what I want in there and he does whatever the heck he wants to do and it always looks great. I've worked with Michael for eight years, and he knows where he can take liberties and where he can't. He knows where changing one thing will alter a story and where it won't. Steve is the same way. I'm lucky to have guys that like the scripts that I give them, and tend to not have a problem with following them. That's the worst thing that can happen to the writer of these things, to write a script and have the artist completely draw somethi﹍﹍﹍ I've been lucky enough to stick with the guys that I like, because they don't do that kind of thing, o﹍﹍﹍ to make a change, they will call me and suggest things. I totally welcome that input from them.

TARGETTING A MEMORY: Bucky is back as the Winter Soldier, a man at odds with his friends, with past, with reality itself… but not with his capacity to kill.